ARTISTS BY THEMSELVES

ARTISTS
BY
THEMSELVES

Artists' Portraits
from the
National Academy
of Design

NATIONAL ACADEMY OF DESIGN

This exhibition was made possible by grants from the
National Endowment for the Arts and the New York
State Council on the Arts and by a generous contribu-
tion from the Mediators, Richard Manney, President.

Contents

Exhibition Itinerary

Foreword

IN 1820, JUST A FEW YEARS BEFORE THE FOUNDING OF THE NATIONAL ACADEMY OF DESIGN, a collection of opinions by Horace Walpole was published in Boston. In section CCXXVII of *Walpoliana* the author addresses the subject of the portrait. He begins . . . "I prefer portraits, really interesting, not only to landscape-painting, but to history." A landscape for Walpole is "an exquisite distribution of wood and water, and buildings. It is excellent—we pass on, and it leaves not one trace in the memory." Historical painting he calls "sublime deception," always falling short of the idea, false as to costume, grouping, and attitude. "But a real portrait we know is truth itself; and it calls up so many collateral ideas as to fill an intelligent mind more than any other species."

Isn't this particularly true of the self-portrait? The special glance of the artist looking out first at himself and then at the world encourages the viewer to penetrate the sitter's most secret thoughts. And when artists paint fellow artists, doesn't the same quest for truth prevail?

Artists By Themselves is drawn from the National Academy's collection of over 1,300 artists' portraits. These works, most of them submitted by the artist members as a condition of their membership in the Academy, offer a view of the painting of portraits in America over a period of 160 years. These are intimate portraits. Absent are heroic poses, swords and spurs, ballgowns and feathers. Instead there are brushes, palettes, engravers' tools.

Patterns of friendship emerge as one examines who painted whom. Were artist and sitter studying together, traveling together? Were they teacher and pupil? Were they related through blood or marriage? The Academy fostered a brotherhood of artists, especially during the first 80 to 100 years of its existence when the art world was a smaller, less complicated place.

Today the Academy still exists to encourage this fraternity among artists, and the same obligation exists to submit a diploma portrait upon election. The work of current members occupies an important place in this catalogue. It is the Academy's hope that the exhibition will focus much deserved attention on a species that, in the years since Walpole wrote, continues "to fill an intelligent mind."

John H. Dobkin
Director

Acknowledgements

IT WAS ONLY LOGICAL THAT THE NATIONAL ACADEMY OF DESIGN ORGANIZE AN EXHIBITION of its artists' portraits, following its exhibition of figure painting in 1979 and landscape painting in 1980. The selection of 72 paintings out of a possible 1,300 presented a great challenge. Dr. William H. Gerdts, Executive Officer, Ph.D. Program in Art History, CUNY, deserves a special thanks for participating in the first round of this process of selection and Michael Quick in the second. Assisting in the preparation of the catalogue were six of Dr. Gerdts' doctoral students. Their names appear at the end of the very fine essays.

Barbara S. Krulik and Dita Amory ferreted out biographical information on all the artists and sitters, Abigail Booth Gerdts and Miss Amory prepared the lists of artists' portraits in the collection, Anne Hoene Hoy and Ms. Krulik edited the catalogue material. Staff members who devoted time over the past year are Betsy Arvidson and James P. Nally.

John Brealey, with his customary concern, continued to advise the National Academy on matters of conservation and supervised work on several paintings in the exhibition.

Richard Manney, charter member of the Advisory Board, has generously supported this project, and for this the National Academy is very grateful.

Help, advice and support came from Peter Beril; Barbara Ball Buff; Doreen Bolger Burke, Metropolitan Museum of Art; Lawrence Campbell, Art Students' League; Mark Davis; Stephen Edidin; Mabel Eng; Dr. William H. Gerdts; Jemison Hammond, Archives of American Art; Ian Highet; Betty Krulik; Sandra Leff, Graham Gallery; Gerry Levin, Forum Gallery; Mary Beth McKenzie; William McNaught, New York Director, Archives of American Art; Sarah Mleczko; Joan Nicholson, Deputy Director, American Academy in Rome; Arleen Pancza, Archives of American Art; Ronald G. Pisano; Dr. Steven Potkin; Thérèse Rosinsky; Cathy Stover, Archivist, Pennsylvania Academy of the Fine Arts.

JHD

Introduction

ALTHOUGH THE NATIONAL ACADEMY'S COLLECTION INCLUDES MANY ARTISTIC TREASURES of American landscape painting, genre painting and other subjects, its collection of artist portraits is even more special. With over 1,200 images, it is one of the half-dozen largest holdings of painted portraits in this country; as a specialized collection of likenesses of artists, it tops even the Uffizi Gallery's famous collection of some 900 self-portraits.

This invaluable collection of portraits of nearly all the major American artists since the Academy's founding arose out of a regulation, appearing first in the revised constitution of 1839, that any artist elected to the rank of Associate of the National Academy would be required to present to the Academy a portrait of himself, before his new status could be confirmed and official. This gift would be in addition to the example of the artist's work that he would present to the Academy if he were later elected a member of the National Academy. The latter presentation, known as a Diploma Work, had a prominent precedent in the practice of the Royal Academy of Arts, the British organization that in many ways served as a model for the National Academy of Design, but the Diploma Portrait did not Nor was the Diploma Portrait customary in the other major art academies with which the Americans were likely to have been familiar.

The minutes of the Council, unfortunately, are silent as to the thinking behind this new requirement. Perhaps there were specific justifications of the moment, but the concept, in any case, expresses one of the basic purposes of an art academy, which is to draw attention to exceptional artists and honor them.

Although the National Academy's collection of artist portraits is unexpected in many ways, it conforms to a long tradition, originating in the Renaissance, of honoring great men through the display of their portraits. Already in the Middle Ages, of course, portrait series had been painted, at first limited to the genealogy of ruling houses or the Papacy. In the fourteenth century, cycles of decoration featuring the nine illustrious men and women of history were painted to honor these exemplary individuals and provide models of valor and virtue. The modern conception of a portrait collection originated under the influence of the learning and broader ideals of the humanists, as Italian decorative art began to develop larger series of likenesses. Between 1367 and 1379, Francesco il Vecchio da Carrara had a *Sala Virorum Illustrium* in his palace of Padua decorated with thirty-six likenesses of famous men of the ancient world, following Petrarch's literary treatment of them. Early in the fifteenth century, such series were expanded to include famous men of the modern world. Federico da Montefeltro extended the humanistic tradition one step further toward the modern sense of a portrait collection in lining his Studiolo at Urbino with individual panel paintings set into the wall (rather than painted on the wall) of twenty-eight famous men, including philosophers, poets, popes and theologians. The tradition approached its modern form yet more closely thanks to Paolo Giovio, Bishop of Nocera (1483-1552), who assembled a collection of almost 400 independent portraits of famous men. His example was widely followed in Italy.

As time passed, artists began to be included among the famous men, but it was the second edition of Giorgio Vasari's *Lives of the Most Famous Artists*, published in 1568 with illustrations, that constituted the first series specifically of artist portraits. It was to set the pattern for numerous later illustrated lives of the artists, including the series, *Pictorum aliquot Celebrium Praecipuae Germaniae Inferioris Effigies,* first published in 1610 by Hendrick Hondius and Simon Frisius. Probably the best known of these publications today is the series of engravings by Van Dyck, published between 1636 and 1641 in the first of many large editions which filled a considerable demand continuing into the nineteenth century. These and many other series of published portraits, which were widely available, firmly established the concept of the collection of artist portraits. In fact, assembling images from these numerous series was itself a minor branch of the tradition of print collecting.

In addition to print series of artist portraits, the conception of a collection of painted portraits, exactly paralleling the collection of the National Academy of Design, was already fully developed in the late Renaissance, at the time of the founding of the first art academy in the modern sense. In the statutes of the Florentine Accademia del Disegno, drafted in 1562-63 by Vasari and Vincenzo Borghini, article 22 proposed that a frieze should be painted on the walls of the academy building representing the most famous Tuscan painters since Cimabue, as well as worthy contemporary artists upon their deaths. This project was never realized, because the academy lacked its own building until the eighteenth century, but around 1573 Vasari painted such a frieze of thirty portraits in his own house.

Following the suggestion in the statutes of the Florentine academy, Federico Zuccari, as first president of the Accademia di San Luca in Rome, opened in 1593, gave the Roman academy his own portrait. A series of copies of portraits of famous artists was then made, and later a series of portraits of contemporary academy members. A somewhat parallel Roman practice was the permission that the Congregazione dei Virtuosi received to erect busts of its deceased members in its chapel in the Pantheon.

Commissioning portraits of members accords, after all, with one of the principal purposes of the early academies, establishing the high status of the artist, and of the members in particular, as men of genius, distinct from members of the craft-oriented guilds and governing themselves. Such an impulse certainly stood behind the impressive memorial services that the organizations held for deceased academicians. In a sense, the presentation pieces that members-elect were required to submit to these first academies also represented them in a kind of memorial gallery.

Even though a collection of members' portraits was a logical part of an art academy, the custom was only intermittently honored in later academies. The Royal Academy of Arts did not accept Sir Henry Raeburn's self-portrait when he presented it in 1815 because a self-portrait was not admissable as a presentation piece, or Diploma Work. On the other hand, the Royal Academy did have a strong sense of its own tradition, later purchasing self-portraits of leading members such as Sir Thomas Lawrence, Richard Westall and Edward Penny. Gifts and bequests, in any case, provided it with an extensive collection of images of members.

Portraits of artists have also had a special interest to collectors other than art academies. There were several extensive collections of artist portraits in Italy during the Baroque period, when Cardinal Leopoldo de'Medici founded the collection exclusively of self-portraits that is now in the Uffizi Gallery in Florence. Inclusion in this world-renowned collection was such an honor that even an artist of Sir Joshua Reynolds's stature gladly gave his portrait. Other examples abound, from the collections of portrait drawings formed by Nicola Pio in the early eighteenth century to the collection of ninety-two portraits of contemporary artists formed by Alexander Macdonald (d. 1884) and his wife and now in the Aberdeen Art Gallery and Museum in Scotland (fig. 1).

Fig. 1. JOHN SINGER SARGENT, *Self-Portrait,* Aberdeen Art Gallery and Museum, Aberdeen

Perhaps an additional influence on the establishment of the National Academy of Design's requirement that Associates present a portrait of themselves was the English tradition of portraits of members of literary and artistic clubs. The term "kit-kat," referring to a portrait roughly thirty-six by twenty-eight inches and showing one or both hands, originated from the choice of that size for the forty-two portraits of the members of the Kit Kat Club that Sir Godfrey Kneller painted between 1703 and 1721. Sir Joshua Reynolds painted two group portraits of members of the Society of Dilettanti between 1777 and 1779. The virtually complete group of portraits of grand masters of the Pennsylvania Masonic grand lodge suggests that such a tradition, in a more limited form, existed in this country already in the eighteenth century.

A conspicuous American precedent for the establishment of the Academy's collection of portraits is the group of depictions of national heroes that had formed the core of the Peale museums in Philadelphia and Baltimore. A similar desire to honor great men, and a corresponding public interest in such portrait series, was reflected in the publication around 1816-18 of Joseph Delaplaine's *Repository of the Lives and Portraits of Distinguished American Characters,* and John Sanderson's *Biographies of the Signers of the Declaration of Independence,* published in 1820-27. Closer at hand was the growing portrait collection in New York's City Hall, honoring mayors, state governors and some presidents of the United States, but also including a series of monumental portraits of naval heroes of the War of 1812 and exceptional commissions such as Samuel F. B. Morse's portrait of the Marquis de Lafayette. The latter painting generated great interest within the art world and general public alike in 1825-26. Also in New York, the National Academy of Design's chief rival, the American Academy of the Fine Arts, supported the publication, between 1834 and 1839, of James Barton Longacre and James Herring's *National Portrait Gallery of Distinguished Americans,* with the understanding that all the original portraits painted as a basis for the engravings would be deposited at the American Academy as a gallery of portraits.

The National Academy of Design's collection of artist portraits began with commissions for the

Fig. 2. Sir Godfrey Kneller, *William Congreve*, 1709, 36 x 28 in., National Portrait Gallery, London.

portraits of its professor of mythology, William Cullen Bryant, and its distinguished professor of anatomy, Dr. Frederick Gore King, which Samuel F. B. Morse carried out in 1825 and 1826. By resolution at the Academy's annual meeting on May 2, 1838, a portrait was commissioned from Charles C. Ingham to honor William Dunlap. At a special meeting on July 12, 1843, to commemorate the death of Washington Allston, it was resolved to inquire into purchasing a bust of the great man. Against this background of honoring distinguished members through portraits, the Academy added to its new *Constitution and By-laws*, published in 1839, the regulation that:

> Every Associate shall, during the first year after his election, present to the Academy his own portrait, to be the property of the Academy, and to be preserved in the gallery of the Institution. A failure to comply with this rule within the time specified, shall make void the election of the candidate elect. (Article V, Section 3.)

The requirement was slow to establish itself within the small academy, even though its membership was dominated by portraitists. The inventory of the Academy's collection, published together with the revised constitution of 1843, lists only eleven artist portraits, most of these the commissioned portraits already mentioned and portraits of members of the Council, who were no doubt setting an official good example. Only four of the twenty-seven associates elected between 1839 and 1842 had complied with the requirement.

Among these eleven paintings was Asher B. Durand's *Portrait of Lewis P. Clover, Jr.*, (p.61) in the exhibition. It is smaller than most of the portraits that were donated later, since the size requirement of thirty by twenty-five inches was first specified in constitutional revisions of 1844. This standardization would have made the close hanging of the portraits neater and more compact and would also have allowed the Council to order frames for them a dozen at a time. This it did on February 26, 1844, ordering another half-dozen on October 21, and more at regular intervals.

On February 17, 1845, the Council took official recognition of the problem of noncompliance and voted to send notices to the delinquent Associates elected in 1844. On April 2, 1845, the names

Fig. 3. GEORGE W. TWIBILL, *Portrait of John Trumbull,* oil on canvas, 27 x 19 in., National Academy of Design, New York.

of members of that group who still had not complied were stricken from the list of the Associates. An example having been made, the officers submitted the names for reelection at the annual meeting of 1845. After that, compliance with the requirement seems to have improved, and, after awhile, the formal acceptance of a Diploma Portrait by the Council and official ratification of the Associate-elect as an Associate appear regularly in the Council minutes. (Only in fairly recent years has this iron rule been relaxed.) The published inventory of August 1, 1852, attests to the success of the enforcement of the requirement, listing seventy-seven artist portraits. With the collection growing swiftly, its very size soon must have presented problems to the Academy. Although the minutes of this Council meeting of November 2, 1846, mention "The Gallery of Portraits of Members," there seems to be no record of how and where the portraits were displayed in the nineteenth century, or which ones were displayed when space got tight. It was presumably a space problem that led to a reduction in the size requirements in the constitution of 1882, from the previous thirty by twenty-five inches to only twenty-one by seventeen inches, or one half the area. Perhaps the optimism over plans for a new academy building led to the restoration of the larger standard size in 1898.

These size limitations and other special circumstances of the Academy's collection have given it a character distinct from that of a typical sampling of the development of American portraiture. Most fundamentally, the size restrictions greatly reduce the options available to the portraitist. For instance, since a life-sized portrait measuring thirty by twenty-five inches usually cuts the figure at about the elbows, the portrait in most cases loses the hands, with their expressive potential, as well as the complete battery of attributes that the hands might have held in a formal portrait. Even the minor adjustment of extending the format to thirty-six inches by thirty inches, as Daniel Huntington did in his self-portrait (p. 35), a later gift to the Academy and therefore not subject to the usual limitations, permits the subject to hold a book of Old Master engravings, suggesting both his learning and the grand artistic tradition that he carries forward. In a thirty by twenty-five-inch painting, the arms must be bent and raised if they are to be shown, making a natural activity difficult to represent (p. 65). The naturalism

IACOBUS DE GEYN, ANTVERP.
PICT. ET SCULPT.

Geinius eximius Scalptor, Pic torque peritus,
Inventor felix, judicioque bonus.
Et Belli et Pacis pingens Insignia, gratus
Ipse Duci Bella qui artibus egregius.
Hondius exc. Cum privilegio. 1610.

Fig. 4. HENDRIK HONDIUS, *Portrait of Jacob de Gheyn II,* 1610, engraving, 8⅛ x 4⅞ in., private collection.

Fig. 5. Unknown, France, 18th Century, *Portrait of Louis de Boullongne* (1654-1733), engraving, 14 x 9¾ in., Los Angeles County Museum of Art, Gift of Irene Salinger in memory of her father, Adolph Stern.

Fig. 6. D. CHADOWIECKI, *Portrait of Pasche Johann Friedrich Weitsch,* engraving, 9⅞ x 6⅝ in., Los Angeles County Museum of Art, Gift of Mr. & Mrs. Stanley Talpis.

of the period prevented portraitists from employing the conventional turned and pointing or gesturing poses of the seventeenth century, as seen, for instance, in Kneller's inventive Kit Kat series (fig. 2). Kneller could easily introduce the hands, whereas nineteenth-century artists could not. The hands can be shown, however, if the artist paints more of a less-than-life-sized figure, as Edith Prellwitz did in her *Self-Portrait* (p. 110), or as George Twibill did in his "full-length in small" *Portrait of Colonel John Trumbull* (fig. 3). Another way to include the hands is to stretch the figure along the diagonal, as in Lawton Parker's imaginatively posed *Portrait of Frederick Frieseke* (p. 41), or Eakins's *Portrait of Edward W. Redfield* (p. 89). With the loss of the hands also goes the possibility for an active portrayal of the figure, another of the forms of characterization or idealization available in the grand-manner tradition of portraiture. The significant special exception to this is, of course, the artist's self-portrait, in which his hands are generally raised to paint and the decided turn of the body suggests an active role.

Cutting the figure at the elbows also tends, as a design principle, to bring it forward to the picture plane, not only eliminating the intervening space, but also making it difficult to establish space (and therefore a setting) behind the figure. The relative bulk of the immediate foreground figure and the resulting tension of the picture surface tend to oppose the construction of an orderly progression into space and thus the creation of a persuasive environment around the subject. When such spatial suggestion is attempted, it is usually by means of turning the figure to establish a diagonal into space, terminating in a wall parallel to the picture plane, as in the self-portraits by Walter Ufer (p. 149) and Robert Brackman (p. 154). Such a sense of setting is achieved only with considerable effort. In most cases, artists confined to a format as small as thirty by twenty-five inches paint an indefinite background.

These size restrictions must seem Procrustean to the public of today, which is familiar through camera reproductions and travel with the great painted self-portraits of the Baroque period

Louis de Boullongne.
Chevalier de lordre de S.Michel Escuyer secret du Roy Peintre de sa
Majesté Directeur et Recteur del Academie Royale de Peinture et sculpture.

which use setting and costume so effectively. A much different body of artist portraits, however, dominated the consciousness of the early nineteenth century. By far the largest and most comprehensive array of artist portraits existed in the graphic tradition, essentially the series of engraved artist portraits that was published either separately or as plates in the various lives of the artists. A limited number of the earlier engravings gave the artist both a studio setting and symbolic attributes (fig. 4), but the large majority of them were bust portraits which indicated the profession and stature of the artist through elaborate enframement (figs. 5 and 6). (Since most of the portrait images were taken from bust-sized portraits in earlier books, an elaborate frame allowed the engraver to add symbols without trying to reconstruct the studio life and costume of the artist. In addition, such frames contributed uniformity to a series of likenesses gathered from different sources.)

Notwithstanding the *trompe-l'oeil* enframement of Rembrandt Peale's various memorial "port-hole" portraits, such explicit symbolism was virtually impossible for nineteenth-century American artists. The typical portrait in the Academy's collection became, for the most part, a simple bust without elaboration. Until the 1880s, in fact, there is little to indicate even that the subjects of the portraits are artists. (It is notable how few three-quarter-length Victorian photographs of artists even include a palette and brush.) The Victorian artist presented himself as a gentleman with a respectable, but unnamed, profession. Neither did he cast himself in the role of the genius. He was a man of property and taste who happened to paint, but did not feel it important to show his brushes in his portrait any more than a surgeon would have held his scalpel or a merchant a fistful of coins. In Christian Mayr's *Self-Portrait* (fig. 7), one does see the example of Van Dyck's artist portraits with their use of the hand, understood to suggest the creative role of the artist (fig. 8). (This motif occurs again in the mid-twentieth-century *Self-Portrait* (p.151)of Walter Stuempfig.) Eliza Greatorex is shown holding her professional insignia of pen and drawing portfolio in her portrait by Ferdinand Boyle (p.65), which

Fig. 7. CHRISTIAN MAYR, *Self-Portrait,*
oil on canvas, 20 x 25 in.,
National Academy of Design, New York.

creates a tone of formality rare in the collection. (In this context, it is interesting to note how the women artists, Edith Prellwitz (p.110), Lilian Hale (p.137) and Gertrude Fiske (p. 140), also make a point of portraying themselves as artists, with their professional tools in hand.) Among works by the more sophisticated artists of the end of the nineteenth century, there are more allusions to the world of art. A consciousness of the tradition is readily discovered in Robert Vonnoh's portrait of his wife (p. 94) in the costume of Mme. Vigée-Lebrun (fig. 9). Does Louis Betts's gesture in shading his eyes in his *Self-Portrait* (p.139) or Robert Philipp's (p.157), recall the peering of Sir Joshua Reynolds (fig. 10)?

Although these few can be pointed out, such allusions and conventions are rare among the earlier portraits of the Academy's collection. For the most part, they present their subjects simply as men—or, in fact, gentlemen, since they wear coats and ties, city clothes that a businessman might wear, until into the early twentieth century. Maxfield Parrish's rolled-up sleeves in Kenyon Cox's portrait of 1905 (p.107) and Charles Hawthorne's open shirt in 1906 (p.83) introduce, within the exhibition, the note of professional informality that is to become the rule in this century as the artist once again represents himself working in his studio milieu.

The single broadest characterization of the portraits in the collection is that they strike a delicate balance between the intimate and the formal. They were intended for public display, so they do not violate standards of decorum for their periods. Among the late nineteenth-century works, one finds no confessional, self-accusing portrayals, with disfiguring distortions that suggest psychic torment, although such private portraits and self-portraits were painted by some European artists of the period. Even the boldest twentieth-century portraits in the Academy collection are still public images.

The Academy portraits are polite, but they are also exceptionally penetrating, and give us in good measure that quality in portraiture known as "presence." They are, after all, portraits of the self or of friends. They therefore reveal that knowledge of a sitter's personality which

PETRVS BREVGEL
ANTVERPLÆ PICTOR RVRALIVM ACTIONVM.

Ant. van Dyck fecit aqua forti.

Fig. 8. ANTHONY VAN DYCK *Portrait of Petrus Bruegel the Younger,* etching, 9½ x 6 in., Los Angeles County Museum of Art, Howard de Forest bequest.

is found in most great portraits. Such knowledge, contained in a small format, creates the feeling of intimate communion that makes the best of these works so absorbing. The market place today seems to avoid portraits that convey a strong sense of personality, preferring instead the decorative portrait that does not intrude upon the psychic poise of the collector. Like a still life, it arranges colors and reproduces textures in an agreeable manner, skillfully rendering physical appearance. But, surely, the genius of portraiture is the ability to evoke a personality, to capture the elusive spirit of an individual, perhaps to penetrate beyond public appearances to the quiet inner life. If this is the measure of the success of a portrait, then the Academy's collection is an exceptional one, since its portraits are so full of that special insight which clearly establishes character. The individuals one encounters in these portraits are distinctly defined as particular personalities, quite different from one another. We see them through their own eyes or the eyes of an intimate, someone who conceived the design of the likeness in the light of his personal understanding of his friend and fellow-artist.

Given that, for the most part, the format precludes symbolic accessories or characterizing backgrounds, what opportunities for expression does the Academy portraitist have left to him? With what means does he achieve his strong sense of himself or of the spirit of his friend?

As a matter of fact, there are many slight adjustments that can help to shape a characterization. Even the slight tilt of the head in Charles Loring Elliott's dashing *Portrait of James Edward Freeman* (p. 73), for instance, goes far toward suggesting the sitter's nonchalance and freedom from convention. In fact, almost any variation from a level, upright head can serve as characterization, as in Asher B. Durand's *Portrait of Louis P. Clover* (p. 61), who seems a little shy. It would be difficult to catalogue all of the ways in which an artist can suggest the personality of his portrait subject, but there are some devices that occur with exceptional frequency within the Academy's collection and perhaps deserve special notice.

Among the most prominent of these design features is the direct gaze of the subject, which

Fig. 9. Marie Louise Elizabeth Vigée-LeBrun, *Self-Portrait*, Uffizi, Florence.

Fig. 10. Sir Joshua Reynolds, *Self-Portrait*, ca. 1748, National Portrait Gallery, London.

is otherwise uncommon in the portraiture of the nineteenth century. In most portraits of the period, the sitter's head is turned about one quarter from frontal view, an angle that balances the full-face and the profile aspect and enhances the three-dimensionality of the head. The sitter generally gazes into the distance or in the general direction of the viewer, but rarely at him, perhaps because a stare can be uncomfortable to the viewer and seem immodest on the part of the subject. But many of the Academy's portraits do project this somewhat challenging direct gaze. This is what the artist sees, of course, when he searches in his mirror for the forms of his self-portrait, so self-portraits tend to seem audacious.

The direction of gaze is related to another important formal feature for portraiture, the position of the body. The self-portraitist is generally turned (away from the mirror) to work on his painting, looking back toward the mirror (and thus the viewer). This turning in order to look gives the gaze in these paintings an additional force, suggesting the intention of seeking out the viewer. Even so, the position is less dramatic than the fully frontal pose,, which gives the impression of total exposure and frankness. Probably for that reason, complete frontality is exceedingly rare in conventional nineteenth-century portraiture. In the small-format paintings of the 1880s and 1890s, such as William Merritt Chase's *Portrait of Robert Blum* (p. 79) and the self-portraits by George de Forest Brush (p. 104) and Irving Wiles (p. 82), the effect of this enforced intimacy is almost startling. A contrasting approach is found in Cecilia Beaux's *Self-Portrait* (p. 38), in which the body is frontal but the head and gaze are turned away, conveying an impression of pointed reserve. The *Portrait of Bessie Potter Vonnoh* (p. 94), in which the sitter turns from a sideways position to look directly at the viewer, is the Beaux self-portrait's psychological opposite.

Another potent device often used in the portraits of the Academy's collection to enhance the impression of intimacy is limited lighting. A fully illuminated background, as in Charles Loring Elliott's *Portrait of James Edward Freeman* (p. 73) or Emanuel Leutze's *Portrait of Wor-*

thington Whittredge (p. 76), gives an impression of space around the sitter, a space open enough to be shared with others. A dark background, on the other hand, generally shortens the distance between subject and viewer and brings them into more of a one-on-one relationship. Within this relative darkness, a spotlighted head, standing out in high contrast against the background, as in William Merritt Chase and Frank Duveneck's joint *Portrait of Frederick Dielman* (p. 36) or George Bellows's *Portrait of Paul Manship* (p. 43), always retains a bit of drama, or a suggestion of that moment of surprise felt in a sudden encounter. While their strong lighting is nominally even harsh in its forceful objectivity, it nonetheless establishes an immediate impression of encounter with the viewer and helps remove barriers to a sympathetic understanding. A dim light, however, is even more conducive to a sense of intimacy. The heavy chiaroscuro of Eastman Johnson's (probably unfinished) *Portrait of Sanford Robinson Gifford* (p. 75) or Julian Alden Weir's *Self-Portrait* (p. 40), for instance, encroaches on the forms and partly dissolves them, requiring the viewer tenderly to search the dimness for the features of the subject, who is very close, yet somehow elusive. A hush falls upon the relationship, evoking a feeling of spiritual communion. There are few thoughtful people who will not sense the aching poignancy of John White Alexander's shadowy *Self-Portrait* (p.119).

This extreme degree of intimacy achieved through chiaroscuro, as in the case of the frontal poses, is unusual in the earlier part of the past century, but is encountered much more frequently after 1885 and increasingly toward the turn of the century, reflecting the Symbolist tendencies of the period, its interest in psychology and the private, somewhat awesome inner life of the individual. The shadows seem to take one into that mysterious larger life of the spirit, although they are never entirely free of the suggestion of the secret and the shameful. The shadows falling across the face of Robert Brackman in his *Self-Portrait* (p.154) ominously bespeak the potency of the dark forces within. The distinct cast shadow in Daniel Garber's expressive *Self-Portrait* (p. 94) seems to embody this other side.

Fig. 11. DANIEL HUNTINGTON, *Portrait of Thomas Cole*, oil on canvas, 20 x 16 in., National Academy of Design, New York.

Another quality of the Academy's portraits that deserves mention is their gravity. The cheerful, smiling faces stand out as welcome exceptions to the unrelenting weight of most of the countenances. In part, this is merely a characteristic of New York portraiture, which predominates in the Academy's collection and, for some reason, as early as the Federal period, seems to smile less than the portraiture of Boston and Philadelphia. It also reflects, in a collection mainly of male images, the fact that the dominant convention of portraiture in the nineteenth century was a male image of direct expression, conveying common sense and stability, contrasting at times with a woman's charm and freer expression of emotion. It should also be added that self-portraits are generally more serious in mood than most portraits.

Although special circumstances have shaped the Academy's collection, imparting a distinct character and encouraging the use of certain artistic devices and kinds of interpretation, one can nevertheless trace in it the main movements of style over the course of American art history in the nineteenth and twentieth centuries.

The collection stretches back to before the Academy's founding to include a youthful *Self-Portrait* (p. 33) of Samuel F. B. Morse, painted about 1809 and typical of the portraiture of the Federal period in its simplicity, emphasis on the silhouette and closeness of the figure to the picture plane. As Morse went on to become the city's foremost painter of the Romantic period, which stretched between about 1820 and 1850, the chasteness of this early work gave way to the opulence of such powerful pictures as his *Portrait of Dr. Frederick Gore King* (p. 58) commissioned by the Academy to honor its professor of anatomy. Its vivid background color, rich blacks, strong contrasts of light and dark, flowing line, dramatic pose and expressive brushwork combine in a forceful image charged with energy and emotion.

Had the portrait requirement been instituted with the Academy's founding in 1826, the Romantic movement would have been better represented in the collection. By 1839 the masters of this phase of American art were already members and thus not subject to the requirement,

Fig. 12. CHARLES LORING ELLIOTT, *Portrait of Mrs. Thomas Goulding,* oil on canvas, 34¼ x 27 in., National Academy of Design, New York.

although, as leaders of the Academy, some of them voluntarily fulfilled the portrait obligation, as Thomas Seir Cummings did, with his portrait by Charles C. Ingham (p.63), and the Academy later was given, or even purchased, portraits of some of its founders. Ingham's work is generally classed with the contemporaneous Romantic movement, although its compact forms and geometric clarity relate more to the Classical style that preceded the more narrowly defined Romanticism and extended into the Romantic period. Its greater mass and more complicated lighting, however, distinguish it from a work of the earlier Federal period.

Some of the best Romantic portraits, ironically, are the youthful works of the very artists who were later to become the leading exponents of the realistic style of the 1850s and 1860s. Daniel Huntington, whose mature style is closer to the realism of his late *Self-Portrait* (p.35) employed a softer and more atmospheric handling in his early *Portrait of Thomas Cole* (fig. 11), whose distant gaze and sparkling eye suggest the visionary imagination of this master of Romantic landscape painting. Charles Loring Elliott's early portraits in the Academy's collection similarly do not represent the forceful realism of a mature work such as his *Portrait of Mrs. Thomas Goulding* (fig. 12), least of all his expressively brushed image of the young Jasper Francis Cropsey (p.71) who likewise casts his gaze upon distant goals. One might think the portrait's coloring, so close to the tones of Cropsey's favorite autumn landscapes, could be a mischievous joke on Elliott's part, were they not also found in the Academy's other portrait of Cropsey by James H. Cafferty.

Much more representative of the High Victorian period of the 1850s and 1860s is the cool clarity found in the style of Emanuel Leutze's *Portrait of Worthington Whittredge* (p.76), dated 1861. In the portraits of this period a lighter background is preferred, both for the impression of lucid objectivity it gives, as well as for the greater sense of mass it imparts to the figure by opening up space around it. Bulky, sometimes dryly literal, the portraits can achieve considerable force of characterization, as in this somewhat stormy image of Whittredge with

Fig. 13. J. ALDEN WEIR, *Portrait of Olin Levi Warner*, 1888, oil on canvas, 21 x 17 in., National Academy of Design, New York.

his arms crossed. On the whole, however, they are less dramatic than the portraits of either the Romantic period that preceded them or the cosmopolitan era that follows. High Victorian portraits, like landscapes and still lifes of the 1850s and 1860s, reveal an interest in an objective truth.

The 1870s were a decade of fundamental change in American art, brought about by the provocative new styles and professional attitudes introduced by a steady stream of young artists returning from periods of study in Europe. Some members of the Academy apparently felt their standing and patronage threatened when these beginners dominated the annual exhibitions, especially in 1877 with the success of the show piece, *Sheepshearing in the Bavarian Highlands* (location unknown) by Walter Shirlaw, who probably completed his dramatic *Self-Portrait* (p.82) around this time. Shirlaw withdrew from the Academy that year, however, to join the leaders of his generation in forming the secessionist group, the Society of American Artists. These artists protested the Academy's new regulations governing the annual exhibition, which they considered unfair to those who were not members. The exhibitions of the new group proclaimed the basic difference in outlook that separated them from the Academy and its patrons. While established American artists still attempted to create a persuasive illusion of reality on the canvas, suppressing any evidence of the artist's hand that would betray the deception, the younger artists prized technique for its own sake, even at the expense of illusion. They were confident of their abilities and proud to demonstrate how beautifully they could handle paint. The Society's early exhibitions were filled with oil sketches, student figure studies and boldly experimental, unfinished paintings, all celebrating the artistic process which was of consuming interest to these recent students. It is characteristic of the division between the two groups that in 1878 J. Alden Weir exhibited a finished portrait of his father at the National Academy and an oil sketch for the painting at the exhibition of the Society of American Artists.

Fig. 14. J. ALDEN WEIR, *Portrait of Albert P. Ryder*, ca. 1902, oil on canvas, 24 x 20 in., National Academy of Design, New York.

While the rivalry soon subsided and before long the exhibitions of the groups began to look alike, it was almost a decade before the leaders of the Society of American Artists began to be welcomed into the Academy as associates. The portraits that were produced as a result of these elections are among the jewels of the collection; they dazzle with the freedom and grace this sophisticated generation could command. Even in the confining twenty-one by seventeen-inch format stipulated for Diploma Portraits between 1882 and 1898, their inventiveness brings the element of surprise to what could have been just a row of heads. William Merritt Chase's full-face *Portrait of Robert Blum* (p.79) represents the kind of startling innovation that only the completely cosmopolitan artist, secure in his taste and eager for expression, could have achieved. Such pictures are also beautifully painted, with a new consciousness of brushwork and color. The series of portraits by J. Alden Weir (p.40, p.129, and fig. 13 and fig. 14) are not only spirited, telling likenesses, but also show pieces of technique to delight the eye of the connoisseur. This group of artists clearly saw the opportunity to paint for an audience of artists in the spirit of bohemian exchange. George de Forest Brush submitted his *Self-Portrait* (p.104) unfinished, arrested in the course of the creative process which would have been familiar and interesting to his comrades.

Their extensive training and exposure to both art traditions and numerous current idioms prepared this generation to paint a wide variety of subjects in a range of styles, a diversity that today's scholarship is only beginning to sort out. They were a generation that revolutionized the use of light and color in American art. But paradoxically, very little of this change is reflected in the main portrait tradition of the period, or, for that matter, in the Academy's collection. Even the masters of American Impressionist landscape—John Singer Sargent, William Merritt Chase and Edmund Tarbell, among others—painted portraits within the universally accepted convention of an artificially lighted, largely dark interior. During a period of profound change in American art, the unvarying Caravaggist format of a strongly illuminated

Fig. 15. DANIEL HUNTINGTON, *Portrait of Asher B. Durand*, 1857, reworked 1887, oil on canvas, 56⅛ x 44 in., The Century Association, New York.

figure against a dark field can be found in paintings stretching over a quarter of a century in the Academy's collection.

The discerning eye, however, can detect an evolution of style within this main approach. The original point of departure is seen in Walter Shirlaw's *Self-Portrait* and the *Portrait of Frederick Dielman* (p.36) by Frank Duveneck and William Merritt Chase. During their student years in Munich, Shirlaw, Duveneck and Chase had been nicknamed the inseparable Holy Trinity of the colony of Americans. Their portraits employ the harsh and dramatic lighting they had learned there. It is an excessively strong light that strikes into the deep darkness with the force of a spotlight. Over the next thirty years to about 1910, one sees this artificial lighting soften and move closer to the natural lighting that already streamed through the windows of American genre painting in the 1880s. It becomes a cooler, more diffused side lighting, filtering through an interior, in the portraits of around the turn of the century. Louis Betts's *Self-Portrait* of 1907 (p.139) and Edith Prellwitz's *Self-Portrait* of 1909 (p.110) exemplify such portraits, with their slight *sfumato* and sense of shadowy interiors reminiscent of Velazquez. They convey a mood of sweet nostalgia and delicate gentility.

In both their softer handling and their more spiritual overtones, these self-portraits reveal the effect of the brief but profound dominance of the Aesthetic movement around the turn of the century. Strongly influenced by the example of James Abbott McNeill Whistler, this movement represented an anti-realist current that gave primacy to formal concerns. The conflict between illusionism and visible technique that raged in American art in the 1870s had climaxed by the turn of the century, and the illusion of three dimensions was sacrificed entirely to the graceful decoration of a two-dimensional surface. The later president of the National Academy, John White Alexander, exemplifies this subordination in the playing-card-thin, profile image in his *Portrait of Edwin Austin Abbey* of around 1901 (p.121). Emil Carlsen's late portrait of his son, Dines (p.42), likewise suppresses modeling and emphasizes

Fig. 16. VINCENT COLYER, *Portrait of Sanford Gifford*, oil on canvas, 30 x 25 in., National Academy of Design, New York.

the surface through a unifying tone. This taste for extreme refinement and aesthetic balance was in turn rejected by the rebels of 1908, the so-called Ashcan School, who returned to the dramatic artificial lighting of the Munich movement in paintings that affirm both the solidity of the illusion and the vigorous energy of the artistic process.

The stability of the portrait tradition during the late nineteenth century and early twentieth century, which hints only obliquely at the profound changes in other genres during that period, completely disintegrated between about 1915 and 1925. Whether the rejection of portrait conventions reflects transformations in society brought about by the Great War or causes within the development of art itself, the change was absolute. After 1925 it was virtually impossible for an artist to paint a formal portrait with the grand-manner trappings that were taken for granted before the war. Not only columns and drapery but darkened interiors are gone forever. The subject is no longer isolated in a universal darkness, reverently and majestically: he is now an ordinary man working in his office. His wife, in an afternoon dress, relaxes at home or in her garden. The bourgeois reality of their everyday environment is accepted without question.

This matter-of-fact presentation and use of setting to characterize the sitter are also seen in the Academy's artist portraits beginning about 1910 (p.41). These works offer a variety of setting and treatment that seems kaleidoscopic after the genteel uniformity of the earlier images. Their special fascination is that they all so completely celebrate the physical and psychological world of the artist.

Of course, there is ample precedent for a studio setting in artists' portraits, especially self-portraits. Descending from the self-portraits of the Baroque period are, within the American tradition, such paintings as Daniel Huntington's *Portrait of Asher B. Durand* (fig. 15), depicting the artist at work at his easel within an extensive landscape, and William J. Whittemore's

Portrait of Charles C. Curran (p.103) showing the subject as an art student painting from a cast. Both are straightforward, naturalistic settings. However, there are also nineteenth-century portraits portraying the artist's world in a way that foreshadows a distinctly different twentieth-century approach. A treatment similar to Huntington's *Durand,* within a more modest format, is Vincent Colyer's *Portrait of Sanford Robinson Gifford* (fig. 16); because of its cropping, it is ambiguous whether the artist is set against a typical landscape motif or one of his own paintings. This uncertainty adds great romance to the portrayal since the poetic sunset not only specifies an environment but seems to characterize the gentle spirit of the artist. In a similar way, the *Portrait of Frederick Ballard Williams* by Elliott Daingerfield includes the excited landscape found in Williams's own paintings and so suggests the sitter's mystical feelings (p.110). Is Williams likewise sitting in front of one of his paintings, or is he dreaming such an image? By making the subject's own art the background for his portrait, the portraitist suggests a projection of the subject's spiritual state. This is the dominant characteristic of the Academy's self-portraits after about 1925.

Depictions of the artist's own work, with its resonant associations, appear in other late nineteenth-century self-portraits painted in a distinctive personal style. J. Alden Weir was identified with still lifes of exotic vessels and flowers in dark interiors at the time he painted his *Self-Portrait* in 1886 (p.40); the porcelain vase in his characteristic style in its background is therefore an emblem of his career as well as a suggestion that such tender images also bespeak his spirit. The point of view expressed in his subject matter and style is felt to constitute his spiritual identity as an artist. This equation, developed tentatively, or in some cases perhaps even accidentally, in nineteenth-century portraits, is a recurring theme in the present century. It is developed at length, for instance, within the similar self-portraits by N. C. Wyeth (p.150), Peter Hurd (p.150) and Andrew Wyeth (p.46), three members of the same tradition and family. Each has chosen for a background a characteristic landscape that could well be a painting before which the artist stands, but here they are actual landscapes in which the artists work, for they are wearing hats or are dressed for out-of-doors. Each stands within one of his paintings—a subtle, but significant, distinction. The artists are also *in character* in their settings, N. C. Wyeth good-humoredly smiling before one of his gently rolling, make-believe landscapes which might illustrate a child's adventure tale; Peter Hurd garbed as a Clint Eastwood type, the Western man of few words; Andrew Wyeth driven before the wind within the overcast, haunted landscape familiar in his art and here echoed in his shadowed face and troubled expression. Likewise, Ivan Le Lorraine Albright (p.153) and Walter Stuempfig (p.151) describe themselves with the language of Surrealist decay and existential isolation that dominates the world vision expressed in all of their art.

Artists of all periods, of course, have expressed their world view in their self-portraits, sometimes in ways that were all the more powerful because of the restricted range of formal expression available to the artist. The twentieth-century artist, in contrast, makes full use of nearly complete freedom, in self-portraits that contrast strongly one with another. In fact, this extremely personal self-interpretation is hard for the modern representational artist to avoid. Because there is no consensus concerning what constitutes a realistic portrayal in the twentieth century, the modern artist must in every case interpret reality in terms of his personal vision. His spirit and style thus approach unity, much more completely and explicitly than in earlier periods of art. The self-portraits by the Academy's twentieth-century artists are fundamentally different from earlier ones in the collection in the degree to which they are able to use this precondition to explore the spiritual identity of the artist. The distinct style and forms that he has developed to express his point of view on the world are now turned upon his own image. We confront the excited spirit (p. 45) that dreams John Costigan's epiphanous landscapes. We feel the isolation of the fragmented, dusky world of Edwin Dickinson (p. 47). There is a confessional frankness to all of these paintings which makes James Wyeth's nakedness in his *Self-Portrait* (p.160) less than shocking. The modern portrait moves from likeness to interpretation. It recognizes as the primary reality that we live more in our feelings than in our houses.

The Academy's collection is not only a record of its membership; it traces the place of the artist in American society, while demonstrating how the artist has come, in the end, to define his social setting through his private point of view. These images trace the ascendancy of style and expression over imitation in American art. They document the steadily increasing subjectivity and emotionality of modern life.

Because these very trends have compromised the traditional role of portraiture and reduced its patronage, many art lovers may be unaccustomed to looking at portraits and may feel ill-equipped to understand and enjoy the subtleties and range of expression they offer. Precisely because the limitations of their format focus our attention on the most basic qualities, the intimate portraits in the Academy's collection afford the modern connoisseur a particularly revealing introduction to this fascinating art form. Their exceptional beauty and power will reward his close attention.

Michael Quick
Curator of American Art
Los Angeles County Museum of Art

Catalogue

Dimensions are given in inches,
with height preceding width.

Key to Abbreviations:
NA   National Academician
ANA Associate of the National Academy
PNA President of the National Academy
HM   Honorary Member

Samuel Finley Breese Morse (1791-1872) N.A. 1826 (Founder),
   P.N.A. 1826-1845, 1861-1862
PORTRAIT OF WILLIAM CULLEN BRYANT (1794-1878) H.M. 1833
Oil on canvas
30 x 20⅞
Unsigned
Commissioned by the Council of the National Academy of
   Design, 1828-29

Eastman Johnson (1824-1906) A.N.A. 1859, N.A. 1860
SELF-PORTRAIT
Oil on canvas
30⅜ x 25
Unsigned

Daniel Huntington (1816-1906) A.N.A. 1839, N.A. 1840,
   P.N.A. 1862-1870/1877-1890
SELF-PORTRAIT
Oil on canvas
36⅛ x 28¹³/₁₆
Signed lower left: D. Huntington / 1891

Frank Duveneck (1848-1919) A.N.A. 1905, N.A. 1906
William Merritt Chase (1849-1916) A.N.A. 1887 N.A. 1890
PORTRAIT OF FREDERICK DIELMAN (1847-1935) A.N.A.
   1881, N.A. 1883, P.N.A. 1899-1909
Oil on canvas
30 x 24⅞
Unsigned
Dated upper right: 1882

Thomas Eakins (1844-1919) A.N.A. 1902, N.A. 1902
SELF-PORTRAIT
Oil on canvas remounted on masonite
30 x 25
Unsigned

Cecilia Beaux (1855-1942) A.N.A. 1894, N.A. 1902
SELF-PORTRAIT
Oil on canvas remounted on masonite
24⅞ x 20
Signed upper right: Cecilia Beaux 1894

John Singer Sargent (1856-1925) A.N.A. 1891, N.A. 1897
SELF-PORTRAIT
Oil on canvas
21 x 17
Signed upper left: John S Sargent
Dated upper right: 1892

Julian Alden Weir (1852-1919) A.N.A. 1885, N.A. 1886,
  P.N.A. 1915-1917
SELF-PORTRAIT
Oil on canvas
21¼ x 17¼
Signed upper left: J. Alden Weir / 1886

Lawton S. Parker (1868-1954) A.N.A. 1916
PORTRAIT OF FREDERICK CARL FRIESEKE (1874-1939)
   A.N.A. 1912, N.A. 1914
Oil on canvas
25⅝ x 32
Unsigned

Emil Carlsen (1853-1932) A.N.A. 1904, N.A. 1901
PORTRAIT OF DINES CARLSEN (1901-1966) A.N.A. 1922, N.A. 1941
Oil on canvas
30 x 25
Unsigned

George Wesley Bellows (1882-1925) A.N.A. 1909, N.A.
  1913
PORTRAIT OF PAUL H. MANSHIP (1886-1966) A.N.A. 1914, N.A. 1916
Oil on masonite panel
30 x 25
Signed lower right: Geo Bellows-

William Glackens (1870-1938) A.N.A. 1906, N.A. 1933
PORTRAIT OF ERNEST LAWSON (1873-1939) A.N.A. 1908, N.A. 1917
Oil on canvas remounted on masonite
30¹/₁₆ x 25¹/₁₆
Signed lower center: W Glackens

John E. Costigan (1888-1972) A.N.A. 1924, N.A. 1928
SELF-PORTRAIT
Oil on canvas
30⅛ x 25⅛
Signed lower right: Self Portrait / By John E. Costigan / 1924

Andrew Newell Wyeth (1917-   ) A.N.A. 1944, N.A. 1945
SELF-PORTRAIT
Oil and tempera on gesso panel
25 x 30⅛
Signed lower left: Andrew Wyeth (script) / Andrew Wyeth
  (printed)

Edwin Walter Dickinson (1891-1978) A.N.A. 1948, N.A.
  1950
SELF-PORTRAIT
Oil on canvas
23 x 20⅛
Signed upper left: 1949 / E W Dickinson ANA

George Tooker (1920-   ) A.N.A. 1968, N.A. 1970
SELF-PORTRAIT
Tempera on gesso panel
24 x 19½
Signed lower right: Tooker 1969

Founders and Friends

THE PORTRAITS BY THE FOUNDING MEMBERS OF THE NATIONAL ACADEMY OF DESIGN WERE ALL produced by artists who attained prominence in New York City during an age of increasing cultural optimism. The National Academy of Design, established in 1826 by and for artists, was a physical expression of the artists' faith in the future of America's role in the development of art. Most of the portraits in this section of the exhibition were added to the Academy's collection shortly after their execution. And most of them were painted specifically for the Academy, either to fulfill the obligation of each member to present a portrait of himself upon his election to the Academy or, as in the case of Samuel F. B. Morse's *Portrait of Dr. Frederick Gore King,* upon commission from the Academy. In any event, the sitters and the artists knew one another, sometimes very well, and because of their mutual association with the National Academy of Design during its initial years, they shared a set of common goals and hopes. From this type of personal relationship then, there were produced a remarkable group of portraits that commemorate not only the skill of the artists—Morse, Durand, Ingham and Inman—but the era in which the pictures were produced.

Samuel Finley Breese Morse (1791–1872) was the guiding force behind the formation of the National Academy of Design, as well as its first president. He was born in Charlestown, Massachusetts, the son of a minister and the nephew of Dr. Samuel Finley, the first president of the College of New Jersey (now Princeton University). Morse attended Yale College and developed an interest in art there. His *Self-Portrait* in miniature, in the present exhibition, is thought to have been painted about 1809, prior to Morse's graduation from college in 1810. The painting is a delicate yet lively rendition of the youth, and it is interesting to note that although Morse had not yet undertaken formal art training, he conceived of himself as an artist, for the portrait shows him holding a painter's palette in his left hand. According to William Dunlap in his *History of the Rise and Progress of the Arts of Design in the United States* (1834), Morse's father was not pleased with his son's inclination towards a career in art, but "finding the passion for painting incorrigible in his son, [he] determined to indulge him in his wishes to take advantage of the means of studying in Europe."

Morse's youthful efforts earned him encouragement from Washington Allston and Gilbert Stuart, and it was arranged for Morse to accompany Allston and his new wife to London so that he could be trained at the Royal Academy under the tutelage of Benjamin West and study paintings of the Old Masters. Morse arrived in England in 1811 and remained there until August 1815. During this time Morse became fast friends with the young Charles Robert Leslie (1794–1854) and took rooms with him in Fitzroy Square. Leslie, although born in England (of American parents), had spent his childhood in Phildelphia and was trained in art only insofar as he was apprenticed to a local bookseller. Like Morse, Leslie desired a proper education in art, so he returned to England in 1811.

Included in the present exhibition is a portrait executed by Leslie of Washington Allston. The sketch, presumably painted while Leslie, Allston and Morse were living in London, shows a youthful optimistic Allston, prior to the early death of his wife and the cultural depletion he felt upon his return to Boston with ambitions as a history painter. Although Leslie returned to America only briefly to work as a professor of drawing at West Point (1833–1834), he remained a lifelong friend and colleague of Morse during his career as a respected artist in London. Leslie and Allston were both elected honorary members of the National Academy of Design in 1827.

During Morse's stay in London, 1811 to 1815, he developed an interest in historical painting. In 1813 his canvas *The Dying Hercules* was exhibited and well-received at the Royal Academy. It was during this London period that Morse executed his portrait of Benjamin West. Already an old man, West is portrayed with reverence and admiration by the artist in his twenties. Dressed in a dark robe and a fine white cravat, West is seated before a large stone column, a grand-manner convention that accentuates the weighty significance of this American president of the British Royal Academy. The upright solidity of the column is paralleled in West's position on the canvas. Morse offers a frontal, almost iconic, rendition of his teacher. Although West's expression is stern, his eyes reveal the kindness and generosity that this master had shown to generations of students. Interestingly, Morse's more accessible advisor in London, Washington Allston, also painted a portrait of the elder West at about this time. This work, in the collection of the Boston Athenaeum, gives a much frailer and less heroic impression of the artist.

When Morse returned to America, he settled in Boston, but he quickly realized that the work available for a history painter was limited, so he established himself as an itinerant portrait painter, traveling first to New Hampshire and then to Charleston, South Carolina. Morse wintered there for a number of years and earned popular—hence, financial—success. According to Dunlap, he completed four portraits a week over a three-month period. By 1823 Morse had returned north and settled in the New York City area with his family. In 1824 he received the commission to paint a full-length portrait of General Lafayette for the New York City Hall Portrait Gallery, thus establishing for himself a significant reputation as a historical portrait painter.

It was in late 1825 that Morse's cultural idealism prompted him to pour his administrative energies into the organization of an art society composed of and for artists. The American Academy of the Fine Arts, already in existence in New York for more than twenty years, had become an inert association of Federalist businessmen. It had ceased to be a vital outlet for the advancement of American artists and their art. Under the direction of the established artist John Trumbull since 1816, the American Academy of the Fine Arts had frustrated young artists in New York City by its lack of facilities for the study and exhibition of new art. In response to the needs of his colleagues, Morse, then an "elder" statesman of thirty-four, helped form the New York Drawing Association in late 1825. In January 1826 this group of artists, who had banded together to advance their artistic education, became the founding members of the National Academy of Design. Samuel F. B. Morse was elected its first president, a position he held for nearly twenty years.

During the formative years of the Academy. Morse painted the portraits of two of his friends and supporters, William Cullen Bryant (1794–1878) and Dr. Frederick Gore King (1801–1829). Although neither man was an artist by profession, each was closely affiliated with the organization of this American artistic society.

Frederick Gore King was one of the first men appointed as an instructor in the art school established by the Academy. He was elected in 1826 to teach anatomy. It is recorded in Thomas Seir Cummings's *Historic Annals of the National Academy of Design* (1865) that "Dr. King was requested to sit for his portrait. It was painted by Mr. Morse, and is an excellent likeness. . . ." Morse painted a handsome portrait of the doctor, depicting him seated at a table in front of a large book, no doubt one of his weighty anatomical texts. The red damask drapery behind the sitter creates a dignified backdrop for this man of science.

William Cullen Bryant—lawyer, poet and editor—was only thirty when the National Academy was organized. Leaving a law practice in Massachusetts, Bryant arrived in New York City in 1825 and shortly thereafter was named assistant editor of the *Evening Post,* New York's leading newspaper. He succeeded the editor, William Coleman, upon his death in 1829 and ran the publication for many years.

Bryant was also a poet—in 1821 he had published his first volume of poetry, which contained his famed *Thanatopsis*—and he remained devoted to literary pursuits throughout his journalistic career. Bryant was an ardent supporter of the goals of the National Academy, and much of the controversy regarding its inception and early art exhibitions was aired in the pages of the *Evening Post.* In 1827 he was asked to become an instructor in the Academy's school of art, where he lectured for many semesters on mythology and antiquities. Bryant was then elected Honorary Member of the Academy in 1833, and he remained an effective spokesman for the organization. When the Academy established its first permanent home on 23rd Street, Bryant was asked to deliver an address at the opening ceremonies. He was again summoned by the Academy to eulogize Morse upon his death.

Morse's portrait of Bryant romantically evokes the vitality and energy of this rising Knickerbocker man of letters. His head, with its fine nose and curling hair, is sensitively positioned in front of a soft blue evening sky. A hint of pink clouds can be seen above a classical ruin. This glimpse of the American romantic landscape is an appropriate stage for a portrait of the poet who admired Wordsworth and revered nature.

Born in Springfield, New Jersey, in 1796, Asher B. Durand began his artistic career in 1812 with a five-year apprenticeship to Peter Maverick, a noted engraver based in Newark, New Jersey. Immediately after his apprenticeship ended in 1817, Durand became a partner in Maverick's engraving company and was installed as the manager of the New York City office of the firm.

By 1820 the beauty and technical mastery of Durand's engravings had earned him a reputation that won him Colonel John Trumbull's commission to engrave his *Declaration of Independence.* The ensuing jealousy between the founding partner and his rising protégé is thought to have led to the dissolution of the partnership, whereupon Durand moved on to form the engraving firm A. B. & C. Durand, Wright & Co. with his brother Cyrus (1787–1868) and Charles Cushing Wright (1796–1854). (The firm was especially involved in the engraving of bank notes.) Succeeding this partnership was yet another engraving firm, Durand, Perkins & Co., which lasted until 1831.

During the 1820s, the decade in which Durand helped establish the National Academy of Design, he worked almost exclusively as an engraver, executing works after paintings by John Vanderlyn, Thomas Sully and Charles C. Ingham. In his *Historic Annals of the National Academy of Design,* Thomas Seir Cummings lists the names of the founding artists, with the designation "Engraver" after Durand's name.

As a painter, Durand is noted for his landscapes, but his earliest work in oil was primarily portraiture. Between 1833 and 1837 Durand executed a number of three-quarter-length portraits, including his likeness of Thomas Cole, painted in 1837 (Berkshire Museum, Pittsfield, Mass.), and a rendition of his patron, Luman Reed, executed in 1835 (New York City Chamber of Commerce).

Durand's *Self-Portrait* in the present exhibition is thought to have been painted during this period, perhaps in 1835. It is a simple rendering, composed within an oval format, but the portrait nonetheless captures the artist's sincerity and intensity of purpose. Painted in dark tones, the figure suggests the strength of character in Durand that was later proven by his election as president and his capable administration of the National Academy of Design from 1845 to 1861.

In 1837 and 1838 Durand's inclination towards landscape painting emerges and portraiture recedes in importance for him. However, it was about this time that he painted a charming, lively portrait of the young Louis P. Clover, Jr. Born only in 1819, by which time Durand had become established as an engraver in New York, Clover was ultimately to study this art under Durand. Interestingly, Clover's father was the owner and proprietor of a mirror and picture frame shop on Fulton Street in lower Manhattan. Opened in 1816, this store became a gathering place for artists seeking supplies and advice. Louis P. Clover, Sr. was the publisher of the William J. Bennett aquatints—views of American cities that represented the finest of American printmaking of the time (1830s). It is quite understandable that Clover would have directed his son to study with a New York artist of such distinction as Asher B. Durand. After a three-year apprenticeship with Durand, the young Clover turned to painting and followed it as a profession in New York and Baltimore during the 1840s. He was elected an associate member of the National Academy of Design in 1840—at which time this portrait of him might have been painted—but he was turned toward the ministry of the Episcopal Church and became ordained in 1850. Subsequently Clover rectored churches in Virginia and Illinois, although he did continue to paint.

Charles Cromwell Ingham (1796–1865) was born in Dublin, Ireland, where he studied painting at the Dublin Society's School, as well as under William Cumming. He exhibited a number of works in Dublin before he emigrated to America in 1816. He established himself as a portraitist and subject painter in New York City and gained a reputation for highly finished portraits of society women. His detailed and polished canvases often provided flattering, idealized renditions of his subjects, so he was able to carry on a successful business of portrait commissions. At times the glazes and sprightly colors of his pictures conveyed such a sense of heightened realism that they stood out at exhibitions and received much popular and critical attention. It is interesting to note, however, that Ingham's *Self-Portrait,* in the collection of the National Academy of Design, utilizes a brushwork style that is freer than most of his commissioned work. The composition of the painting is unfinished, suggesting the sitter's intense personality rather than delineating his countenance. The example of Ingham's work in the present exhibition is more characteristic of the artist's style, with fine brushstrokes applied to the image of his fellow Academician Thomas Seir Cummings (1804–1894.)

Cummings, like Ingham, was one of the original members of the New York Drawing Association, the organization of artists that preceded the National Academy of Design by several months. Cummings, in fact, was one of the young art students at the American Academy of Fine Arts' gallery of plaster casts when the incident described by William Dunlap in his book occurred. It involved a dispute between the keeper of the plasters and students who complained that they were denied access to the Academy to sketch the collection of casts, although they had arrived during the posted hours of admittance: 6 A.M. to 9 A.M. The complaints of the young, enthusiastic artists about the difficult rules were overheard by the president of the American Academy, John Trumbull, who met the youths at the door and told them that "beggars are not to be choosers." Dunlap states that this incident had a catalyzing effect on the younger generation's decision to post a petition that resolved for "the formation of a Society for Improvement in Drawing."

Cummings was involved with the establishment of the National Academy of Design and its early administration perhaps even more than Ingham. Cummings—born in England, but brought to America at a very early age—was a miniature portrait painter by profession. He had early training in the drawing academy of John R. Smith, but later he became a pupil of Henry Inman (who was only three years his senior). After studying with Inman for several years, Cummings went into partnership with him, a relationship that lasted until 1828. Cummings and Inman would often paint the same sitter, Cummings executing a miniature rendition and Inman doing the portrait-in-large. From 1826 until 1864 Cummings was the treasurer of the National Academy of Design. Prior to his death in 1894 he was the last surviving founder.

The present portrait, painted by Ingham in 1844, shows a handsome man of forty conveying a clear-eyed sense of purpose. Ingham depicts Cummings in formal dress, with a lustrous black velvet robe draped over his left shoulder. Although executed eighteen years after the founding of the Academy, the work was probably painted in response to the organization's request for portraits of all elected associates.

Henry Inman (1801–1846) was born in Utica, New York, but he moved with his parents to New York City at the age of eleven. His desire to pursue a career in art was furthered by the initiation in 1814 of a seven-year apprenticeship to John Wesley Jarvis (1780–1840), one of New York's leading portraitists. Jarvis received a number of important portrait commissions from the New York City Hall to commemorate the heroes of the War of 1812, and Inman often worked with him on such commissions, aiding in the execution of the backgrounds and costumes. Inman also worked on miniature portraits during this partnership. An 1822 letter published in Henry T. Tuckerman's *Book of the Artists* (1867) recalls "Jarvis and his pupil coming to Boston. Henry's beautiful little watercolor likenesses were a source of some profit."

By 1823 Inman had established himself as a painter of portraits-in-large, cabinet portraits and miniatures. He accepted Thomas Seir Cummings as a pupil, and by 1827 (by which time Cummings had become his partner) Inman agreed with Cummings that he should give up painting "in little." Conversely, Cummings agreed to pursue a career of miniature portraiture, leaving behind work "in oil." In the present exhibition, Inman's miniature work is represented by his portrait-in-small of Charles Cushing Wright (1796–1854).

Wright, also a founding member of the National Academy of Design, was an engraver and medallist. While a partner with Asher B. Durand in 1826–27, Wright executed portrait medallions of such distinguished Americans as George Washington, Thomas Paine and DeWitt Clinton. Inman's rendition of Wright, probably executed in the mid-1820s, is a watercolor miniature in oval form. Darker and, in a sense, more masculine than Morse's miniature in this exhibition, Inman's portrait focuses on Wright's handsome features and self-assured personality. Wright's olive skin, glinting eyes and wavy, almost unruly, hair transmit to the viewer an image of a man of a confident age.

Kathleen M. Burnside

Benjamin West

Born in Springfield, Pa., of Quaker heritage, the son of innkeeper who emigrated from England at early age. First instruction from a minor English portrait painter, William Williams, whom he met in Philadelphia. Studied assiduously on his own and, with financial support of friends, traveled to Italy in 1760, perhaps the first American to study there. Visited France and England; so warmly welcomed that he remained in England for life. Immediately assumed an unrivaled position of leadership in London as a history painter. His studio became very popular, the first American art school for aspiring Colonial painters, including Washington Allston, Charles Willson Peale, Gilbert Stuart, John Trumbull, Rembrandt Peale, Thomas Sully and Samuel F.B. Morse. 1768, King George III made him charter member of Royal Academy of Arts. 1772, appointed "Historical Painter" to the King, a position he held until 1811. Beginning 1771, engravings after West's historical pictures, such as *The Death of General Wolfe,* were widely distributed, providing him fame and a generous income shared with his publisher. 1780, commissioned by George III to design a major biblical series, the *History of Revealed Religion,* for a small private chapel to be built at Windsor Castle. To West's great disillusionment, project later cancelled. Patronage of George III rendered useless by 1810, as monarch suffered increasing mental disorder. 1792, appointed to succeed Sir Joshua Reynolds as second president of Royal Academy, a position he held, excepting one year, until his death. West continued to guide young American artists, securing their professions as portraitists. British patronage of his historical painting continued until his death in 1820 on March 10, when he was mourned as one of England's great artists and accorded full honors at his burial in St. Paul's Cathedral, London, 1820.

DA

William Cullen Bryant

Born in Cumington, a small town in western Mass., a physician's son. Early training in local district schools and reading in well-stocked family library. 1806, left home to learn Latin from Rev. Thomas Snell of North Brookfield; 1807, learned Greek from Rev. Moses Hallock. Attended Williams College for one year, 1810-11, then transferred to Yale. Left Yale for lack of tuition, decided to study law. 1808, Dr. Bryant published son's first satirical piece entitled "The Embargo," an assault on President Jefferson. Essay received much attention, later republished. Admitted to the bar in 1815, although he disliked the profession. Continued to write poetry, but without publishing or circulating writings. 1821, married Frances Fairchild and settled as a lawyer in Great Barrington, Mass. His poem "Thanatopsis" published in *North American Review,* 1817, his father having found several manuscripts in his son's desk and sent them all for publication. Bryant's talents immediately recognized in American literary world. Invited to read the Phi Beta Kappa poem at Harvard's commencement, 1821. 1824-25, period of great productivity when he emerged as America's great poet. Left family in 1825 to go to New York to assume co-editorship of the monthly *New York Review and Atheneum Magazine.* 1826, undertook editorial work on the *Evening Post.* 1828-1838, appointed Professor of Mythology and American History at National Academy of Design, where Bryant elected Honorary Member in 1833. Academy commissioned Samuel F. B. Morse to paint portrait of Bryant in 1828. 1832, publication of collection of his poems hailed as best volume of American verse ever assembled. *Post* editor died and Bryant succeeded him, holding editorial position for almost half a century, though production of written verse reduced to very little. Newspaper prospered in 1840's, becoming a leading Democratic force in nation. Bryant traveled to the South, to Europe and to Cuba, anonymously publishing his travel correspondence in paper. 1866, printed Lincoln's Cooper Union speech. To escape depression resulting from wife's death in 1865 began translating the whole of Homer, project of 1866-1871. Wrote of morality in poem, "The Flood of Years," followed by his autobiographical meditation, "A Lifetime," the last of his works, 1876. After delivering an oration at a statue unveiling in Central Park, Bryant fell, sustained a concussion and died soon afterwards in June, 1878. Had been everywhere regarded as the first citizen of New York, generously supporting its social and charitable causes. (*See color, page 33.*)

DA

Dr. Frederick Gore King

Born in England, the youngest son of Rufus King, emigrated to U.S. with family when very young. Excelled at Cambridge College, Mass. before traveling to New York to begin medical studies under a Dr. Post. Early interest in anatomy, later the focus of his career as professor. Graduation thesis on neurology published in part in the *New York Medical and Physical Journal.* After earning medical doctorate, married Dr. Post's daughter and spent one year at New York Hospital as house surgeon. Appointed demonstrator of anatomy at New York's College of Physicians and Surgeons where his father-in-law was professor. 1825, compiled and published *Catalogue of the Anatomical Museum in the College of Physicians and Surgeons, New-York.* Some time after 1825, succeeded Dr. John Wakefield Francis as professor of anatomy at American Academy of the Fine Arts, New York. When dissident artists from Academy formed the "Society for Improvement in Drawing," King offered to lecture on anatomy. In 1826, these artists formed National Academy of Design, electing King professor of anatomy. Also gave a series of lectures on various medical subjects at New York's Atheneum. Traveled abroad several times to care for ailing family members, visiting Italy to study the arts and sciences and Paris to continue anatomical research and collect French medical books. Fall, 1828, returned to New York to resume medical practice. Contracted fever from which he never recovered. Died in New York on Apr. 24 at age twenty-eight.

DA

Samuel Finley Breese Morse (1791-1872) N.A. 1826 (Founder),
  P.N.A. 1826-1845, 1861-1862
PORTRAIT OF BENJAMIN WEST (1738-1820)
Oil on canvas
30 x 25
Unsigned
Purchased by the National Academy of Design, 1944

Samuel F.B. Morse

Born in Charlestown, Mass., the eldest of three sons of Reverend Jedidah Morse, one of the great nineteenth-century Calvinist preachers, and Elizabeth Ann Breese, granddaughter of Dr. Samuel Finley, Calvinist president of College of New Jersey (later Princeton University). Attended Phillips Academy in Andover, Mass., and Yale University, graduating from there in 1810. Determined to become an artist, at first against his family's wishes. Studied academic techniques with Washington Allston in Boston before traveling with him to London in 1811. Enrolled at Royal Academy schools where he studied in life and antique drawing classes under guidance of Allston and Benjamin West. 1815, his parents unable to support him any longer, Morse returned to America convinced of supremacy of history painting as vehicle of intellectual expression. 1816, to support himself, traveled to New Hampshire as itinerant portrait painter. 1818, married Lucretia Pickering Walker and soon afterwards traveled to Charleston, S.C. seeking portrait commissions. Painted President James Monroe in Washington. 1821, Morse a founder of South Carolina Academy of the Fine Arts. Exhibited painting, *House of Representatives,* in New Haven, without much success, 1823 and in New York at American Academy of the Fine Arts in 1825. Won commission from City of New York to paint the Marquis de Lafayette in 1825, an honor that advanced his career and guaranteed future portrait assignments, Governor DeWitt Clinton and William Cullen Bryant among them. Same year, Morse joined New York Drawing Association, precursor to National Academy of Design, which Morse and other artists founded in 1826. Morse served as Academy's first president, 1826-1845, and assumed the role again after the death of Durand, 1860-61. Lucretia Morse died in 1829 and Morse sailed that year to Europe, financing his trip with prearranged commissions from American patrons. Traveled to England, France, Italy, and Switzerland. 1831-32, in Paris to paint large canvas depicting the Louvre's Salle Carré. When picture indifferently received in New York exhibition, 1833, attention shifted from career in art to invention of electromagnetic telegraph. 1833, first demonstrated his invention; 1838, developed Morse Code; 1844, first long-distance telegraphic communication. A gifted lecturer on art theory in America, Morse was appointed Professor of Literature of Arts of Design at University of City of New York (later New York University). Devoted much time to National Academy from 1835 to 1845, expanding its schools, collections, exhibitions, and influence. 1837, very disappointed to have lost bid to paint one of the murals of the U.S. Capitol rotunda. Went to Europe a third time in 1838 to get patent for telegraph. 1839, met Louis Daguerre in France and introduced the daguerreotype to America. Politically controversial, ran for mayor of New York 1836 and 1841. In old age, a generous philanthropist to National Academy. Following his death in New York City, April 2, Congress held memorial services and William Cullen Bryant delivered a eulogy.

DA

Henry Inman

Born in Utica, N.Y., on Oct. 20. Was instructed in drawing as a boy in Utica; 1812 moved to New York, apprenticed for term of seven years with portraitist John Wesley Jarvis. Spent these years traveling to Boston, Philadelphia, Baltimore and New Orleans, where Jarvis had portrait commissions. 1822, married Jane Riker O'Brien; soon afterwards, set up studio on Vesey Street in New York as a painter of portraits, miniatures and genre pieces. 1826-28, in partnership with Thomas Seir Cummings with whom he took leading role in organization of National Academy of Design. Served as its first vice-president, 1827-1830, and again 1838-1844. 1829, commission for full-length portrait of Martin Van Buren for City Hall established him as leading New York portraitist. 1831, having resigned as officer of National Academy, took a studio in Philadelphia; settled nearby on an estate in Mount Holly, N.J., 1832. Became a director of Pennsylvania Academy of the Fine Arts and a partner in the lithography firm of Childs and Inman. Also recognized for portraiture in Philadelphia. Late 1834, returned to New York, where he remained except for visit to England in mid-1840's. From 1840, success and health declined, owing to his asthma condition. 1844, commissioned by friends James Lenox, Edward L. Carey and Henry Reed to go to England to paint William Wordsworth and other literary figures. Wordsworth painting met with much success. Precarious health obliged him to return to New York in 1845. Commissioned by Congress to paint a series of historical paintings for Capitol. While at work on first of these, died of heart disease in New York, January 17. National Academy members honored him with funeral procession and with memorial exhibition of his portraits, landscapes and genre paintings.

DA

Charles Cushing Wright

Born in Damariscotta, fifty miles east of the Kennebec River in Maine. 1814, apprenticed to John Osburn, a jeweler and watchmaker in Utica, N.Y. Remained with Osburn until age twenty-one, working at the silversmith's forge. As engraver, fashioned his own tools for copperplate engraving. He later designed medals, using intaglio process in steel. Traveled to Albany in 1818, then to New York City, then Savannah, Ga., remaining there until the fire of 1820. Spent four years in Charleston, S.C., where he executed a number of dies and portraits cut in steel, among them the portrait of Charles Cotesworthy Pinckney. Wright also undertook xylographic and copperplate engraving to expand his enterprise. 1824, returning to New York, formed die-sinking business of Wright and Bale; also undertook engraving of banknotes and watchcases. Later became one of first manufacturers of steel pens in U.S. A founding member of National Academy of Design in 1826, Wright was its first treasurer, designer of Academy's seal and lecturer on art of medal engraving. 1840, formed partnership with Asher B. Durand in banknote engraving business. Among his most notable achievements were portrait medals of Gilbert Stuart, John Trumbull and Washington Allston for the American Art-Union; the Independence medal of George Washington; and the 1849 medals commissioned by Congress to commemorate the victories of Generals Winfield Scott and Zachary Taylor in war with Mexico. Latter so successful that Wright was considered (though not appointed) to office of Chief Die-Sinker to U.S. Mint. Recognized as a pioneering American medalist, he died in New York, June 9.

DA

Samuel Finley Breese Morse (1791-1872) N.A. 1826 1901
   (Founder) P.N.A. 1826-1845, 1861-1862
SELF-PORTRAIT
Watercolor on ivory
3¼ x 2⅝
Unsigned
Donated by: Samuel P. Avery; John G. Brown; Thomas B.
   Clarke; Lockwood De Forest; Daniel Huntington; James C.
   Nicoll; and Harry W. Watrous

Samuel Finley Breese Morse (1791-1872) N.A. 1826 (Founder),
    P.N.A. 1826-1845, 1861-1862
PORTRAIT OF DR. FREDERICK G. KING (1801-1829)
Oil on canvas
34⅝ x 27⅜
Unsigned
Commissioned by the Council of the National Academy of Design, 1827

Henry Inman (1801-1846) N.A. 1826 (Founder)
MINIATURE PORTRAIT OF CHARLES CUSHING
    WRIGHT (1796-1854) N.A. 1826 (Founder)
Watercolor on ivory
3 x 2½
Unsigned

Charles Robert Leslie (1794-1859) H.M. 1827
PORTRAIT OF WASHINGTON ALLSTON (1779-1843) H.M. 1827
Oil on canvas
26 x 18
Unsigned
Gift of Samuel F. B. Morse, 1865

Asher Brown Durand (1796-1886) N.A. 1826 (Founder)
  P.N.A. 1845-1861
SELF-PORTRAIT
Oil on canvas remounted on masonite
30⅛ x 25¼
Unsigned

Asher Brown Durand (1796-1886) N.A. 1826 (Founder) P.N.A. 1845-1861
PORTRAIT OF LEWIS P. CLOVER, JR. (1819-1896)
  A.N.A. 1840
Oil on canvas remounted on masonite
20 x 16
Unsigned

Washington Allston

Born in Georgetown, S.C., November 5. Spring, 1787, went to Newport, R.I., to study classics and literature in preparation for admission to Harvard College. Instruction in painting from provincial artist Samuel King. 1794, established close relationship with artist Edward Greene Malbone. 1796–1800 attended Harvard. May, 1801, determined to pursue art, traveled to London with Malbone. Studied at Royal Academy schools under supervision of Benjamin West. Exhibited paintings at Royal Academy annual exhibitions of 1802 and 1803. Then traveled to Paris via Low Countries with close friend John Vanderlyn. Both in 1804 Salon, first American artists to exhibit in Paris. 1804–08, studied Roman and Venetian painting in Rome, where he formed lasting friendships with Washington Irving and Samuel Taylor Coleridge. 1808, returned to Boston to establish himself as professional painter. 1808–1811, high productivity in portraiture. Anxious to work on a more ambitious scale than his American patronage warranted, sailed to England in 1811 with wife, Ann Channing, and pupil Samuel F. B. Morse. 1811–18, period of greatest success; many of his major historical works commissioned by England's leading patrons. *Dead Man Restored to Life by Touching the Bones of the Prophet Elisha*, critically acclaimed at Royal Academy in 1813 and British Institution in 1814, established his prominence. Painting later purchased by Pennsylvania Academy of the Fine Arts for record sum paid to an American painter. June, 1814, one-man show in Bristol, one of first exhibitions in England to celebrate a living artist. Again painted portraits, but chose friends, Benjamin West among others, and family as subjects. 1815, deeply depressed at death of his wife. 1817, contributed two comic illustrations to *Knickerbocker's History of New York* by Washington Irving. August, 1818, left England for America. Soon after departure, elected an Associate of Royal Academy and, three years later, considered for election to full Academician to fill place vacated by the deceased Benjamin West. Promotion later rejected because Allston had returned to America and it was thought he might never visit England again. 1820s and 1830s, Allston one of best patronized aritsts in America, celebrated by Boston aristocracy. 1828, served as influential member of committee that organized memorial exhibition at Boston Athenaeum of portraiture of Allston's good friend, Gilbert Stuart. In later years, concentrated much time on completion of *Belshazzar's Feast*, a large picture begun in London, 1817. Painting still unfinished when artist died in Boston on January 9.

DA

Charles Robert Leslie

Born in Clerkenwell, England on Oct. 19 to Robert and Lydia Baker Leslie, Americans then visiting Great Britain. 1799, family returned to U.S., settling in New Jersey. Father, formerly a watchmaker from Philadelphia, sent son to local New Jersey school, urged him to study drawing. Charles later attended University of Pennsylvania; 1808, apprenticed to booksellers Bradford & Inskeep. Submitted five theatrical watercolors to 1811 annual exhibition of Pennsylvania Academy of the Fine Arts, there honored in 1816 with one-man show, an unusual tribute to such a young artist. 1811, sponsored by wealthy Philadelphia patrons, his employer, and Pennsylvania Academy, traveled to England to study painting. Shared living quarters with Samuel F.B. Morse and attended evening classes at Royal Academy, working from antique casts. Immediate success in England earned him two silver medals from Royal Academy for drawings rendered in antique class of Henry Fuseli and life class of John Flaxman. In London, met and advised by Washington Allston and Benjamin West. By 1816, his reputation as a portraitist well established; commissioned to paint portraits of American Ambassador to England, John Quincy Adams, and his wife, Louisa Johnson Adams. Continued to receive important commissions from wealthy English patrons throughout his life. 1817, traveled to Paris with Allston and English painter William Collins, then visited The Netherlands. Washington Irving engaged Allston and Leslie to illustrate two comic works, *History of New York* and *The Sketch Book*. Later Leslie painted many genre subjects, illustrating themes from Shakespeare to Molière. 1821, elected Associate of Royal Academy, London; 1826, elected an Academician, the first of Benjamin West's students to receive honor. 1825, married Harriet Stone of London. 1833, accepted an appointment to teach at the U.S. Military Academy, West Point, but stayed only a few months, returning to England in 1834 to remain there for life. 1843, wrote *Memoirs of the Life of John Constable Esq., R.A.* 1847, appointed professor of painting at Royal Academy, publishing his lectures of four years of instruction as *A Handbook for Young Painters*. 1855, his biography of Sir Joshua Reynolds completed posthumously by literary executor. Died in London, May 5.

DA

Asher Brown Durand

Born in Jefferson, N.J., on August 21. 1812-17, apprenticed to engraver Peter Maverick, principally making copies of English book illustrations for American publishers; 1817-20, partnership with Maverick. 1821, married Lucy Baldwin. Hired by John Trumbull to engrave *The Signing of the Declaration of Independence*. The project lasted until 1823, helping to establish Durand's reputation as printmaker. Activities in portrait, gift book and bank-note engraving for the next decade. Ca. 1827, initial member of Sketch Club, New York. Widowed in 1830, married Mary Frank of New York in 1834. Through patronage of Luman Reed, began to develop interest in portraiture and landscape painting. Early 1830's, Reed commissioned a series of portraits of all the Presidents of the United States. At suggestion of Thomas Cole, traveled to White Mountains, Adirondacks, Berkshires and Catskills to draw and paint. 1840-41, traveled to Europe with painters John William Casilear, John Frederick Kensett and Thomas Pritchard Rossiter, visiting England, Lowlands, France, Germany, Switzerland and Italy. Met English painters Sir David Wilkie, J. M. W. Turner and American painter Charles Robert Leslie in London, visited current exhibitions. Returned to America to pursue landscape painting almost exclusively. Served as second president of the National Academy, 1845-1861. Exhibited there for many years, each time his landscapes attracting more attention. Continued to take sketching trips to White Mountains, Lake George and area near his Catskills home. Upon Thomas Cole's death 1848, became acknowledged leader of American landscapists. 1849, painted *Kindred Spirits* representing Cole and William Cullen Bryant; gave picture to Bryant as a tribute to their mutual friend. 1855, Durand's views, "Letters on Landscape Painting," published in *The Crayon*, the art periodical published by his son. 1869, retired from New York to his birthplace. Ceased to paint in 1878, died on Sept. 17, 1886. Grolier Club held comprehensive exhibition of his graphics in 1895, with catalogue listing 237 works.

DA

Charles Cromwell Ingham (1796-1863) N.A. 1826 (Founder)
PORTRAIT OF THOMAS SEIR CUMMINGS (1804-1894)
   N.A. 1826 (Founder)
Oil on canvas
30 x 25
Signed on reverse: T.C. Cummings painted by C.C. Ingham
   1844

Lewis P. Clover, Jr.

Born New York City on Feb. 20. (Father owned frame and artists' supply store in lower Manhattan.) Studied engraving and painting with Asher B. Durand, 1838-1845. Exhibited continuously National Academy of Design, mainly figure, genre, and portrait paintings. Also exhibited at American Academy and American Art Union, Apollo Association, Pennsylvania Academy of the Fine Arts and Boston Athenaeum. In 1850, ten years after his election to membership in National Academy, gave up painting for ministry of Episcopal churches in Virginia. About 1860, in Springfield, Ill. painted portrait of Abraham Lincoln. Returned to New York and died there Nov. 9.

BSK

Charles Cromwell Ingham

Born in Dublin, Ireland. Age 13, enrolled at Royal Dublin Society to study drawing. Trained four years in studio of William Cumming, a noted woman's portraitist. During this time painted *Death of Cleopatra* which won Dublin Academy award and later appeared in first exhibition of American Academy of Fine Arts, New York. 1816, exhibited two works at the Dublin Academy before emigrating with his family to New York. In time recognized as successful portraitist of women and children; also painted several eminent male figures, the Marquis de Lafayette in 1825, the scholar Guilian C. Verplanck in 1830, and Governor DeWitt Clinton, ca. 1825. Also painted miniatures on ivory. One of original founders of National Academy of Design in 1826, frequently a member of its council, taught at its school, and served as vice-president, 1845-1850, 1859-1861. Active member of Sketch Club, of which he was a founder in 1847. Died in New York on December 10.

DA

Thomas Seir Cummings

Born in Bristol, England, on August 26; emigrated to New York as an infant. At fourteen, began drawing lessons with English itinerant painter Augustus Earle who had rented part of family's house. Later enrolled in drawing school of John Rubens Smith. 1821, a pupil of Henry Inman, studying techniques of oil, watercolor and miniature painting. 1824-27, partnership between the two artists, Inman concentrating almost exclusively on oil painting, Cummings principally on miniatures. 1822, married Jane Cook, also of British descent. Influential figure in founding of National Academy of Design, 1826, serving as Treasurer, 1827-1864, and Vice-Presi-dent, 1850-58. For several years conducted a private school of design in New York. Helped organize New York Sketching Club in 1844. Active in military affairs, rising in Second Regiment of New York Light Infantry from private to colonel and in 1838 to brigadier-general. His copy of Gilbert Stuart's *Martha Washington* presented to Queen Victoria in 1851 and gracefully acknowledged by Lord Palmerston. 1863, National Academy resolving to build on its 23rd Street property, Cummings made chairman of building committee. 1865, costly and ornate structure dedicated; Cummings published *Historic Annals of the National Academy of Design*, a detailed history of Academy to that time. Retired from professional activities, living first in Mansfield, Conn., and from 1889 in Hackensack, N.J., where he died on Sept. 24.

DA

Ferdinand Thomas Lee Boyle

Born in Ringwood, England, and brought to America as a child. Studied portraiture and miniature painting under Henry Inman. Lived in New Rochelle, N.Y., before moving to New York City in 1844. 1855, moved to St. Louis where he was one of founders of Western Art Academy. Served in Civil War, returning to reside in New York in 1866. There painted portraits of Charles Dickens, Archbishop Hughes, General Grant and Edgar Allan Poe, among others. Served for many years as professor at Brooklyn Institute of Art and as head of Art Department of Adelphi College. Lost his membership at the National Academy in 1888 because he had failed to exhibit, a principal condition for membership. Brooklyn was his home in later years. Died in 1906.

DA

Eliza Greatorex

Born in Manor Hamilton, England, on December 25. With her family, emigrated to New York in 1840. 1849, married the prominent New York City musician, Henry Greatorex (1816-1858). After his death in 1858, became a professional artist, studying in New York under William W. Wotherspoon, James M. Hart and William Hart. Later studied in Paris and Munich. Best known for her views of New York City, she was also a landscape painter and etcher. 1869, first woman elected to Associate membership at National Academy of Design, where she remained an Associate until 1887. 1871, distinguished herself as founder of first art colony in Rocky Mountains, in Colorado Springs. During later years, spent much time in Europe with two daughters, Kathleen Honora and Elizabeth Eleanor, both of whom became artists. Died in Paris, on February 9.

DA

Ferdinand Thomas Lee Boyle (1820-1906) A.N.A 1849
DIPLOMA PORTRAIT OF MRS. ELIZA GREATOREX
  (1819-1897) A.N.A. 1869-1888
Oil on canvas
30⅛ x 24⅜
Signed lower left: F.T.L. Boyle / 1869

Leaders at Mid-Century

American portraiture continued as an important art form through the mid-nineteenth century. By the 1840s American-trained Charles Loring Elliott and Daniel Huntington had become preeminent. Emanuel Leutze and Eastman Johnson followed, displaying the influence of their European academic training. These four painters fostered their careers by painting portraits of themselves, their families and important public figures, and by becoming distinguished members of the National Academy of Design.

Born in 1812 in western New York, Charles Loring Elliott was the son of a builder and architect. Though he aspired to be a painter, his ambition was not favored by his father, whose goal was for his son to become an architect. Elliott mastered mechanical drawing in an effort to please his father. But in 1829, Elliott's desire to become a painter prevailed, and he journeyed to New York City to seek guidance from Colonel John Trumbull, president of the American Academy of the Fine Arts. Trumbull was not to be the advocate he had hoped he would be. He advised Elliott to accede to his father's wishes and pursue a more financially rewarding architectural career. Elliott was undaunted by the revered Trumbull's advice, however. Finally, the aging master relented and allowed Elliott to enter the Academy to draw from the Antique Gallery's plaster casts.

After several months Elliott left the Academy, because, although he gave generously of his time and direction, Trumbull persisted in advocating that he give up painting for architecture. Elliott then sought out John Quidor, a genre painter devoted to illustrating the stories of Washington Irving, and, after moving into Quidor's studio, he began to paint dramatic and literary genres.

By 1833 he had made his way as an itinerant portraitist to Clinton, New York, the home of Hamilton College. Elliott painted portraits of Hamilton's faculty and students, and he befriended Daniel Huntington, who was a student at the college at that time.

Elliott painted portraits almost exclusively. In fact, his prolific ouevre exists as a documentary of distinguished Americans. In 1846 after the death of Henry Inman, Charles Loring Elliott replaced Inman as the leading portraitist in New York. He specialized in painting older gentlemen in the grand-manner tradition.[1] However, in the collection of the National Academy of Design are two fine examples of more intimate, collegial portraits of his fellow academicians, James Edward Freeman, and Jasper Francis Cropsey.

The *Portrait of James Edward Freeman* (ca. 1850) is slightly more formal than the *Portrait of Jasper Francis Cropsey* (1845-46). The distinguished Freeman sits gazing directly at the viewer, with his right arm bent at the elbow, resting upon the chair arm. Elliott has captured the serious, yet pleasant, expression of the sitter, who, with a slight tilt of the head, receives the viewer quite directly. Cropsey, on the other hand, is rendered with a youthful, starry-eyed treatment. He does not confront the viewer directly, but looks off into the distance, full of the dreams and visions of a twenty-two-year-old landscapist.

Charles Loring Elliott and Daniel Huntington shared equal regard as portraitists during the middle of the nineteenth century. While Elliott achieved slightly greater fame, Huntington celebrated a longer and more versatile career, for his virtuosity as a painter extended beyond painting likenesses to include landscape and history painting. Nevertheless, the majority of Huntington's works were still portraits, perhaps as many as one thousand.

Huntington, born in New York in 1816, had the more formal training of the two. He spent a year at Yale University, and in 1832, at the age of sixteen, he entered Hamilton College, where he first met Elliott. At this time Huntington had yet to pursue his painting career formally. Under the guidance of his new friend, who was four years older, Huntington began to paint with supplies borrowed from his new mentor.

In 1836 Huntington left college and returned home to New York City, where he entered the studio of Samuel F. B. Morse, president of the National Academy and professor of painting at New York University. After leaving Morse's studio he spent several months painting landscapes in the Catskills. He returned to New York City to continue his training at the studio of Henry Inman.

By 1838 his exhibition career was well underway. He exhibited that same year at the American Art-Union—then the Apollo Gallery—and by 1839 was elected one of the youngest associates of the National Academy. Two sojourns to Europe followed, one in 1839 to Rome, Florence and Paris, and another, during 1842–45, which he spent in Italy. Between his trips abroad, he was elected (1840) as an academician to the National Academy.

An indication of Huntington's popularity as a painter was the invitation by the American Art-Union in 1850 to exhibit his work in a major exhibition.[2] The range of Huntington's work in this exhibition represented his versatility during the first twenty years of his career. Thereafter, portraiture dominated his work.

Huntington's *Self-Portrait* (1891) in the National Academy's collection is an impressive and commanding image befitting the position of an Academy president. Huntington is seated, and appears interrupted by the viewer, as he studies a volume of prints. The page to which he has turned, appears to be a print after Titian, displays a kneeling figure with right hand at her breast, looking upward in a virtuous, beseeching pose, similar to his allegorical fantasies of the 1840s.[3] Huntington regards the viewer with a direct, quiet stare as he turns from his book. His gray beard is softly waved, and his thin face has been sensitively rendered. Huntington has captured the stately bearing of his seventy-five years.

Much more than just a leading artist of the mid-nineteenth century, Huntington was a major founder and leader of the fine arts. In addition to his twenty-one-year tenure (1862–1870 and 1877–1890) as president of the National Academy; he was also one of the founders of the Century Association, serving as its president for sixteen years after the death of William Cullen Bryant, as well as vice president of the Metropolitan Museum of Art from 1870 to 1903.

At mid-century Elliott and Huntington were the leading portraitists of New York, alike stylistically because of their similar training and influences. Two of their contemporaries, Emanuel Leutze and Eastman Johnson, also made fine contributions to American portrait study, in part because of the influence of their European academic training.

Born in a small town near Stuttgart, Germany, in 1816, Emanuel Leutze emigrated to America with his family and settled in Philadelphia when he was nine years old. At sixteen he began to take drawing lessons, and by 1834 he had become a proficient portraitist. After a short-lived commission, painting portraits for the National Portrait Gallery of Distinguished Americans in 1836, Leutze was an itinerant portrait painter, working exclusively in Virginia, Maryland and Pennsylvania. His budding success led him to travel to Düsseldorf, where in 1841 he enrolled in its famous Academy. It was at Düsseldorf in 1849 that Leutze began the master scheme for what was to become his most renowned work: *Washington Crossing the Delaware* (Metropolitan Museum of Art, New York).

Leutze achieved such fame as a history painter that in his own time he was considered to be a major force in this most revered category of painting. As a portraitist, however, he was no less successful. His German portraits are a survey of his circle at the time. He painted numerous portraits of his wife, Juliana Lottner, and her family. Perhaps the best examples of his three-quarter-length portraits are those of his father-in-law, Colonel Heinrich Lottner of 1853, and of his brother-in-law, Friedrich Lottner of 1852.[4]

Leutze's circle in Düsseldorf included many American painters seeking academic training.[5] Of his compatriots, Worthington Whittredge remained the longest in Düsseldorf (1849–1856) and became Leutze's closest friend. They were both in New York in 1859 and were elected to the National Academy of Design at almost the same time, Leutze in 1860 and Whittredge in 1861. During the 1860s they both took studios at the 10th Street Building in New York City.

Many of Whittredge's fellow artists chose to paint his portrait. Leutze painted several of Whittredge, the most compelling being his 1859 portrait in the National Academy's collection. In this portrait Whittredge is a striking subject, displaying a sturdy countenance and projecting a sense of self-assurance as he stands, hands folded across his chest, and gazes piercingly at the viewer. The simplicity of the composition and the clean, hard-edged rendering of the figure add to the portrait's forthright nature. Compared to Leutze's *portrait d'apparat* of Whittredge—the Academy portrait captures the character and expression of the sitter in order to create a direct psychological relationship with the viewer, whereas his later portrait *Worthington Whittredge in his Tenth Street Studio*, collection of Barbara B. Lassiter of 1865 shows Whittredge painting at his easel, well-fitted with the accoutrements of his craft.

Leutze's Düsseldorf studio was a haven for young American artists. Many of these painters were witness to—and some even participated in the production of—Leutze's major opus, *Washington Crossing the Delaware*. Whittredge was an important model for the figure of Washington:

> I suppose there is no artist now living who is as familiar as I am with the assembly of his great picture of "Washington Crossing the Delaware". . . . He found great difficulty in finding American types for the heads and figures. . . . He caught every American who came along. . . . I was seized and made to do service twice, once for the steersman with the oar in my hand and again for Washington himself.[6]

Among the young Americans in Leutze's atelier who witnessed *Washington Crossing the Delaware* in progress was Eastman Johnson. Johnson, most famous for his genre scenes, began and ended his career as a portrait painter. Born in Lovell, Maine, in 1824, Johnson was the son of Phillip C. Johnson, Maine's secretary of state. He studied lithography in Boston for two years, and by 1842 he was an itinerant portrait painter in Maine, doing crayon portraits of family and friends. Determined to become an established portraitist, Johnson, through his father's political connections, settled in Washington, D.C. In 1845 he was busy compiling a portfolio of contemporary portraits of distinguished Americans. His fame and popularity as a portraitist grew quickly. In 1846 he was commissioned by Henry Wadsworth Longfellow to paint portraits of Longfellow's family and friends, including such *literati* as Emerson and Hawthorne.

Johnson desired formal academic instruction, so in 1849 he left for Europe and enrolled in the esteemed Düsseldorf Academy. In January 1851, after a year and a half at the Academy, he entered Emanuel Leutze's studio, where he was quickly assimilated into Leutze's circle of compatriots. But after staying with Leutze for only six months, Johnson traveled to London for the Crystal Palace Exhibition and then settled in the Netherlands. He returned to Düsseldorf in 1854, however, and executed a brilliant portrait of Worthington Whittredge (Detroit Institute of Fine Arts), which is obviously indebted to recent Dutch influence. In 1855 Johnson moved on to Paris to study with Thomas Couture. After several months, he returned to the United States—the end of his academic sojourn.

Johnson's *Self-Portrait*, ca. 1859, in the National Academy's collection was painted at the time of his election to associate in 1859. It is one of many self portraits that followed in his later years. The young, self-assured artist reflected in this portrait, which is rendered with subtle modeling and soft light, is a man about to take on the challenge of his New York career. During the 1880s Johnson turned exclusively to portraiture and painted until the age of seventy-six.

Joan Darragh

Notes

1. For a discussion of grand-manner portraiture of this period, see William H. Gerdts, "Natural Aristocrats in a Democracy, 1810–1870," *American Portraiture in the Grand Manner: 1720–1920* (exh. cat., Los Angeles County Museum of Art, 1981).

2. See American Art Union, *Catalogue of Paintings by Daniel Huntington, N.A., Exhibiting at the Art Union Building, 497 Broadway* (exh. cat., New York, 1850).

3. For an in-depth discussion of Huntington's early allegorical works, see William H. Gerdts, "Daniel Huntington's Mercy's Dream: A Pilgrimage through Bunyanesque Imagery," *Winterthur Portfolio,* vol. 14 (1979), pp. 171–94.

4. For a discussion of *Colonel Heinrich Lottner,* see Gerdts, "Natural Aristocrats."

5. For a detailed listing of Leutze's studio and circle, see Worthington Whittredge, "The Autobiography of Worthington Whittredge, 1820–1910," ed. John I. H. Baur, *Brooklyn Museum Journal,* vol. 2 (1942), pp. 7–68, and John I. H. Baur, *Eastman Johnson, 1824–1906: An American Genre Painter* (Brooklyn Institute of Arts and Sciences, 1940). For an in-depth discussion of Leutze's *Washington Crossing the Delaware,* see Barbara S. Groseclose, *Emanuel Leutze, 1816–1868: Freedom Is the Only King* (exh. cat., National Collection of Fine Arts, Smithsonian Institution, 1975).

6. Whittredge, *op. cit.,* p. 22

Charles Loring Elliott

Born in Scipio, Cayuga County, N.Y., in December to architect Daniel Elliott. Family moved to Syracuse, N.Y. in 1827, where Elliott attended district school and later received some training as an architect, drafting for his father. Father at first discouraged his study of art, but sent him to New York in 1829 with letter of introduction to John Trumbull. Trumbull permitted him to draw from casts at American Academy of Fine Arts but advised a career in architecture. Studied painting with John Quidor and worked in studio of William Rimmer, the latter apparently giving no instruction. Spent ten years as itinerant portrait painter in central and western New York State. Painted portraits of faculty members of Hamilton College and there befriended student Daniel Huntington whose portrait he also painted. 1839, began exhibiting at National Academy of Design, earning a meager living in New York. Work steadily improved, especially after he met painter Henry Inman in 1844. 1845, success of Elliott's portrait of Captain John Ericsson at National Academy exhibition secured his reputation. After Inman's death early in 1846, Elliott became New York's leading portrait painter, exhibiting successfully again that year at National Academy. 1854, moved to West Hoboken, N.J., but kept a studio in New York, continuing to paint in or near the city till his death in Albany August 25. In lifetime had produced over 700 portraits, many of them important full-length commissions.

DA

Jasper Francis Cropsey

Born in Rossville, Staten Island, N.Y. on February 18. 1837-1842, apprentice to New York architect Joseph Trench. Also studied watercolor drawing with Edward Maury, an Englishman. 1843, exhibited first painting at National Academy of Design. Set up architectural office in Granite Building, New York, using architectural commissions to support himself while concentrating on landscape painting. Paintings favorably received by Henry Inman and William Sidney Mount. 1845, wrote essay "Natural Art" for the Art Union, New York. Attended life classes at National Academy. Married Maria Cooley, sailing with her to Europe in 1847. Traveled extensively through England and Scotland, then south to Switzerland and Italy where they lived for awhile in Thomas Cole's old studio. 1849, left Italy for England and Wales by way of France, where he sketched at Fontainebleau and Barbizon. 1849, back in New York, painted from his European drawings; also painted landscape views, sketched in Vermont and in White Mountains, N.H.

Shared studio with Thomas Hicks. Summer sketching trips in New York State and New England. 1854, elected Honorary Professional Member of Pennsylvania Academy of the Fine Arts. Sketching excursions as far west as Michigan and as far north as Canada. 1855, wrote of importance of working from nature in article entitled "Up from the Clouds" issued in the art magazine, The Crayon. 1856-1863, in England, became acquainted with John Ruskin, Sir Charles Eastlake, Lord Lyndhurst and Daniel Huntington. Exhibited Indian Summer Morning in the White Mountains at Royal Academy, 1857. Illustrated collections of poetry by Edgar Allan Poe and Thmas Moore. Queen Victoria appointed Cropsey to American Commission for 1862 International Exposition in London where he exhibited Autumn on the Hudson and received a gold medal. 1863, returned to New York. Began to accept occasional architectural commissions again. 1867, exhibited two paintings at Universal Exposition, Paris; helped found American Watercolor Society. Completed construction of his house "Aladdin" in Warwick, N.Y., 1869. Exhibited regularly at National Academy and American Watercolor Society, 1869-1890. Exhibited three paintings at International Exhibition of 1876, the Philadelphia Centennial; also designed stairways, waiting rooms and platforms for Sixth Avenue Elevated. 1884, financial circumstances forced sale of "Aladdin". Bought house in Hastings-on-Hudson where he spent much time painting landscape, 1885-1890. 1892, made a fellow of London Society of Science, Literature and Art. Suffered a stroke the following year, died June 22.

DA

James Edward Freeman

Born on Indian Island, New Brunswick, Canada. 1826, although poor, determined to train as an artist; in New York, applied to painter William Dunlap for instruction. On Dunlap's recommendation, entered National Academy of Design. Briefly resided in ancestral home of James Fenimore Cooper before leaving for Italy in 1836, where he remained for rest of life. 1840-49, served as American consul in Ancona, although he generally lived in Rome and discharged his minor duties through an agent. Married sculptress Augusta Latilla, 1845. Paintings rarely exhibited in America, although his last picture shown in National Academy exhibition of 1868. Published two volumes of memoirs, Gatherings from an Artist's Portfolio, 1877, and Gatherings From an Artist's Portfolio in Rome, 1883. Died in Rome, on November 21.

DA

Charles Loring Elliott (1812-1868) A.N.A. 1845, N.A. 1846
PORTRAIT OF JASPER FRANCIS CROPSEY (1823-1900)
    A.N.A. 1841, N.A. 1851
Oil on canvas remounted on masonite
22 x 19
Signed lower left center: C.E. to S.P.A.
Gift of Samuel P. Avery

Eastman Johnson

Born in Lovell, Me. on July 29. Grew up in Freyburg and later Augusta, Me., where father held various positions in state government. Eastman showed early aptitude for art, age sixteen began a two-year employment in Boston lithography shop. Dissatisfied with lithography, returned to Maine to begin painting crayon portrait sketches. Father was then Maine's Secretary of State, provided son with prominent sitters. 1844, after some time as itinerant portrait draftsman in New England, Johnson moved to Washington, D.C., there assembling portfolio of drawings of national figures, Dolly Madison and John Quincy Adams among them. At invitation of Henry Wadsworth Longfellow, moved to Cambridge, Mass., to continue his portrait work; Ralph Waldo Emerson, Nathaniel Hawthorne and Josiah Quincy, President of Harvard University among his subjects. 1849, went to Düsseldorf to study painting formally, first in anatomy classes at Royal Academy and, in 1851, in studio of Emanuel Leutze. Traveled to London to see Crystal Palace exhibition before moving to The Hague to study the Old Masters. Remained there until 1855, establishing himself so successfully in portraiture that he was offered position of court painter, an honor he refused. 1855 moved to Paris, entered studio of Thomas Couture. Less than a year later, returned to U.S. at death of mother. 1855-58, after spending time in Washington, D.C., Superior, Wis., and Cincinnati, Johnson moved to New York and took a studio in University Building. 1859, exhibited *Life in the South (Old Kentucky Home)* at National Academy of Design, the genre picture that established his reputation and secured his election as Associate to National Academy. Followed Union army on several campaigns during early years of Civil War. Taught at National Academy in fall, 1868, and spring, 1869. Married Elizabeth Buckley of Troy, N.Y. Summered in Nantucket with family for rest of active life, where he painted and sketched. Spent summer of 1875-1880 on imagery of cranberry picking. 1881, began to paint fewer genre scenes and more portraits. By end century, considered a leading portrait painter; President Benjamin Harrison was his subject in 1895. Died in New York City on April 5.
See color, page 34.   DA

Sanford Robinson Gifford

Born in Greenfield, Saratoga County, N.Y. Attended Brown University, 1842-44. Left Brown to study painting in New York with John Rubens Smith, a watercolorist and son of English engraver John Raphael Smith. Following sketching tour of Catskills and Berkshires in summer 1846, turned to landscape painting in tradition of Thomas Cole. 1847, began exhibiting at National Academy of Design. 1855-57, first trip to Europe, traveling to England, France, Germany, Austria, Switzerland and Italy. In Rome, associated with Worthington Whittredge and Albert Bierstadt among other American artists. Returned to New York and set up studio in 10th Street Studio Building, where he remained for life. In defiance of vogue for lavish studio furnishings, occupied a sparsely decorated room with only essential painting equipment; always lived modestly, despite indulgent support of family. Continued to spend much time sketching in Catskills and Adirondacks with artist-companions Jervis McEntee, John Kensett and Worthington Whittredge. 1859, went abroad with Jervis McEntee. At outbreak of Civil War, joined New York Seventh Regiment, serving in campaigns of 1861, and 1863-64. Returned to Europe in 1868, visiting Italy, Syria, Greece, Turkey,

Lebanon and Palestine. Several paintings from European and Near Eastern travels exhibited at 1876 Centennial Exposition, Philadelphia, where he won medal for excellence in landscape painting. 1870, traveled with Whittredge and Kensett on F. V. Hayden's surveying expedition to the Rocky Mountains of Wyoming. 1874, returned West, touring Alaska, British Columbia, Oregon and California. 1877, married at age fifty-four. His health declining, went with wife to Lake Superior region hoping to regain strength. Condition worsened and he died in New York City, on August 29. Metropolitan Museum of Art held memorial exhibition of 160 paintings; 1881, published a "memorial catalogue" listing complete corpus of paintings.

DA

Worthington Whittredge

Born on his father's farm near Springfield, Oh., May 22. Went to Cincinnati in 1837 as a house and sign painter. Began to study art, first painting portraits and later landscapes. Exhibited three landscapes at Cincinnati inaugural exhibition, 1839. After learning the daguerreotype process in Cincinnati moved to Indianapolis in 1840 to open a studio. Despite failure, stayed in Indianapolis for a year, living with Henry Ward Beecher and painting portraits of Beecher family, including Harriet Beecher Stowe. Returned to Cincinnati in 1843 when he gave up portraiture to become a landscapist. Exhibited many landscapes in Cincinnati in 1840's, sending seven to Cincinnati Academy's second annual exhibition, 1841. His painting *View of the Kanawha Morning* shown at National Academy of Design and praised by president, Asher B. Durand. With money from commissions by Cincinnati patrons, traveled abroad in 1849, sketching during summer in Belgium and Germany and renting a studio in Paris the next winter. Went to Düsseldorf, befriending Emanuel Leutze and posing for several figures in *Washington Crossing the Delaware*. Stayed in the home of German landscape painter Andreas Achenbach for one year. Work of this period reflects influence of Düsseldorf Academy painters, Achenbach, Carl Friedrich Lessing and Johann Schirmer. Sketching trip to Switzerland in summer, 1856, accompanied by Leutze and William S. Haseltine. Joined on Lake Lucerne by Albert Bierstadt, who then went with him to northern Italy. Spent next three years in Italy, settling in Rome, Bierstadt and Sanford Gifford his constant companions. Returned to New York in 1859, settling in 10th Street Studio Building in 1860. Joined with fellow artists and the aged philosopher Emerson at The Century Association to honor William Cullen Bryant's seventieth birthday, 1864, an occasion that profoundly impressed Whittredge and other mid-century painters. Accompanied General John Pope on tour of Colorado and New Mexico, making many field sketches. Married Euphemia Foot in Geneva, N.Y., 1867. Again in West 1870, traveling to Colorado and Wyoming with S. Gifford and John Frederick Kensett. Returned a third time to Platte River region, Colorado, 1871. Elected president of National Academy, serving 1874-77. Spent later life in Summit, N.J., where Calvert Vaux designed a house for him. Continued sketching, traveling frequently to Catskills, Newport, R.I., Gloucester and Ipswich, Mass. Traveled to Mexico in 1893 and again in 1896 with Frederic Church. Exhibited 125 paintings at The Century Association, March 1904. Completed autobiography in 1905. Died in Summit, N.J., Feb. 25.

DA

Charles Loring Elliott (1812-1868) A.N.A. 1845, N.A. 1846
PORTRAIT OF JAMES EDWARD FREEMAN (1808-1884)
   A.N.A. 1831, N.A. 1833
Oil on canvas
30⅛ x 25⅛
Unsigned

Emanuel Leutze

Born in Schwabisch-Gmund, near Stuttgart, Germany, on May 24, emigrated with family to Philadelphia in 1825. 1834, drew from casts in John Rubens Smith's art classes, rapidly developing skills in portraiture. Commissioned in 1836 to paint portraits of public figures in Washington, D.C., from which engravings would be printed for publication, *National Portrait Gallery of Distinguished Americans.* Project collapsed in the depression of 1837; Leutze then worked as an itinerant portraitist in Virginia and Maryland. 1839, settled Philadelphia to paint literary subjects in addition to portraits. 1841, group of Philadelphia patrons sponsored his trip to Düsseldorf to study at art academy; distinguished himself as painter of historical subjects, his principal concern for next twenty years. Left Düsseldorf Academy several years later, scornful of plodding routine and long period of apprenticeship required. Traveled to Italy, returned to Düsseldorf in 1845 to marry Julia Lottner, daughter of Prussian army officer. 1848, promoted founding of Malkasten, a coalition of artists who had recently left Academy and sought the unification of German states. Leutze wished to politicize the group further, encouraging the promulgation of democratic thought. 1849, began working on *Washington Crossing the Delaware,* this first version damaged in studio fire. Second version painted soon afterwards and exhibited in New York and Washington to much admiration. Petitioned Congress in April, 1852, to commission replica of this work with pendant, *Washington Rallying the Troops at Monmouth;* pendant completed 1854. Returned to Düsseldorf in 1852, continuing to paint historical subjects. 1856, helped organize a pan-Germanic congress of artists, the "Deutsch Kunstgenossenschaft." Returned to U.S. with prospect of commission in Washington, D.C. Completed mural *Westward the Course of Empire Takes Its Way* in U.S. Capitol, 1862. Family permanently returned to U.S. Leutze spent remaining years dividing time between New York and Washington, working on both history paintings and portraits. Died in Washington, D.C., on July 18.

DA

Thomas Moran

Born in Bolton, Lancashire, England on Jan. 12, the son of Thomas Moran and Mary Higson Moran. Emigrated with family to America in 1844, settling in Philadelphia where he apprenticed to a wood engraver for two years. 1856, shared studio with his brother, Edward, began painting in watercolors, then in 1860 in oils. Met and received advice from marine painter James Hamilton. 1862, briefly in England, copied Turner's paintings at National Gallery, London. Turner's technique and palette greatly influenced evolution of Moran's style as landscape painter. April, 1862, married one of his pupils, Mary Nimmo, of Strathaven, Scotland. 1866-1871, again in Europe, visited England, France and Italy and copied Old Master paintings. 1871, joined U.S. Geological Expedition under F.V. Hayden to Yellowstone region. 1873, second Western exploration with Major John Wesley Powell, to Rockies and Grand Canyon of Colorado River. 1874, again with Hayden, traveled to Mountain of the Holy Cross, Colorado. Sketched extensively on all expeditions. Painting of Mountain of the Holy Cross won medal at Centennial Exhibition in Philadelphia, 1876. Panoramic paintings, *Grand Canyon of Yellowstone,* 1871, and *Chasm of the Colorado,* 1873, provided first pictorial record of still unknown western scenery, purchased for large sum by Congress for U.S. Capitol. Moran's contributions to exploration commemorated by naming of Mount Moran, Teton Range, Wy., and Moran Point, Ariz. Lived in Philadelphia until 1872, then in Newark, N.J., until 1881, then New York City. 1884, built studio in East Hampton, Long Island, N.Y., where he had already spent several summers. Vis-

ited England and Mexico in 1880's, Italy in 1886 and 1890, and Pacific Coast several times. Although primarily known for expansive landscape paintings also executed etchings and illustrations. Elected to the British Society of Painter-Etchers and praised by John Ruskin for his graphic work. 1916, moved to Santa Barbara where he painted till his death at age ninety, Aug. 25.

DA

Hamilton Hamilton

Born in Middlesex, England on April 1; his family emigrated to Cowlesville, Wyoming County, N.Y. As youth determined to become a painter, against his parents' wishes. After self-training at home, moved to Buffalo in 1872 where he opened studio as portrait painter. 1875, visited Rocky Mountains, painted the Laramie Peaks. The painting *Laramie Peaks* shown at Philadelphia Centennial Exhibition, 1876. 1878, traveled to Paris to further his art training; a few months later joined American colony in Pont-Aven, Brittany. Remained in Brittany for a year, returning to Buffalo in 1879. Spent two years there before moving to New York where he became acquainted with Thomas Moran, Robert Burn and Winslow Homer. Frequently visited studios of William Merritt Chase and Birge Harrison. Visited England in 1895, where he met John Ruskin. Briefly toured Colorado in 1896, returning to New York where he resided till his death. Although best known for his landscapes, recognized in the 1890's for his pictures of young women. Died in Silvermine, near Norwalk, Conn., on January 4.

DA

Daniel Huntington

Born in New York City on October 14. Showed early interest in art at private school in Rome, New York. 1830, entered Smith's Academy, New Haven, in preparation for Yale University. Attended Yale for one year before transferring to Hamilton College where itinerant artist Charles Loring Elliott painted his portrait. Encouraged by Elliott and several professors to consider career in art, applied to Art Department of New York University, recently established under direction of Samuel F.B. Morse. Studied under Morse and later with Henry Inman. 1836, commission to draw Hudson views led to interest in landscape, in addition to portraiture, genre and still life. Exhibited portrait of his father in annual exhibition of National Academy of Design, 1838. Traveled to Europe in 1839, studying assiduously in Italy where he shared evening life classes with other young American artists. Returned to New York in 1840, already enjoying considerable patronage. A year later began work on *Mercy's Dream;* Inman enthusiastic about preparatory charcoal drawing for painting, urged Huntington to prepare finished composition by laying paint directly over charcoal without altering original sketch. 1842, married Sophia Richards of Brooklyn; and subsequently returned to Europe; in Rome for three years. 1850, William Cullen Bryant and other friends organized retrospective exhibition of Huntington's paintings, for which artist assembled catalogue. 1851, returned to Europe, visiting the Crystal Palace in London and painting portraits of prominent British figures, among them the Archbishop of Canterbury and Sir Charles Eastlake, President of the Royal Academy. 1858, returned home, commission to paint *The Republican Court,* a composition of forty figures. Completed in eighteen months; painting later sent to Universal Exposition in Paris. 1862, elected president of National Academy, a position he held longer than anyone in institution's history, 1862-69 and 1877-1891. Also served as vice-president of Metropolitan Museum of Art, 1870-1903, and president of Century Association, where he was honored with a memorial exhibition in 1908. Died in New York on April 18.

See color, page 35.

DA

Eastman Johnson (1824-1906) A.N.A. 1859, N.A. 1860
PORTRAIT OF SANFORD R. GIFFORD (1823-1880)
  A.N.A. 1850, N.A. 1854
Oil on canvas
26⅜ x 22¼
Signed lower left: E.J.
Gift of Mrs. Eastman Johnson, 1907

Emanuel Leutze (1816-1868) H.M. 1843, N.A. 1860
PORTRAIT OF WORTHINGTON WHITTREDGE (1820-
1910) A.N.A. 1860, N.A. 1861
Oil on canvas
30 x 24⅝
Signed lower right: E. Leutze / 1861

Hamilton Hamilton (1847-1928) A.N.A. 1886, N.A. 1889
PORTRAIT OF THOMAS MORAN (1837-1926) A.N.A. 1881, N.A. 1884
Oil on canvas
30⅛ x 25
Signed lower right: Hamilton Hamilton / 1881

The American Artists Trained in Munich

From the late 1840s, foreign training was a trend for an increasing number of American artists. In the 1850s, the leading centers for American students were the academy at Düsseldorf and the ateliers of Paris. The Civil War only temporarily interrupted this development, and after the war, improved transatlantic travel was one of the factors accelerating the movement toward art training abroad. In the 1870s, the art academy of Munich supplanted that of Düsseldorf in importance, while Paris, as an art center larger than both of them, attracted many times the numbers of students who went to Germany. For a brief period early in the decade, however, the disruption of the Franco-Prussian War and the Commune made Paris inaccessible, and Munich won the best of a small generation of students. The most brilliant of these were Frank Duveneck, William Merritt Chase and Walter Shirlaw.

Duveneck, Chase and Shirlaw were closely associated as leaders among the American students in Munich, who called them the inseparable "Father, Son and Holy Ghost," and they sent major works to the New York exhibitions of 1876, 1877 and 1878. After their return to the United States, Chase and Shirlaw led the group of young artists who seceded from the National Academy of Design in 1877, forming the Society of American Artists.

Because almost all art training in Munich was concentrated in the Royal Academy, and most Americans went through a certain number of classes together, the work of the returning students struck American critics as having a distinct "look" that identified it. In its broadest terms, the Munich manner can be characterized as a style of realism based upon a study of the appearance and techniques of the Caravaggist painters of the early seventeenth century. Walter Shirlaw's *Self-Portrait* (p. 82) and the *Portrait of Frederick Dielman* (p. 36), a fellow student in Munich, painted jointly by Frank Duveneck and William Merritt Chase, show how dramatic and forceful this approach could be. In both, the figure is placed against a background of complete darkness. A strong, directed light strikes the figure from above and to the side, brightly illuminating part of the face, but leaving the rest in shadow. The effect is one of a harsh, bracing realism that arrests attention.

While this general description applies to both paintings, closer examination reveals distinct personal variations in technique. Shirlaw's forms are smoother than the faceted shapes wrought with the blocky brushwork in the portrait of Dielman. (The seamless painting appears to have been finished by Chase on an armature of form by Duveneck.) In fact, there was a continuous development within this general Caravaggist approach during the decade of the 1870s, and each of the three artists went on to change further soon after leaving Munich. Chase's portrait of Thomas Dewing of 1887 (p.81), a leading figure in the Aesthetic style in the United States, and his portrait of the cosmopolitan Robert Blum of 1889 (p.79) are quite different again, particularly in the texture of their brushwork, although they share a family resemblance in their lighting, and, above all, in their masterly command of technique. Their excellent technical training and intense study of the Old Masters while in Munich equipped these artists to handle paint effectively and gracefully in a range of styles over the course of their careers.

It was no doubt this love of the method of painting that made Duveneck and Chase such effective teachers to a generation of American students. Although Irving Wiles also studied with Carolus-Duran in Paris, he must be considered a disciple of Chase and therefore an heir to the tradition of art instruction in Munich. The evocative, rich darks and fluency of technique in his striking *Self-Portrait* (p.82) are worthy of that generation of virtuosi.

Michael Quick

Frank Duveneck

Born Covington, Ky., Oct. 9. Began painting as a child in Latrobe, Pa., and Quebec, Canada; apprentice church decorator in Covington, 1862. 1870, traveled to Munich to study at Royal Academy; drawing from antique casts and painting under Wilhelm von Diez. Influenced by Wilhelm Leibl, also teaching at Royal Academy. 1872, returned to U.S.; 1872-75 frequent travel between Cincinnati and Boston. Returned to Munich, 1875, and began school of painting. Taught in Munich and artists' colony called Polling. American students included Chase, White Alexander, Blum, Twachtman, Shirlaw and Dewing, called "The Duveneck Boys."

Duveneck and "Boys" move to Italy; winters spent in Florence, summers in Venice. Shared studio with James Abbott McNeill Whistler in Venice, 1879-1881. Traveled to England, and returned to Italy to work, 1881-85. 1886, married painter Elizabeth Booth. Frequent trips to Paris from Florence. Elizabeth died in Paris, 1888. Returned to Cincinnati, taught painting at Cincinnati Art Museum during winters, 1890-92. Traveled to Spain with Charles Forbes and Julius Rolshoven, 1894. Joined faculty of Art Academy of Cincinnati, 1900. Served on International Jury of Awards for Panama-Pacific Exposition, San Francisco, 1915, and given special exhibition of paintings and etchings, awarded gold Medal of Honor. Received honorary LL.D. from University of Cincinnati, 1917. Died in Cincinnati on Jan. 3.

BSK

Frederick Dielman

Born Hanover, Germany, Dec. 25. Came to U.S. as a child. Graduated from Calvert College, Baltimore, Md. Worked as topographer and draftsman with U.S. Engineering Corps 1866-1872. Returned to Germany to study at Royal Academy, Munich, under Wilhelm Diez, 1872-76; classmate of Frank Duveneck. Established studio in New York upon his return, 1876. Taught at the Art Students' League, 1878-1886. Lectured on perspective at National Academy School, 1889-1900. Commissioned to design mosaic decoration in Library of Congress building, completed 1897. Also commissioned to design mosaics for Pennsylvania State Capitol, Albany Savings Bank, New York, and Iowa State Capitol in Des Moines. First European-born artist to serve as President of National Academy, 1889-1909. Elected to Society of American Artist, 1905. Resumed teaching at Art Students' League, 1897-1903. President of Fine Arts Federation and professor of drawing at College of City of New York, 1903-1918. Director of Art School of Cooper Union, 1903-1931. Died in Ridgefield, Conn., on Aug. 15. *See color, page 36.*

BSK

William Merritt Chase

Born Williamsburg, Ind., Nov. 1. Family moved to Indianapolis 1861. Chase began drawing using family and friends as subjects, 1865-66. Chase's father took him for first professional art instruction under Barton S. Hays, 1867. Chase enlisted in Navy, where he served for only three months and returned home, resumed study with Hays. With encouragement from Hays and Jacob Cox, went to New York to study with Joseph O. Eaton, and at National Academy of Design, 1868-69. 1870-71, exhibited still lifes and portraits at National Academy; visited family in St. Louis. Businessmen financed Chase's study abroad in exchange for a painting each. Enrolled in Royal Academy, Munich, under Alexander von Wagner, Karl von Piloty and Wilhelm Leibl. Became a friend of Frank Duveneck, Walter Shirlaw and J. Frank Currier, 1872. Sent canvases to U.S. for exhibition, 1874-77. 1877-78 traveled to Venice with Duveneck and John Twachtman; while in Italy received invitation to teach at Royal Academy, Munich, which he declined. Returned to New York to teach at Art Students' League. Established studio on 10th Street where he also taught privately. Studio became meeting place for artists, including Julian Alden Weir, Edwin Austin Abbey, Winslow Homer and Elihu Vedder, 1878. Traveled back and forth on painting expeditions to Europe, meeting and working with American painters Weir, Robert Frederick Blum, J. Carroll Beckwith and H.S. Mowbray; and European artists Alfred Stevens and Giovanni Boldini, 1881-84. 1885, elected President of Society of American Artists; met Whistler in London and they painted portraits of each other. Same year traveled with him to Belgium and Holland to see mutual friends Alfred Stevens, Jules Bastien-Lepage and Robert Blum; first one-man exhibition at Boston Art Club, painted landscapes in New York and Brooklyn. Married Alice Gerson, 1886. Artists elected to membership in National Academy with Chase were Robert Blum, George de Forest Brush, Charles C. Curran, William H. Low, Robert C. Minor Mowbray, Augustus Saint Gaudens, Olin Warner, 1888. At party in Chase's 10th Street Studio arranged by John Singer Sargent and Mrs. Jack Gardiner of Boston Spanish dancer Carmencita entertained and inspired paintings by Sargent and Chase. Opened summer school in Shinnecock, Long Island, 1891. 1895, resigned presidency of Society of American Artists after ten years; gave up 10th Street Studio; purchased house on Stuyvesant Square. Auction of contents of 10th Street Studio was financial disaster. Resigned teaching posts in Brooklyn Art School and Art Students' League. 1896, opened Chase School of Art in New York City and began commuting to Pennsylvania Academy of the Fine Arts to teach. Took class to Madrid, 1896. Taught and exhibited extensively in United States and Europe, 1897-1901. 1902, final summer at Shinnecock Art School, traveled to London to sit for portrait by Sargent, commissioned by Chase's students. Purchased villa near Fiesole, Italy, 1907; commissioned by Italian government to paint self-portrait for Uffizi Gallery; elected to American Academy of Arts and Letters. Resumed teaching classes at Art Students' League, 1908. Exhibited in important international exhibitions Exposición International de Bellas Artes, Chile, 1910; Panama-Pacific Exhibition, San Francisco 1915, as well as one-man shows at Vose Gallery, Boston, 1909; National Arts Club, New York, 1910, and traveling exhibition to Detroit and Toledo museums, 1916. Continued traveling in Europe, 1909-16. Saw Futurist exhibition in Paris and Armory Show in New York, disapproved of modernist tendencies. Died in New York Oct. 25.

BSK

Robert Frederick Blum

Born Cincinnati, Oh., July 9. Studied under Frank Duveneck at McMicken School of Design, classmate of Kenyon Cox. 1876, Traveled with Cox to Philadelphia for Centennial Exhibition. Studied at Pennsylvania Academy of the Fine Arts under Thomas Eakins. Moved to New York and shared studio with Cox, 1879. 1879-1880 traveled to Europe: London, Paris, Genoa, Rome; in Venice, met Duveneck and Whistler. 1881, again in Europe; visited Venice and went to Spain to study Velázquez, with William Merritt Chase and writer William Baer; in 1882 in Antwerp, Brussels, Haarlem and Zandvoort. 1882-85 worked in Holland; visited by Chase and Whistler, 1885. Returned to New York and took over Julian Alden Weir's studio, working there 1885-1893. In Japan 1889-1891, on commission by *Scribner's Magazine* to illustrate Sir Edwin Arnold's *Japonica*, published 1890-91. Returned to New York; commissioned to paint murals for Mendelssohn Hall, New York, executed *Mood to Music* and *Vintage Festival*, 1893. Murals completed, 1898 (studies at National Academy, murals now in Brooklyn Museum). Died in New York on June 8.

BSK

William Merritt Chase (1849-1916) A.N.A. 1888, N.A. 1890
PORTRAIT OF ROBERT BLUM (1857-1903) A.N.A. 1888, N.A. 1893
Oil on canvas
21⅛ x 17⅛
Signed center right: Chase.

Thomas Wilmer Dewing

Born Boston, Mass., May 4. Worked as lithographer and took some classes at Boston Art Club; classmates included James Wells Champney, Francis Millet, Edwin Weeks. Traveled to Paris to study at Académie Julian under Gustave Boulanger and Jules Joseph Lefèbvre, 1876. Joined Edwin H. Blashfield and Walter Gay in studio of Léon Bonnat. Established friendship with William Sartain and William Merritt Chase. Moved briefly to Munich to study with Frank Duveneck, 1876-78. Returned to U.S., began teaching as assistant in evening class at Museum of Fine Arts, Boston. Exhibited at Society of American Artists, 1878. Became friends with Abbott Handerson Thayer who introduced him to Maria Oakley, New York painter (whom he married in 1881); elected to Society of American Artists, 1880. Taught composition at Art Students' League, 1881-88. Exhibited regularly at Society of American Artists and National Academy of Design, 1879-1896. His friend Chase painted portrait of him for National Academy of Design a year before Chase's election. Established studio at 3 Washington Square North 1886-95. Other artists in studio building were Will and Mary Fairchild Low and E.L. Henry. Traveled to Europe, 1883. Summered in Cornish, N.H., 1885-1903; other artists located there were Abbott Thayer, George de Forest Brush, Augustus St. Gaudens and Kenyon Cox. Resigned from Society of American Artists, 1898. Became member of American Impressionists' group known as "The Ten," 1898. 1900, commissioned to design program of stained glass for Rogers Church in Fairhaven, Mass.; painted murals for New York Appellate Courthouse; Library of Congress, Washington, D.C.; Boston State House; and U.S. Pavilion at Paris Exposition. Elected to National Institute of Arts and Letters, 1908.

BSK

Walter Shirlaw

Born in Paisley, Scotland, Aug. 6. Emigrated to United States, 1841, settled in New York City. Quit public school at age twelve, 1850, to pursue training in art. Apprenticed himself to bank note engraver, worked as engraver, then designer for several years. Studied at National Academy of Design. Opened a studio in New York and began exhibiting at National Academy, 1862. Moved to Chicago to take position as designer in bank note company, maintained studio there. Active in founding of Art Institute of Chicago. Traveled to Europe to study, first to Paris, then to Munich, 1870. Enrolled in Royal Academy under Johann Rabb, Arthur Georges Ramberg, Paul Wagner and Wilhelm Lindenschmidt (the younger). Awarded medal at Royal Academy in Munich and scholarship of studio space and free use of model. Moved to Polling, Germany, to work with Frank Duveneck and William Merritt Chase, the three becoming known as "the Father, the Son, and the Holy Ghost" of the "Duveneck Boys," 1877. Also there were John White Alexander, John Twachtman, Thomas Dewing and Robert F. Blum. Exhibited at Centennial Exhibition, Philadelphia, where he received a medal, 1876. Traveled through Europe, visiting and working in France, Holland, Italy, England and Spain. Exhibited regularly in National Academy exhibitions. Upon his return to New York, 1877, elected an Associate of National Academy. Resigned to found the Society of American Artists; served as first President for a term of two years, 1879-1881. Taught at Art Students' League, 1877-1881. Re-elected Associate of National Academy, 1887. Exhibited at Paris Exposition, 1889. Commissioned to paint murals for World's Columbian Exposition, 1893, and Library of Congress, 1896, as well as murals in private residences. Awarded silver medals at Pan-American Exposition, Buffalo, 1901, and St. Louis Exposition, 1904. Member of Century Association, National Association of Mural Painters, and Artists' Aid Society. Died in Madrid, Dec. 26.

BSK

Irving R. Wiles

Born in Utica, N.Y. on Apr. 8. At early age, moved with family to New York City where painter-father maintained studio on Washington Square. Father encouraged his enrollment at Art Students' League, after one year allowed him to choose between career as artist or violinist, 1880. Studied under J. Carroll Beckwith and William Merritt Chase at the League. Chase was to become greatest influence and close friend. Traveled to Paris, at urging of Beckwith, to study with Charles Emile Auguste Carolus-Duran, 1882. Returned to New York, 1883, supported himself with commissions for illustrations in *Century, Harper's* and *Scribner's* magazines. Married Mary Lee, 1887. Taught painting at Art Student's League 1890s and 1900s, The Chase School and in his own studio. Exhibited watercolors at Paris Salon, received Honorable Mention, 1889. Received Bronze Medal at World's Columbian Exposition, Chicago, 1893. Established summer art school with father at Peconic, Long Island, N.Y., where friend and artist E.A. Bell had summer home, late 1890's. Awarded Shaw Prize, Society of American Artists; Bronze Medal, Paris Exposition, 1900. Traveled to Holland and Spain with William T. Smedley to study work of Frans Hals and Velázquez, 1904-05. First one-man show of portraits held at Knoedler Galleries; traveled to Italy; Gold Medal at Exposición International de Bellas Artes, Buenos Aires, 1910. Traveled with daughter, Gladys, to England, 1912. Exhibited and received awards at Pennsylvania Academy of the Fine Arts, National Academy, American Artists Professional League, Lotos Club and American Watercolor Society. Died in Peconic, N.Y., July 29.

BSK

Charles W. Hawthorne

Born in Lodi, Ill., Jan. 8. Came to New York, 1890. Worked during day at various jobs, on docks and at stained-glass factory; studied painting at night at Art Students' League under Frank Dumond, 1893; under George de Forest Brush and Henry Siddons Mowbray, 1894-95. Began studying with William Merritt Chase at Shinnecock, L.I., summer 1896. Fall 1896, helped Chase organize Chase School of Art, Manhattan (from 1898 called New York School of Art), and worked as assistant; met wife-to-be Ethel Marion Campbell, also a Chase student and Corresponding Secretary at Chase's school, summer 1897. Traveled to Holland, living in Zandvoort, near Haarlem. Greatly influenced by Frans Hals's fluent brushwork, but to subdue strong impulse to copy it, worked exclusively with palette knife, summer 1898. 1899, back in New York; discontinued association with Chase; opened own summer school, Provincetown, Mass. on Cape Cod. First one-man show at Clausen Gallery, 1902. Married Ethel Marion Campbell, 1903. Traveled to Italy with financial assistance from collectors, including John Gellatly. Influenced by psychological aspect of Italian Renaissance portraiture. Discovered formula for Tintoretto's medium, 1906 (subsequently manufactured in New York, called Hawthorne Medium). Spent winters in Bermuda or Paris, summers in Provincetown, 1907-1919. Influential teacher of artists such as Edwin Dickinson and Raphael Soyer. Elected Société Nationale des Beaux-Arts, Paris, 1913. Taught at National Academy of Design, Art Students' League, Art Institute of Chicago, and John Herron Art Institute, Indianapolis. Died in Baltimore, Md., Nov. 29. Wife published *Hawthorne on Painting*, 1938.

BSK

William Merritt Chase (1849-1916) A.N.A. 1888, N.A. 1890
PORTRAIT OF THOMAS WILMER DEWING (1851-1938)
  A.N.A 1887, N.A. 1888
Oil on canvas
20⅞ x 17¼
Signed center left: Chase / 87.

Walter Shirlaw (1838-1909) A.N.A. 1887, N.A. 1888
SELF-PORTRAIT
Oil on canvas remounted on masonite
30⅛ x 25
Unsigned

Irving R. Wiles (1861-1948) A.N.A. 1889, N.A. 1897
SELF-PORTRAIT
Oil on canvas
22⅛ x 18
Signed upper right: Irving R. Wiles / 1897

Charles Webster Hawthorne (1872-1930) A.N.A. 1908, N.A.
  1911
SELF-PORTRAIT
Oil on canvas remounted on masonite
30 x 25
Signed upper right: C.W.H. / CWHawthorne

Painters in Philadelphia

1876 WAS A PROUD YEAR FOR PHILADELPHIA AND AN AUSPICIOUS MOMENT FOR THE VISUAL ARTS THERE, as well. The city, which a century before had witnessed the signing of the Declaration of Independence, appropriately hosted the nation's Centennial Exposition, and the only permanent building erected on the Centennial site was designated the new Pennsylvania Museum and School of Industrial Art (now the Philadelphia Museum of Art and the Philadelphia College of Art).

More pertinent to the Philadelphians represented in the present exhibition was the sumptuous rehousing, as part of the centennial celebration, of the Pennsylvania Academy of the Fine Arts, then as now the oldest American art academy extant. About its designer, Philadelphian Frank Furness, it has been remarked that "Perhaps no individual architect better epitomizes the independence, exuberant invention and plastic strength of the 70's and 80's."[1] Curiously, the same could be said of Thomas Eakins (1844–1916), the Philadelphia artist who, inside Furness's structure, developed the most inventive, thoroughgoing art school curriculum of the day.

Whereas New York's National Academy of Design and the newly established Boston Museum School offered cast and life drawing and anatomy lectures along traditional lines, Pennsylvania Academy students painted and modeled with clay from life and actually dissected humans and animals. Eakins's novel approach, now termed "naturalism," taught students to observe and experience forms inside-out and thereby to grasp them substantively, in order to recreate them in paint exactly as they are in life. Eakins's *Self-Portrait* (ca. 1902) in the National Academy is the quintessential expression of his doctrine. By building his bust in paint, layer upon layer—rather than outlining it and filling in the color, as was taught in contemporary French academies—Eakins, with great anatomical knowledge, could forge a likeness of staggering corporeal truth.

From Eakins's tenure through the early twentieth century, the thrust of the Academy's teaching remained the same, though decreasingly so after he left in 1886. Fundamentally, the curriculum was based on the belief that "students should gain accurate information rather than merely the knack of representing something."[2] As expressed by Eakins's successor, Thomas Anshutz (1951–1912), "to lead the student to reproduce all the facts of nature he can see is to give him the power to choose his own road."[3]

Anshutz first attended the National Academy, then its Philadelphia counterpart. His experiences there clarify a crucial difference in art instruction at the two institutions. "It was not until some time after I had come to Philadelphia . . . that I learned the essential difference between making a careful copy of lines and forms which express some action and trying to express the action itself."[4] Notably, too, the Pennsylvania Academy placed more emphasis on its school, while the National Academy stressed exhibitions. Students in Philadelphia saw far more of their professors than did their peers in New York and at the latter enjoyed much more impressive studios occupying the entire first floor, in contrast to the National Academy's basement facility.

For ten years at the Pennsylvania Academy, first as Eakins's pupil, then as his assistant professor, Anshutz was immersed in Eakins's system, as *Ironworkers Noontime* (ca. 1880–82), Anshutz's best-known canvas, plainly reveals. This image of about two dozen brawny workmen arranged alongside an iron mill, each in a distinctly different pose, is a textbook example of Eakins's anatomical precepts. Yet, as such, the painting underscores the chief pitfall of Eakins's teaching methods: they were so exhaustive that students were left with little time or energy to apply his principles toward their own ends. Instead, at cross-purposes with the Academy's aims, Eakins's means became their end. Indeed, Anshutz's ironworkers, with their taut musculature, suggest as much about the school's intense atmosphere under Eakins as they do about the artistic fundamentals he stressed.

It is ironic that Anshutz, having signed a petition in 1876 urging Academy directors to let Eakins teach life classes in the new building, helped draft a letter a decade later soliciting his dismissal. Eakins resigned, but his memory did not. His diploma *Self-Portrait* bluntly and bitterly communicates the repeated rejection he suffered both as an educator and as an artist. Anshutz remained on the faculty, and the prodigious list of artists he taught is a sure barometer of his success as a teacher. In fact, the Academy's 1909 annual exhibition included works by nearly one hundred Anshutz students.

Whereas Eakins had dwelled intently upon the subject at hand and the sensory and technical aspects of reproducing it accurately, Anshutz also scrutinized his students to elicit their individual talents, as the broad range of subjects and styles in their mature work reflects. Significantly, Eakins had used his own paintings as references in class, while Anshutz exalted the students' work. In a sense, Anshutz retained the posture of a student, sketching alongside his pupils, one of whom, Edward W. Redfield (1869–1965), described Anshutz as "one of the crowd."[5]

As for the curriculum, Anshutz, according to another of his students, John Sloan, had "the same things [as Eakins] to say about observation of life, character of forms, striving for solidity, and plain painting with no bravura."[6] Anshutz, however, was more flexible about such particulars as media and subject matter. Unlike Eakins, he did not force students into an early use of oils. In 1899 he was quoted as believing that "it didn't make much matter what medium one used or what one chose to portray so long as one was learning how to paint."[7]

This attitude grew, in part, from Anshutz's year of study, at age 42, at the Académie Julian in Paris. There he responded to new stimuli with the same curiosity that distinguished his teaching. The tense muscularity of his pre-Paris figure drawings relaxed, in favor of broader, looser handling. His absorption with oils and earthy pigments under Eakins gave way to equal involvement with pastels, watercolors and brighter hues. Yet the core of Eakins's instruction—his emphasis on form—remained paramount in Anshutz's late works: experimental compositions uniting "a traditional respect for fact with a fresh insight into spatial volumes. . . . By curious coincidence, crudely but intellectually, the theoretical concerns of Cézanne are reached for, the formalization of form beyond Impressionism."[8]

Anshutz apparently found Eakins's approach to portraiture definitive; for his diploma likeness (1910) and other late portraits scarcely differ technically from those painted before his excursion abroad. As his *Self-Portrait* looks back, so, strangely, does Anshutz within it. Leslie Katz remarked considering his haunting countenance, "Honesty requires us to conclude in the face of ironical fact that Thomas P. Anshutz now appears to have been, as painter as well as teacher, Eakins' most accomplished pupil, and experimental craftsman, evolving from the past, preparing for the future, a key figure of transition."[9] Surely one venerable mark of the modesty which made him so effective a catalyst is that his portrait derives from two 1906 portrayals of Anshutz by his *student*, Robert Henri.

Eakins's principles were highly regarded even by a Philadelphia portraitist who did not study with him, Cecilia Beaux (1855–1942). Wary, though, of his "unrivalled sway"[10] over Academy students, Beaux took life classes instead with Eakins's lifelong friend William Sartain. Although their educations were similar, Sartain, unlike Eakins, had studied in Munich, where—of consequence for Beaux—fluid brushwork was championed. Through Eakins's students Beaux gleaned the essence of his anatomical reasoning, and his portraits impressed her with his "unerring eye for the ultimate instant in action and in the drama of a head."[11] Likewise, Sartain "always insisted upon the proportions of the head, in view of its power of content, the summing up as it were,—of the measure of the individual."[12]

Beaux's studied and incisive rendering of her own head in the diploma Self-Portrait (1894) manifests this early training. The buoyant touch and the pastel tones of her dress, however, point to concerns awakened during her nineteen-month sojourn abroad during 1888–89. At the Académie Julian, Beaux was encouraged to paint with "greater vivacity, resonance and brilliance."[13] Impressionist canvases may have impelled her toward more liberal handling of paint, but ironically a summer in Brittany with Philadelphia expatriate Alexander Harrison seems to have been most directly responsible for her transformed palette. Beaux noted his attraction to opaline color schemes, and after her contact with him they turned up in her own paintings. Befitting a former Eakins student and an engineer, Harrison's "method was searching and had the quality of science."[14] It must have reinforced in Beaux the slow, exacting work process that she, too, had formulated in Philadelphia.[15]

Returning there, she worked with pastels to increase her color expertise. A new confidence in controlling brush and color in the portraits she painted between 1893 and 1895 comes across readily in her poised diploma likeness, as does the tenacity which guided her from the outset in assimilating technical skills from various sources without ever being dominated stylistically by any of them.

One of the many Anshutz students whose work disclosed the effectiveness of his teaching is Edward Redfield, who, in accord with Academy goals, applied fundamentals espoused by Eakins and Anshutz toward an independent aesthetic. In 1889, after four rigorous years at the Academy, Redfield—inclined, if anything, toward portraiture—left to attend the Académie Julian. Apparently disenchanted with the Paris school, he moved on later that year to Brolles, a tiny village near the Forest of Fontainebleau, where he began painting winter landscapes, thereafter the principal subject of his oeuvre.

Like Monet and Pissarro, whose landscapes he admired, Redfield painted outdoors, using swift, pasty brushstrokes. As one astute critic realized in 1910, however, "his work is a reflection of the methods of the impressionists which he has adapted to his own uses."[16] True to his Philadelphia training, Redfield employed their animated brush to seize forms all the more forcefully and tactilely in paint, rather than to decompose them as Monet sought to do. The qualities reviewers appreciated in his landscapes—"uncompromising, searching strokes,"[17] "tree and ground forms . . . vigorously drawn . . . local color . . . acccurately stated"[18]—place Redfield squarely in the Eakins-Anshutz lineage. Yet his Impressionist application of their dogma was, at the time, a novelty in America. Exclaimed a 1916 exhibition pamphlet, "His study of his subject is carefully analytic, but his execution once begun is rapid almost beyond belief."[19]

Most of Redfield's landscapes were painted near the farm he settled on the Delaware River in Bucks County, Pennsylvania in 1898, two years after returning from France. His motifs—snowy roads and terrain, old buildings, bare trees, icy streams and the Delaware River itself—have a "homely native flavor,"[20] as do Eakins's and Anshutz's. It seems fitting that Eakins should have painted the diploma portrait (ca. 1904) of an artist with whom he shared so many personal traits. Both Eakins and Redfield have been repeatedly characterized in print as forthright, rugged, hard-working, outdoor-loving, parochial, analytical and tenacious; their paintings and diploma likenesses project this better.

By way of explaining Eakins's resignation, the Academy's 1886 annual report stated, "The Committee on instruction were of the opinion that better results would be obtained and a broader teaching follow from the influence of several minds in the school rather than from the influence of one."[21] The Academy implemented its new policy by engaging leading artists from other cities as visiting faculty. One of these artists, Robert Vonnoh (1858–1933), was principal instructor in portrait and figure painting from 1891 to 1896.

Noted for his versatility as a painter, Vonnoh represented the kind of new blood Academy directors endeavored to introduce. A typical description reads, "Mr. Vonnoh excels as a painter of portraits, landscapes and figures; he holds fast to academic tradition and at the same time may be reckoned with those who are in the vanguard of progress."[22] Apparently the board sought artists with sound, academic underpinnings and a modern, impressionistic outlook. Other faculty selections—Beaux, Theodore Robinson, Joseph DeCamp, Julian Alden Weir and William Merritt Chase—support this view and amplify the gap between the school's longstanding concentration on form and the more precocious exploration by art schools elsewhere of composition and brushwork, independent of form.

While studying with Vonnoh, for instance, Henri's "weakness for meticulous drawing" was apparently surmounted by a "certain surety and dash."[23] Notably, though, Vonnoh's underlying philosophy agreed with the Academy's. "My teaching has been general, not specific. My aim has been to give the student fundamentals to which he can always hie back for reference, natural laws which serve as a point of departure."[24] Perhaps Vonnoh's diploma *Self-Portrait* (1899) best illustrates what he imparted to Academy students: a vivid characterization, soundly crafted, it seems in the same breath fluent and facile.

Beaux moved to New York in the 1890s, but she returned to Philadelphia periodically from 1895 to 1915 to teach portrait painting and drawing as Vonnoh's successor. Like Eakins, Beaux emphasized solid construction of the head and disciplined students to hard work. In her estimation, "Eakins had no follower of his own metal there, but the tradition of his day remained and much very sincere work was done."[25]

Daniel Garber (1880–1958), a landscape and figure painter and a favorite student of Anshutz's, became assistant professor in 1909, as Anshutz had previously been to Eakins. Until 1950, when he retired, Garber perpetuated the nineteenth-century aesthetic values and curriculum of Anshutz and Beaux, and like them he was known as a firm disciplinarian. This continuity stabilized the school and offset the varied instruction provided by temporary visiting faculty.

When Garber, an Indiana native, enrolled at the Academy in 1899, fourteen years after Redfield, he was already drawn toward landscape painting, a fact that highlights the rise and westward spread of Impressionism in America during the intervening years. As early as high school Garber revered the American Impressionist J. Alden Weir, to the extent that he signed his name *J.* Daniel Garber until 1900. Before entering the Pennsylvania Academy, he took life and illustration classes at the Art Academy of Cincinnati, where he encountered landscapes by major Cincinnati-born painters Frank Duveneck, John Twachtman and others.

In Philadelphia, Garber worked with Anshutz, Beaux, Chase and, presumably, Weir, who taught there between 1899 and 1905 (the years of Garber's schooling) and whose proclivity toward sun-drenched summer scenes Garber grew to share. In 1905 Garber went to London, and the paintings he executed there exhibit his diversified training. He painted his father-in-law "entirely within the Eakins-Anshutz tradition," while "apart from this portrait . . . Garber's work in England demonstrates the most wholeheartedly Impressionist moment in his career."[26] Rather than undergo further formal study abroad, Garber toured England, Italy and France for two years, before returning to Philadelphia.

Perhaps inspired by his colonial Pennsylvania ancestry, Garber, like Redfield, moved to historic Bucks County, where his paintings accented its trees, hillsides, quarries and rivers. Curiously his landscapes span the seasonal range from summer to late fall, that period which Redfield's scenes of winter and early spring miss. Occasional exhibitions paired the two artists, where Redfield's "sharper tang of reality" was contrasted with Garber's "eye for patterns,"[27] reflecting his background in graphic illustration. One reviewer deemed Garber's art "golden age"[28] realism. As the label implies, it was an Impressionist captivation with radiant light, rather than rapid brushwork, that styled his expression. Yet, Garber's light, like Redfield's paint texture, heightens, rather than breaks down, reality; "forms are not at all dissolved, but they are seen in splendid light."[29]

Whatever devices, Impressionist or otherwise, enhanced and differentiated the art of these Philadelphians, it was an impulse toward form and toward essential realities—effectuated at the Pennsylvania Academy by Eakins and perhaps rooted in Philadelphia itself—that remained at the heart of their aesthetic. Beaux wrote of Eakins, "No one who studied under him ever forgot his precepts, or could be interested in any principles of Art that did not include his. They were rock-bottom, fundamental, but somehow reached regions by research, that others could not gain by flight."[30] The independent presence of these Philadelphians within the present exhibition is a striking manifestation of the ultimate significance of her remark.

Mary Wayne Fritzsche

Notes

1. Daniel Mendelowitz, *A History of American Art* (New York: 1970), p. 252

2. Fairman Rogers, "The Schools of the Pennsylvania Academy of Fine Arts," *The Penn Monthly,* vol. 12 (June 1881), p. 458

3. Letter from Anshutz to PAFA President Edward Coates, May 15, 1893

4. Quoted by Sandra Denny Heard in *Thomas P. Anshutz, 1851–1912* (exh. cat., Philadelphia; PAFA, 1973), p. 6

5. *Ibid.,* p. 10.

6. *Ibid.,* pp. 8–10.

7. Francis J. Ziegler, "An Unassuming Painter—Thomas P. Anshutz." *Brush and Pencil,* vol. 4 (Sept. 1899), p. 279

8. Leslie Katz, "The Breakthrough of Anshutz," *Arts Magazine,* vol. 37 (March 1963), p. 29

9. *Ibid.*

10. Cecilia Beaux, *Background with Figures* (Boston and New York: 1930), p. 96

11. *Ibid.,* p. 97

12. *Ibid.,* p. 89

13. Monsieur Julian, quoted by Frank H. Goodyear, Jr., in *Cecilia Beaux, Portrait of an Artist* (exh. cat., Philadelphia: PAFA, 1974), p. 26

14. Beaux, *op. cit.,* p. 149

15. In general, it is essential to recognize that the Philadelphians discussed in this essay associated, while studying abroad, with Pennsylvania Academy-trained colleagues.

16. J. Nilsin Lauvrik, "Edward W. Redfield—Landscape Painter." *International Studio,* vol. 51 (Aug. 1910), p. 36

17. *Ibid.,* p. 29

18. Royal Cortissoz, unidentified clipping, Edward Redfield Papers, Archives of American Art

19. Grand Rapids Art Association, *Exhibition of Paintings by Edward W. Redfield* (exh. cat., Grand Rapids, Mich.: Oct. 1916)

20. Lauvrik, *op. cit.,* p. 29

21. Edward Coates, "Report of the Committee on Instruction", *Eightieth Annual Report of the Pennsylvania Academy of the Fine Arts* (Philadelphia: 1886)

22. Anon., "The Art of Robert Vonnoh," *Art and Progress,* vol. 4, (June 1913), p. 999

23. Bennard B. Perlman, *The Immortal Eight* (New York: 1962), p. 83

24. Quoted in May Brawley Hill, "Robert William Vonnoh," unpubl. CUNY paper (Sept. 1982), p. 22

25. Beaux, *op. cit.,* p. 226

26. Kathleen A. Foster, in *Daniel Garber, 1880–1958* (exh. cat., Philadelphia: PAFA, 1980), p. 21

27. *Art Digest,* (Dec. 18, 1932). Archives of American Art, Roll n55, fr. 791

28. Brooklyn *Daily Eagle,* April 5, 1925

29. William H. Gerdts, in *American Impressionism* (exh. cat., Seattle: Henry Art Gallery, University of Washington, 1980), p. 99

30. Beaux, *op. cit.,* p. 96

Thomas Eakins (1844-1919) A.N.A. 1902, N.A. 1902
PORTRAIT OF EDWARD W. REDFIELD (1869-1965)
  A.N.A. 1904, N.A. 1906
Oil on canvas
20 x 26
Unsigned

Thomas Eakins

Born in Philadelphia, on July 25 to Benjamin Eakins, writing master and teacher of penmanship. 1857, entered Central High School, well known for advanced curriculum and emphasis on science. Excelled in drawing class, learning rudiments of perspective and technique. 1861, B.A.; worked with father teaching penmanship, probably for several years. 1862, registered at Pennsylvania Academy of the Fine Arts to draw from antique casts; 1863, attended life classes and anatomy lectures; probably continued to study drawing there until 1866. 1864-65, observed demonstrations in anatomy classes at Jefferson Medical College, Philadelphia. 1866, to France; 1866-69, studied at Ecole des Beaux-Arts, Paris, first in atelier of Jean Leon Gérôme, then with sculptor A. A. Dumont and painter Léon Bonnat. 1868-69, traveled to Italy, Germany, Belgium and Spain, where he spent several months. 1870, returned to Philadelphia; began painting domestic genre scenes, sporting subjects, portraits of family and friends. 1876, exhibited several oils and watercolors in Centennial Exhibition, Philadelphia, but *Portrait of Dr. Gross (The Gross Clinic)* rejected as unsightly; painting finally shown at U.S. Army Hospital during Centennial. 1876-77, worked as unpaid assistant to Christian Schussele, Professor of Drawing and Painting, Pennsylvania Academy. When Academy directors resolved that Schussele could not delegate authority, Eakins left Academy to teach at Art Students' Union, newly formed by dissatisfied Academy students. 1877, exhibited for first time in National Academy of Design Annual; undertook first known commission, from Union League of Philadelphia for portrait of President Rutherford B. Hayes (now lost). 1878, Pennsylvania Academy directors rescinded resolution concerning Schussele; Eakins again volunteered to assist him; became Professor of Painting and Chief Demonstrator of Anatomy. 1879, Schussele died, Eakins succeeded him as paid professor, teaching first of his perspective lectures in 1880. 1884, married his pupil Susan Hannah Macdowell. Devoted much time to anatomy lectures at Pennsylvania Academy, Brooklyn Art Association and Art Students' League, New York. Inspired by motion photography of Eadweard Muybridge, began photographing figures in motion, using more advanced technical methods. 1886, because of opposition to Eakins's teaching methods, specifically his use of nude male model in women's life class, Pennsylvania Academy directors dismissed him. Protesting students organized Art Students' League of Philadelphia with Eakins as instructor. 1888-1895, lectured on anatomy at National Academy of Design. 1889, students of University of Pennsylvania School of Medicine commissioned portrait of Dr. D. Hayes Agnew. 1891, exhibited at Pennsylvania Academy for first time since 1885, but *The Agnew Clinic* rejected on a technicality. 1892, resigned from Society of American Artists after three years' rejection of his paintings. 1895, anatomy lectures at National Academy and Drexel Institute, Philadelphia, canceled because of opposition to nude male model in life class. Lecturing on anatomy ceased after 1894-95 season. Early 1900's, painted fourteen portraits of members of Catholic clergy. From 1904, exhibited at National Academy every year except two, and at Society of American Artists, 1902-06, when Society and Academy merged. With increasing recognition in early 1900's, produced many more works than in 1890's; all of these later paintings were portraits. 1904, recipient of Temple Gold Medal, Pennsylvania Academy. 1910, poor health and failing eyes; last portraits of any distinction. On June 25, Eakins died. 1917, Metropolitan Museum of Art mounted memorial exhibition; Pennsylvania Academy, yielding to pressure, opened large exhibition in his honor. *See color, page 37.*

DA

Edward W. Redfield

Born in Bridgeville, Del., on Dec. 18. At age seven exhibited a rendering of a cow at Centennial Exhibition in Philadelphia, 1876. Encouraged at early age to pursue art, studied at Pennsylvania Academy of the Fine Arts before traveling to Paris in 1886, to study with academician William Adolphe Bouguereau. Met American painter Robert Henri, with whom he traveled to Venice in 1891. 1898, returned to U.S., acquired farmhouse in Center Bridge, near New Hope, Pa. One of first artists to settle in Bucks County area, spent many years painting local scenery. Also painted in Boothbay Harbor, Me. where he summered. Given many honors between 1900 and 1930, winning almost every prize eligible for landscape painting at Pennsylvania Academy. Also recognized internationally, earning awards from Paris Salon, 1900 Paris Exposition and 1910 Buenos Aires Exposition. Temperamental in nature, resigned from National Academy of Design in 1910 because letters were wrongly addressed to him through a clerical error; he was later reinstated. 1953, held one-man show in New Hope, an area he helped establish as an arts center. Died in Center Bridge, Oct. 19.

DA

Cecilia Beaux

Born Philadelphia to family of some wealth. Began drawing at home at early age; by 1872, an accomplished draftsman, having studied with Dutch artist Adolf van der Whelen. 1875, United States Geological Survey commission to make fossil drawings. 1877–79, studied at Pennsylvania Academy of the Fine Arts; in 1879, exhibited for first time. 1881–83, received classroom instruction in Philadelphia from William Sartain. Her work well received, she painted several notable portraits before traveling to France in 1888. Enrolled that year at Académie Julian in Paris; encouraged by academic masters Tony Robert-Fleury and William Adolphe Bouguereau. Summer with American colony at Concarneaux, then travel to Italy. 1889, returned to Paris to attend evening classes at Académie Colarossi and work in atelier of Benjamin Constant. 1889, visited London before returning to Philadelphia. 1893, elected to Society of American Artists; awarded the Dodge Prize from National Academy of Design, the first of many awards for her paintings. 1895–1915, taught at Pennsylvania Academy of the Fine Arts. 1896, visited France and England, principally to see six of her paintings on exhibition at Champs-de-Mars, Paris. Acquainted with John Singer Sargent in London and Monet in Giverny. 1897, first large exhibition, at St. Botolph Club, Boston. 1898, awarded Gold Medal of Honor by Pennsylvania Academy of the Fine Arts. 1899, painted double portrait *Mother and Daughter*, which won several awards and established her as a preeminent American portraitist. Subsequently received many distinguished commissions and exhibited widely in America. 1904–1924, traveled to Europe intermittently. Ceased nearly all painting in 1930, the year her autobiography, *Background with Figures*, was published. 1935, American Academy of Arts and Letters opened largest exhibition of her work shown during her lifetime. Died on September 7, in Gloucester, Mass., her summer home for many years. *See color, page 38.*

DA

Thomas Pollock Anshutz (1851-1912) A.N.A. 1910
SELF-PORTRAIT
Oil on canvas
30 x 25⅛
Signed lower right: Thomas Anshutz

Thomas Pollock Anshutz

Born Newport, Ky., on Oct. 5. Family moved to Philadelphia, 1871. Anshutz went to New York to study at National Academy of Design under Lemuel Wilmarth, 1872. At Pennsylvania Academy of the Fine Arts, studied with Christian Schuessle in 1876 and Thomas Eakins, 1879-1882. Began teaching at Pennsylvania Academy of the Fine Arts, 1881, as assistant to Thomas Eakins. Succeeded Eakins as instructor in anatomy, drawing and painting, 1886. Married Effie Shriver Russell; took sabbatical from Pennsylvania Academy of the Fine Arts to travel in Europe. Lived in Paris and studied at Académie Julian in classes of Henri Lucien Doucet and William Adolphe Bouguereau, 1892. Returned to United States, rejoined faculty of Pennsylvania Academy, 1893. Other faculty members, William Merritt Chase and Cecilia Beaux. 1898, established Darby School of Painting with Hugh Breckenridge in Fort Washington, Pa. Students include Robert Henri, Edward W. Redfield, William Glackens and Daniel Garber. Traveled to London, 1900. Became Director of Pennsylvania Academy of the Fine Arts after Chase resigned, 1909. Elected Associate of National Academy of Design, 1910 (his student Garber also elected that year). President of Philadelphia Sketch Club, 1910-12. Died in Fort Washington, June 16.

BSK

Bessie Potter Vonnoh

Born in St. Louis, Mo. Aug. 17. Family moved to Chicago, 1874. Enrolled as a student at Art Institute of Chicago, 1890. Later studied and worked in sculptor Lorado Taft's studio where she met Robert Vonnoh. Had First exhibition 1891. Exhibited in Women's Building of the World's Columbian Exposition, 1893. Established her own studio, 1894. Her sculpture was critically well received by mid-1890's, reputation established outside Chicago area. Traveled to France, 1895, and Italy, 1896. Married Robert Vonnoh, 1899. Won Gold Medal at Paris Exposition, 1900. Member of Society of American Artists; exhibited and won Gold Medal at St. Louis Exposition, 1904. Lived in artists' colony in Lyme, Conn. Became Associate of National Academy of Design, 1906, when Society of American Artists merged with National Academy of Design. Had several two-person shows with husband: including Montross Galleries, 1913, and Ainslie Galleries, 1923. Received Academy Gold Medal, 1921. Commissions for Roosevelt Bird Bath, Oyster Bay, Long Island, N.Y., and monument in Central Park, New York City. Robert Vonnoh died, 1933. 1948, remarried to Dr. Edward L. Keyes and widowed again within one year. Continued to live and work in N.Y. where she died on March 9.

BSK

Robert William Vonnoh

Born in Hartford, Conn., Sept. 17. Worked in lithographic firm before entering Massachusetts Normal Art School, Boston, where he studied 1875-79. Taught at Massachusetts Normal Art School, Roxbury Evening Drawing School and Thayer Academy, 1879-1881. Studied in Paris at Académie Julian under Gustave Boulanger and Jules Joseph Lefèbvre. In Giverny, 1883. Returned to Boston, 1883, and resumed teaching at East Boston Evening Drawing School and Cowles Art School until 1885. Worked on figure paintings and portraits, became principal instructor at Museum of Fine Arts, Boston, 1885-87. Traveled to Europe, 1887-1891. Exhibited in Paris Salon, 1889. Principal instructor in portrait and figure painting at Pennsylvania Academy of the Fine Arts, 1891-96. Exhibited at World's Columbian Exposition, Chicago, 1893, and in Stockholm, 1896. Married sculptor Bessie Potter, 1899. Served on National Jury for American Section of Paris Exposition, 1900. Abroad 1907-1911. Taught composition and figure painting at Pennsylvania Academy 1918-1920; students include Robert Henri, William Glackens, Maxfield Parrish and Edward Redfield. Lived in artists' colony of Lyme, Conn. with Childe Hassam and in Grez, France, 1920-1933. Weakened eyesight curtailed painting activity from 1923. Served on advisory committee of Tiffany Foundation, 1923. Died at Riviera art colony in Nice, France, Dec. 28.

BSK

Daniel Garber

Born North Manchester, Ind., Apr. 11. Studied at Cincinnati Art Academy with Vincent Nowottny, 1897-98. Moved to Pennsylvania to study at Darby School under Thomas Anshutz and Henry Breckenridge in summers. Enrolled at Pennsylvania Academy of the Fine Arts under Anshutz, William Merritt Chase and Cecilia Beaux, 1899-1905. 1901, married Mary Franklin; worked as portrait painter and illustrator, studying at night until 1904. Began teaching drawing classes at Philadelphia School of Design for Women (Moore College of Art), 1904. 1905 awarded Cresson Fellowship from Pennsylvania Academy, with award money traveled to Europe; visited London, Florence, and staying in Paris. 1907, back in U.S., settled in Lumberville, Pa. Joined faculty of Pennsylvania Academy as assistant to Anshutz, teaching cast drawing, still life, and figure painting, 1909. Exhibited at Carnegie Institute, Pittsburgh; Corcoran Gallery of Art, Washington, D.C.; International Exposition, Buenos Aires; and St. Botolph Club, Boston. Summers at Tiffany Foundation, Long Island, 1921-23. Commissioned to do murals for Pennsylvania Building at the Sesqui-Centennial Exhibition, Philadelphia, 1926. Continued to exhibit regularly in national exhibitions, 1920s-1942, until serious heart condition and convalescence caused hiatus in painting activity. Major retrospective at Pennsylvania Academy of the Fine Arts, 1945. Elected to American Academy of Arts and Letters, 1947. Retired from teaching at Pennsylvania Academy of the Fine Arts 1950. During teaching career, students included Abraham Rattner, Francis Speight and Walter Stuempfig. Died after fall in Lumberville, Pa., July 5.

BSK

Robert William Vonnoh (1858-1933) A.N.A. 1899, N.A. 1906
SELF-PORTRAIT
Oil on canvas
24 x 20
Signed lower left: Vonnoh 1900

Robert William Vonnoh (1858-1933) A.N.A. 1899, N.A. 1906
PORTRAIT OF BESSIE POTTER VONNOH (1872-1955)
  A.N.A. 1906, N.A. 1921
Oil on canvas
23 x 27
Signed lower center: Vonnoh 1915

Daniel Garber (1880-1958) A.N.A. 1910, N.A. 1913
SELF-PORTRAIT
Oil on canvas
30¼ x 25¼
Signed upper right: DANIEL GARBER / SELF PORTRAIT /
  FOR THE NATIONAL ACADEMY / OF DESIGN

Late Nineteenth Century Idealists

Iℕ ᴀɴ ᴇssᴀʏ ᴏɴ Aʙʙᴏᴛᴛ Tʜᴀʏᴇʀ, ᴛʜᴇ ᴄʀɪᴛɪᴄ Rᴏʏᴀʟ Cᴏʀᴛɪssᴏᴢ ʀᴇᴄᴀʟʟᴇᴅ ʜɪs ꜰɪʀsᴛ ɪᴍᴘʀᴇssɪᴏɴs of the artist: "His eyes seemed to me then to burn with an essentially spiritual light, and his voice to have in it, when it was warmed by emotion, a finer timbre than one ever recognized among other men. Above all, his whole being seemed permeated by a tremendous earnestness."[1] All who knew Thayer were impressed with his vitality, intensity and intellect, qualities that characterized him from his youth. As a student in the Paris studio of the artist Jean Léon Gérôme, he was known as "l'homme serieux" for his hard work and high-mindedness.[2] To George de Forest Brush, a fellow artist and lifelong friend, the Thayer home in Paris was a bulwark against what seemed the shocking immorality of life in the Latin Quarter. Another friend and colleague, Maria Oakey Dewing, wife of the artist Thomas Dewing, noted that even as a young man Thayer was deeply thoughtful and committed to high ideals in art and life. He was so preoccupied with these ideals that he seemed to her lacking in humor and strangely unselfconscious. Throughout his life there was an innocence and naïveté in Thayer's idealistic nature that, combined with his extraordinary intensity, set him apart from others and often inspired their admiration and wonder.

Thayer was born in Boston in 1849 and moved with his family to Keene, New Hampshire, in 1856. He returned to Boston in 1864 to attend school and to begin his study of art with a local painter. He then joined his family in Brooklyn, where they had moved in 1867, and he attended the Brooklyn Art School and the National Academy of Design.

While he was still a teenager, he revealed remarkable artistic talent painting animal subjects with amazing facility from as early as age sixteen. In 1875 he married and moved to Paris to study at the Ecole des Beaux-Arts. He studied first with Henri Lehmann and then in the studio of Gérôme, where he remained for four years. Although he was inspired by Gérôme's teaching, he did not follow his method of precise drawing and carefully delineated form. Thayer painted in a broader, more impressionistic manner, characterized by variations and inconsistencies in the paint surface and a bold lack of finish. This manner, which remained a feature of his work throughout his career, was frequently criticized by his contemporaries. They accused him of poor technique and a lack of craftsmanship, but they excused these faults because of the powerful impact of his work, which they attributed, in part, to his unusual methods. The strength and individuality of Thayer's work is clearly evident in his *Self-Portrait*. The power of his personality, forcefully expressed in the penetrating eyes and broad, furrowed brow, seems to coalesce out of an explosive environment of pigment slashed and scumbled onto the planes and features of his face. It was typical of Thayer to concentrate on the face, the focus of the spirit and character of his subject, and to render other parts of the painting in less detail. As Cortissoz noted, "There are parts of some of his things which look unfinished. But they are never the essential parts. The beauty which he set out to express is always there."[3] This beauty was directly linked to Thayer's idea of the spiritual significance of his subject.

Thayer's greatest challenge as an artist was to capture the qualities of nobility or exaltation that he perceived in figures or landscape—or projected onto them from his inner vision. In his *Self-Portrait*, the stark frontality of the image, the emphasis on the piercing eyes and the nimbus-like shadow behind the head give an impression of heightened spirituality, reminiscent of religious icons. Although Thayer did not support organized religion, he had an innately religious nature and considered art to be a kind of worship. As he explained to his friend and pupil William James, Jr., "It is as if there were a circle in the centre of which there is an altar, an eternal flame. . . . the true artist . . . has always been laying his humble offering before that shrine in the centre."[4]

This attitude led Thayer to become dissatisfied with commissioned portraiture, in which he specialized early in his career, and to address more personally meaningful and elevated themes. In the mid-1880s he began concentrating on the subject of young women, usually represented in classical drapery, often with angel's wings. These monumental figures were for him the embodiment of a spiritual ideal, which came to the fore at about the time of his wife's illness in 1888 and was intensified after her death in 1891. Although Thayer remarried, he seems never to have lost his reverence for his first wife, who, in part, inspired these paintings.[5]

Thayer's heroic women were likened by contemporaries to Olympian goddesses: embodiments of all that is good and noble in humanity, symbols of the triumph of the soul. They are not only spiritual, however; they are also very substantial creatures, their solid flesh rendered in thick, palpable pigment. Thayer's attitude towards nature was at once mystical and sensuous, and this duality is reflected in his work. Like Emerson, whom he greatly admired, he felt a holy presence in nature. But he also reveled in the visual beauty of the changing seasons and took physical delight in participating in them. After 1901 he lived in rural New Hampshire year round, with few amenities and no central heating, and found the challenge of this rugged life exhilarating. He not only lived close to nature but he studied it seriously all his life. By 1896 he was a recognized authority on ornithology, having made important contributions to the understanding of protective coloration in animals. The synthesis of the earthy and other-worldly was an important feature of Thayer's personality and added to the strength of his art.

Thayer's idealization of women was not only an expression of his own temperament and esthetic, it was also characteristic of the age in which he lived. Turn-of-the-century America witnessed an almost universal idealization of women, reflected not only in the arts but in all aspects of society. In his *History of American Painting* (1905), Samuel Isham noted, "The American Girl is placed upon a pedestal and each offers worship according to his abilities. . . . "[6] George de Forest Brush—Thayer's closest friend and former fellow student, both in Gérôme's studio and at the National Academy of Design—spent most of his career celebrating the glory of motherhood in idealized images of his wife and children. Born in Shelbyville, Tennessee, and brought up in Danbury, Connecticut, Brush was sent to New York in 1871, when he was sixteen, to study at the National Academy. In 1874 he went to Paris for further training. His mature works recall Italian Renaissance Holy Family groups and reflect his admiration for this school of painting. Throughout most of his career he spent part of every year in Florence, where he carefully studied the styles and techniques of the Old Masters. Along with many of his contemporaries, he valued the classical heritage of the Renaissance and was strongly opposed to avant-garde developments in art. He studied the *Book of the Art of Cennino Cennini* and told his students, "We must not run after new things. We must find out what the masters knew."[7]

Brush's concern for craft and painstaking execution can be seen in his *Self-Portrait*. A work of extraordinary delicacy, this painting suggests both Northern and Italian Renaissance prototypes. Indeed, Brush's contemporaries variously compared his work to that of Van Eyck, Leonardo, Dürer, Holbein and Ter Borch.[8] The precise modeling, minutely drawn features and exquisite finish of the head are a tribute to the teaching of Gérôme, with whom Brush studied for six years. Unlike Thayer, whose art he admired but whose perfunctory methods he did not,[9] Brush was a true disciple of Gérôme, adopting the linear definition, technical refinement and surface polish characteristic of his master's work. This was especially evident in the paintings executed during the decade after his return from Paris in 1880, when he specialized in American Indian subjects. This theme, inspired by his personal experiences living among Indians in the American West and Canada, was analogous to the exotic, Near Eastern subjects often treated by Gérôme, and it was approached with similar technical control and anecdotal charm. These early paintings were not a commercial or critical success, however. In 1890 Brush painted the first of the family groups, featuring his wife and one or more of his eight children, that brought him substantial fame and fortune thereafter.

Brush favored quasi-religious subject matter for its historical pedigree, derived from traditional Western European sources, and because of its universal appeal. He was not a member of a church nor was he a conventionally religious man, but he had strong socialist sympathies and believed that art should serve the needs of a wide public. He felt that, by treating themes of universal significance, the artist could subordinate his individuality to the interests and expectations of society as a whole.[10] He viewed religion as a great unifying force, and he appreciated the contribution it made to the history of art, not only by inspiring great works but by providing artists with subject matter that was both popular and elevating.[11] Brush deplored the tendency of some modernist art to mystify or offend the average viewer. In 1919 he observed:

> Artists are producing canvases today for which they ought to be arrested. Ten years ago, if an effort had been made to exhibit some paintings being shown today the police would have been called in. Real art is on the wane; it has become so enmeshed in the mad whirl and swirl of modern times that true artistic sense is deadened.[12]

Brush's conservative viewpoint was characteristic of artists associated with the so-called American Renaissance, a movement prevalent from the mid-1870s to about the time of World War I. It was inspired by the admiration for Old World culture shared by artists like Brush and Thayer, who trained abroad, and their wealthy, cosmopolitan patrons. They wished to introduce its graces and advantages into America and to continue its traditions here. They identified strongly with this culture, both in their approach to art and in their image of themselves. Thayer wrote to Cortissoz in 1916, for instance, "Oh you and I are Mantegnas and Gozzolis, not Yankees!"[13] He would have agreed with Bernard Berenson, the famous American connoisseur of the Renaissance, when he wrote to the artist Kenyon Cox ". . . wherever two or three are gathered in the name of art, there is Italy for me."[14] Berenson spent most of his life abroad, but those who remained in America worked hard to advance their cause. They made paintings, sculptures and monuments, wrote books and articles, designed buildings and cities, and founded institutions—all in emulation of European models. They saw a new chapter in European cultural history being written in America: a rebirth on American soil of the classical tradition. In an often-quoted statement, Kenyon Cox presented their point of view:

> . . . it desires that each new presentation of truth and beauty shall show us the old truth and the old beauty, seen only from a different angle and colored by a different medium. It wishes to add link by link to the chain of tradition, but it does not wish to break the chain.[15]

Kenyon Cox was born in Warren, Ohio, in 1857, to a distinguished family. His father was a lawyer, scholar and writer, and he served as a major-general in the Civil War, about which he wrote a history. He later became governor of Ohio, secretary of the interior under Grant, and president of the University of Cincinnati. Cox's maternal grandfather was Dr. Charles G. Finney, the first president of Oberlin College. In his youth Cox was so often ill that he attended school infrequently. He developed an interest in art at an early age and went to art school in Cincinnati, where his family settled in the 1870s. In 1876 he visited the Centennial Exhibition in Philadelphia and remained there for a year to study at the Pennsylvania Academy of the Fine Arts. The following year, at the age of twenty-one, he went to Paris, studying first with Carolus-Duran and then at the Ecole des Beaux-Arts with Cabanel and Gérôme. He also attended classes at the independent Académie Julian. He returned to America in 1882, and soon after he established a studio in New York.

Cox specialized in the human figure, particularly the idealized, academic nude, which he had mastered as a student in Paris. Although this was a common and acceptable subject for Parisian artists, Cox was criticized for his devotion to it in this country, where Puritan values were still prevalent. Since these works did not sell, Cox turned to illustration and to writing for such journals as *The Nation, Scribner's Magazine* and *Harper's Weekly*. In the 1890s he began to do mural painting and distinguished himself in this field. He did murals for major buildings throughout the country, including the Library of Congress. These paintings depicted allegories of Justice, Peace, Hope, Industry, Commerce or Law, in the form of monumental figures in classical drapery or other historical dress. Grand in scale and conception, Cox's murals were patterned after the great mural paintings of the Renaissance. They fulfilled his ideal that art should reflect "love of beauty," "reverence for tradition" and a return to "the permanent and the eternal."[16]

Cox was a prolific writer, known in his day as much for his writing as for his painting. As an outspoken defender of tradition in art, he established his reputation as a staunch conservative early in his career. In a tribute published in *Scribner's* at the time of his death in 1919, Frank Jewett Mather, Jr., described him as

> . . . an embodied conservative conscience, a stalwart and dreaded champion of the great traditions in painting, a dangerous critic of successive new schools and fads, a formidable foe of every sort of sloppiness. . . . His death must have caused relief if not rejoicing among the wild-eyed inspirationalists of Greenwich Village. For them he was an uncomfortable person to have around.

One can understand why this might have been so after reading his comments on modernist art. Painters such as Van Gogh, Picasso and Matisse were described as madmen, charlatans, impostors and savages, decadent and corrupt destroyers of art.[17] "Here is a set of men," he said, "whose art is so crazy that anything which formerly seemed eccentric pales to bourgeois commonplace in the comparison."[18] In an article in *Harper's Weekly* on the Armory Show of 1913, the international exhibition that introduced European modernism into America, he warned the public:

> Do not allow yourselves to be blinded by the sophistries of the foolish dupes or the self-interested exploiters of all this charlatanry. Remember that it is for you that art is created. . . .
> If your stomach revolts against this rubbish it is because it is not fit for human food.

While he excoriated the evils of modernism, Cox celebrated the achievements of Renaissance and Baroque masters and of those of his contemporaries whom he could respect. Among the Americans he often praised were Thayer and Brush. He declared that their art was truly classical and worthy of the work of the great masters.[19] Like Brush, Cox believed that art should appeal to a wide audience and express universal ideals. He noted that "A living and a healthy art never has existed . . . except through the mutual understanding and co-operation of the artist and his public. Art is made for man and has a social function to perform."[20]

If, for Cox, the art of Thayer and Brush performed this social function, so did that of his friend Maxfield Parrish. For Cox included illustration among those art forms which naturally fulfill a public need and have broad popular support. Parrish was the most popular and successful illustrator in early twentieth-century America. From 1895, when he designed his first cover for a national magazine, through the 1930s, he was the most sought-after commercial artist in the country. He not only designed covers and illustrations for such major periodicals as *Scribner's, Century, Collier's, Life* and *Harper's Weekly*, but he was a leading advertisement, poster and calendar designer, a prolific children's book illustrator and a mural painter. By the 1920s there was a vast market for color reproductions of his paintings, and with the publication of *Daybreak* in 1922 Parrish became a national celebrity.

Parrish was born in Philadelphia in 1870 and was educated at Haverford College. His father, Stephen Parrish, who was a well-known painter and etcher, encouraged his son's interest in art. From 1892 to 1894 Parrish studied at the Pennsylvania Academy of the Fine Arts and attended classes at the Drexel Institute given by the illustrator Howard Pyle. In 1898 he moved to Cornish, New Hampshire, an artist's colony frequented by many celebrated people, including Woodrow Wilson and Ethel Barrymore. He built a home near that of his father, who had also moved to Cornish, and remained there for the rest of his life. Cox had a vacation home in Cornish, and he and Parrish saw each other often.

Parrish's characteristic works depict an idyllic world of youth and beauty, suspended in perennial well-being. Slim and graceful young people, engaged in tranquil discourse or solitary reverie, inhabit enchanted landscapes, free from care and pain. "The dawns were rose-colored and the twilights silver. The girls against backdrops of imperishable rocks appeared imperishable, ethereal. The skies were a sleek dreamy blue. . . ."[21] Thus was Parrish's universe described at the time of his death at the age of ninety-five. Through the 1920s prints of his work hung in almost every home, reviving, as another critic noted, "the abandoned dreams of everyone's youth about life as it could or should be."[22]

In addition to his poetic works, Parrish produced witty and whimsical illustrations, as well as advertisements and murals that have an almost Rabelaisian expressiveness. Gnomes, goblins and other fantastic creatures, knights and knaves from an imaginary Middle Ages and men and women with all kinds of physiognomic idiosyncracies inhabit his *Mother Goose* illustrations, his *Old King Cole* mural and his Jello advertisements. The humor and playfulness of these works reveal the droll side of Parrish's nature, which is echoed in a letter that he wrote to Cox in 1905 about his portrait:

> It is very good indeed of you to want to take my likeness for the Academy, and out of 407 applicants I accept you. It says that I must comply with the requirements of Article 4, Section 5, of the Constitution; the latter has not arrived yet, but I don't suppose it is anything very dreadful; they probably knock out your front teeth and tattoo A.N.A. on your bosom, but maybe it won't hurt much.[23]

Cox's portrait of Parrish captures this lively good humor. It also suggests something of the appearance of Parrish's work. To give legibility to his designs, which often had to capture the attention of a casual viewer and be read from a distance, Parrish frequently used profile or strongly silhouetted images. This was not uncommon in commercial art of the time, but it became almost a hallmark of Parrish's style. Parrish also often placed his figures in very relaxed, unselfconscious poses. Cox's profile portrait recalls, in fact, a cover design Parrish did for *Harper's Round Table* in which two young men flank a mantelpiece that frames the magazine's table of contents.[24] In the design, first published in 1897, Parrish using photographs of himself served as a model for both figures. The figure at the left, wearing a bow tie and shirt-sleeves rolled up to his elbows, stands with right arm akimbo, facing his companion. The faces of both figures are seen in profile and resemble, in both features and expression, the portrait Cox painted of Parrish eight years later. The slight smile and the suggestion of a twinkling eye, the casual, jaunty pose and costume and the dapper, boyish appearance of the artist remind one as much of Parrish's work as of Parrish himself. There is nothing of Cox's grand manner here. The likeness is surprisingly natural and direct and very freely executed. It reveals none of Cox's concern for historical precedent or idealism in art. Although the profile portrait was popular in the Renaissance, and Cox and others revived it in recognition of this source, these images tend to be rather austere and aristocratic. The portrait of Parrish has a spontaneity and immediacy that give it a very contemporary feeling. It is not a nostalgic recollection of the past, but a fresh response to the present.

Elliott Daingerfield, an artist oriented as much to the past as to the present, was another friend and admirer of Cox. They had studios in the same building in New York, held similar views on art and moved in the same circles, Brush being a mutual friend. In 1930 Daingerfield wrote an article praising Brush's work, especially his adherence to the technical standards of the Old Masters.[25] He believed in what he called the "Principle of Beauty" in art, and he was opposed to the frank, unidealized subject matter that was being introduced by realist artists, such as the Ashcan School, into early twentieth-century painting. He proudly declared that "The morgue, the gutter, and the slum are not significant of a people who are at once clean, wholesome, and optimistic."[26]

Daingerfield specialized in religious subjects executed in a Renaissance mode and in loosely painted, imaginative landscapes, which often included allegorical figures. His most important commission (1902) was for a series of murals for the Lady Chapel in the Church of Saint Mary the Virgin in New York. Since he was an active churchgoer and very religious, both his landscapes and his religious paintings spring from the same mystical source.

Daingerfield was born in Harper's Ferry, Virginia, in 1859, but he was reared in Fayetteville,

North Carolina, where his father moved in 1861 to serve in the Confederate Army. He decided to become an artist while he was a boy, and he studied with local artists in North Carolina and Virginia. In 1880 he moved to New York, where he worked as a studio assistant for the artist Walter Satterlee, who criticized his work in payment for his services. He also studied from time to time at the Art Students' League. In 1884 he left Satterlee and set up his own studio. He then became friendly with the painter George Inness, whose work he greatly admired. The shimmering surfaces of Daingerfield's paintings, achieved by alternating opaque colors with transparent glazes and varnish, reflect the influence of Inness. Daingerfield also shared Inness's visionary response to nature, and he wrote a book about Inness's art. An active writer, Daingerfield also wrote a book on the work of Ralph Albert Blakelock, as well as many critical and theoretical articles.

In 1911 he went on a short expedition to the Grand Canyon, sponsored by the Santa Fe Railroad Company. Its purpose was to promote railway travel by introducing the public to the beauty of the terrain through artists' interpretations of it. This trip was an important inspiration for him, and he continued to treat the subject of the Grand Canyon in allegorical and poetic landscapes for several years.

Among the five artists on the expedition was Frederick Ballard Williams, whose National Academy diploma portrait Daingerfield painted in 1907. Williams was born in Brooklyn, in 1871. He studied art at Cooper Union, the Institute of Artist Artisans and the National Academy of Design. He specialized in watercolor until about 1896, when he turned to oil painting. He lived much of his life in New Jersey, where he remained active in local and national art institutions, such as the Montclair Art Museum and the American Artists Professional League, which he founded.

Williams's art conforms to Daingerfield's ideal of beauty, although it is not spiritual in any profound sense. His paintings typically feature landscapes graced by pretty women in old-fashioned frocks, which won him the title "The American Watteau." His works were also compared to those of Rubens, Turner and other masters of loose brushwork and high color.[27] The decorative, romantic effects of the colorful, painterly surfaces, as well as the picturesque imagery, were highly admired in his time.

The settings of many of Williams's paintings are coastal scenes, similar to the one depicted in the background of the portrait of him painted by Daingerfield. The small, bright dabs of color seen at the right and left suggest the figures of women that often appear in Williams's work. These figures have been described as "beautifully gowned in shimmering whites, greens, and reds, and most times grouped upon high-colored rocks, and usually with a touch of the distant sea to lend added poetry to the composition."[28] Daingerfield's portrait is a tribute both to Williams's art and to his own, for the richly impasted surface, articulating the dramatic landscape of dense rocks and trees beneath the bright sky, evokes the spiritual tone of Daingerfield's work as much as the decorative quality of Williams's. The artist's sober image before this wild, fanciful setting forms a telling contrast with it and seems an apt metaphor for the character of American Idealist art, for it was inspired by the dreams of nineteenth-century Americans for the grandeur and beauty of times and places very different from their own.

Leslie Yudell

Notes

1. Royal Cortissoz, *American Artists* (New York, London: 1923), pp. 27-28.
2. Nelson C. White, *Abbott H. Thayer, Painter and Naturalist* (Hartford: 1951), p. 26.
3. Cortissoz, *op. cit.*, p. 35.
4. White, *op. cit.*, p. 232.
5. See Ross Anderson, *Abbott Handerson Thayer* (Syracuse: 1982), pp. 22, 63, 72; and Thomas B. Brumbaugh, "The Monumental Art of Abbott H. Thayer," *Antiques* (1973), p. 1136.
6. Samuel Isham, *The History of American Painting* (New York: 1936), p. 471. See also Anderson, *op. cit.*, pp. 72-74; and The Brooklyn Museum, *The American Renaissance 1876-1917* (New York: 1979), pp. 46-50.
   7. Nancy Douglas Bowditch, *George de Forest Brush: Recollections of a Joyous Painter* (Peterborough, Noone House: 1970), pp. 77-78.
7. Nancy Douglas Bowditch, *George de Forest Brush: Recollections of a Joyous Painter* (Peterborough, Noone House: 1970), pp. 77-78.
8. Cortissoz, *op. cit.,* pp. 72-73; Isham, *op. cit.,* p. 492; and Charles H. Caffin, *The Story of American Painting* (New York: 1907), p. 181.

9. Bowditch, *op. cit.*, pp. 186-87.

10. Herbert L. Jillson, "George de Forest Brush," *The Art Interchange*, 46 (April 1901), pp. 75-77.

11. Sadakichi Hartmann, *A History of American Art*, vol. 1 (Boston: 1901), p. 266.

12. Obituary, *The New York Times*, April 25, 1941.

13. White, *op. cit.*, p. 165.

14. Letter, Bernard Berenson to Kenyon Cox, March 13, 1904, Columbia University, Avery Library, Kenyon Cox Papers (citation transcribed from microfilm).

15. Kenyon Cox, *The Classic Point of View* (1911; repr. New York, London: 1980), p. 4.

16. *Ibid.*, p. 22.

17. *Ibid.*, pp. 20-21, 150; Kenyon Cox, *Artist and Public* (New York: 1914), pp. 23-24, 28-42, 98.

18. Cox, *Classic*, pp. 153-54.

19. Kenyon Cox, *Concerning Painting* (New York: 1917), pp. 197, 225-27; *Old Masters and New* (New York: 1905), p. 147.

20. Cox, *Artist and Public*, p. 41.

21. Obituary, *The New York Times*, March 31, 1966.

22. G. Elizabeth Gillett, "Maxfield Parrish at Ninety-Three," *Saturday Review* (March 14, 1964), p. 130.

23. Letter, Maxfield Parrish to Kenyon Cox, May 15, 1905, Columbia University, Avery Library, Kenyon Cox Papers (citation transcribed from microfilm).

24. Coy Ludwig, *Maxfield Parrish* (New York: 1973), fig. 35.

25. Elliott Daingerfield, "George de Forest Brush," *Art in America*, 18 (June 1930), pp. 214-18.

26. Elliott Daingerfield, "Nature vs. Art," *Scribner's Magazine*, 49 (Feb. 1911), p. 256.

27. Clippings of reviews of Williams's work, Scrapbooks of Edwin C. Shaw, Archives of American Art, 1125 frame 1222-1256.

28. *Ibid.*, frame 1222.

William J. Whittemore

Born in New York City, Mar. 26. Early schooling at New York City private schools. Studied at Art Students' League under J. Carroll Beckwith, 1885, and at National Academy of Design under William Hart and Lemuel Wilmarth, 1882-86. Traveled to Paris with Charles C. Curran and Charles Chapman. Enrolled at Académie Julian. Received criticism from Benjamin Constant and Jules Joseph Lefèbvre. Traveled in French countryside with Curran and Chapman. Upon return to New York, established himself at Mendelsohn Studio Building. Other artists there were Irving Wiles. Thorne Sherwood, John White Alexander, Julian Alden Weir, Thomas Hovenden; met Frank Benson, Edmund Tarbell and Joseph DeCamp. Received Silver Medal at Paris Salon, 1889, and Bronze Medal at Atlantic Exposition, 1895. Married first wife, 1895. Moved to East Hampton, Long Island, N.Y., traveled annually to Europe, 1895-1910; visited Italy, Scotland and England. After first wife's death, lived primarily in New York City. Represented by Macbeth Gallery, New York. Traveled to Russia, Belgium and Germany. Returned to New York, established new studio in Sherwood Studio Building. Won Proctor Prize, National Academy of Design, 1917. Member of American Watercolor Society, American Society of Miniature Painters, Lotos Club, Century Club and MacDowell Colony. 1921, second marriage, to painter Helen Simpson, whom he had known since 1893. Lived in La Mesa, Cal., and East Hampton, Long Island, N.Y. Died in East Hampton, on Feb. 7.

BSK

Charles Courtney Curran

Born Hartford, Ky., Feb. 13. Studied at Cincinnati School of Design, later at National Academy of Design under Lemuel Wilmarth 1883-86, and at the Art Students' League. Traveled to Paris to enroll at Académie Julian under Benjamin Constant, Jules Joseph Lefèbvre and Henri Lucien Doucet. Fellow classmates from New York with him in Paris included William J. Whittemore and Charles Chapman, with whom he visited the French countryside. Returned to New York, received the third Hallgarten Prize, National Academy of Design; subsequently elected to Society of American Artists. Received Honorable Mention in Paris Salon, 1890. Received medal at World's Columbian Exposition, Chicago, 1893. Exhibited at important juried exhibitions such as Salon Paris; Corcoran Gallery of Art, Washington D.C.; Society of American Artists, National Academy of Design, New York; Pan-American Exposition, Buffalo, 1901; and St. Louis Exposition, 1904. Traveled and painted with family for several months in Switzerland, 1900. 1904, began spending summers in Cragsmoor, artists' colony he developed with other artists, including Helen Turner, E.L. Henry and Edward Gay. Taught at Cooper Union and National Academy; maintained a studio in New York City throughout career. Traveled to China to visit daughter, 1936; painted series of Chinese temples, subsequently exhibited in U.S. cities. Served as recording secretary at National Academy of Design, 1911-20, and corresponding secretary-treasurer, 1920-1942. Academy honored Curran and wife on his seventy-fifth birthday with book of sketches by many fellow members, 1935. Died Nov. 9.

BSK

George de Forest Brush

Born Shelbyville, Tenn., Sept. 28. Family returned to previous home of Danbury, Conn., 1856, where Brush spent his youth. Showed early interest in photography, music and art, encouraged by his mother. Commuted from Connecticut to attend classes at National Academy of Design under Lemuel Wilmarth, 1871-73. (Classmates include Abbott Handerson Thayer, Julian Alden Weir, and Charles Melville Dewey.) Accepted contribution from anonymous benefactor to travel to Paris, and enrolled at Ecole des Beaux-Arts under Jean Léon Gérôme, 1874. Thayer and Douglas Volk enrolled in same studio, became lifetime friends. Returned to United States briefly upon death of mother, 1875. Back in Paris until 1880. Began to establish career in New York by exhibition with Society of American Artists, 1880. Traveled with brother to San Francisco and American west, 1881-85. Began teaching at Art Students' League, member Society of American Artists, 1882. Met Mary Taylor Whelpley, Brush's student, whom he married, 1886. Couple move to Canadian province of Quebec, where Brush painted Indian subjects. After two years, returned to New York, resumed teaching at Art Students' League. Returned to Paris with family, 1889. Stopped painting Western themes and began using family as subjects, took portrait commissions. Again in New York, taught at Art Students' League, 1892. Exhibited at World's Columbian Exposition, Chicago, 1893. 1892-95, summers in Cornish, N.H., with Augustus St. Gaudens and Thomas W. Dewing. Takes family to England, staying briefly in town of Broadway with Edwin Austin Abbey and Francis Millet, 1898, then on to Paris and Florence. Thayer and Brush go to Venice. 1899-1903, Brush family spent winters in Scarborough, N.Y., and summers in Dublin, N.H. The Thayers and Volks, Edmund Tarbell, Frank Benson and Birge Harrison lived nearby. Moved to Villa il Gioiello, Galileo's last home in Florence, summers spent in Courmayeur, at foot of Mont Blanc, 1903-05. Returned briefly to Dublin, met Samuel Clemens (Mark Twain), back to Florence, 1905. Artists Barry Faulkner, Robert Pearmain and Brush's daughter studied with Brush in Florence in studios previously occupied by American sculptors Hiram Powers and Thomas Ball. In Rome, met Elihu Vedder for whose work Brush had great respect. Returned to New York, studio on MacDougal Street. Elected to American Academy of Arts and Letters and Century Association, 1910. Brush family travel again to Italy to return shortly after outbreak of World War I, 1913-14. New York and Dublin, N.H., 1914. Worked with Thayer on theories of protective coloration and camouflage, visiting Washington, D.C., and seeing ambassadors to Italy on Thayer's behalf. Spent next ten years in New York and Dublin. Retrospective organized by Century Association, 1922. Some travels to Italy and Spain. Honorary degree conferred by Yale University, 1923. One-man shows at Grand Central Art Galleries, 1930 and American Academy of Arts and Letters, 1933. Died in Hanover, N.H. on Apr. 24.

BSK

William John Whittemore (1860-1955) A.N.A. 1897
PORTRAIT OF CHARLES C. CURRAN (1861-1942)
    A.N.A. 1888, N.A. 1904
Oil on canvas
17⅛ x 21½
Signed upper right: Wm. J. Whittemore 1889 / Paris

George de Forest Brush (1855-1941) A.N.A. 1888, N.A.
 1901
SELF-PORTRAIT
Oil on canvas remounted on masonite
18½ x 14
Unsigned

Abbott Handerson Thayer (1849-1921) A.N.A. 1898, N.A.
SELF-PORTRAIT
Oil on canvas remounted on masonite
20 x 16
Unsigned

Abbott Handerson Thayer

Born in Boston, Mass. Aug. 12. Received art instruction from Henry D. Morse, jeweler and amateur animal painter, 1865. Moved to Brooklyn and attended Brooklyn Art School, 1867. Enrolled in school of National Academy of Design, met classmate Maria Oakley. Through her friendship with Helena DeKay, met Kate Bloede. Exhibited in annual exhibition, 1868. 1875, married Kate Bloede and sailed to Europe. In Paris, enrolled in Ecole des Beaux-Arts under Henri Lehman. Established friendship with English painters Everton Sainsbury and Thomas M. Dow and American painter George de Forest Brush. Thayer's home became meeting place for single American artists seeking familiar atmosphere and escape from bohemianism of Latin Quarter. Began studying with Jean Léon Gérôme, 1875-76. Became member of Society of American Artists. Summers spent at Guernsey, 1877. Traveled to Germany with family, 1878. Returned to United States, 1879, and established New York studio. Received first commission from *Scribner's Magazine,* to paint portrait of Mark Twain. Death of son, Harry, 1880, and death of second son, Ralph Waldo, 1881. Family moved often in New England and New York State. Son Gerald born. Elected Vice-President, then President of Society of American Artists, 1882-83, resigned presidency 1884. Wife Kate hospitalized after attack of melancholia. Emma Beach and Mary Amory Greene became close friends of Thayers, both providing emotional stability to distressed family, 1885-90. Thayer drew on his children and close friends as subjects for idealized paintings, 1886-89. Death of wife; marriage to Emma Beach, 1891. Met Charles Lang Freer, who became Thayer's patron, 1892. Travel to Europe, visited old friends Dow and Sainsbury in England, then to Germany, Switzerland and Italy, 1884. Published "Thayer's Law," theory of coloration of animals in nature, addressed conferences of ornithologists in U.S. and England, 1889-98. Traveled with two youngest children and Brush to Canada to hunt, 1899. 1901, traveled extensively in Italy; moved permanently to Dublin, N.H., after twelve years of winters in Scarborough and summers in New York. Met John Gellatly, who became his second patron, 1903. Continued studies in naturalism, conducted painting classes in Dublin studio with students such as Rockwell Kent working as copiers and assistants. Adapted theory of natural coloration and camouflage to use by the military, American and British, with aid from John Singer Sargent in England and George de Forest Brush in Italy, 1904-15. Refused honorary degree from Yale University because of requirement that he accept in person, 1916. Committed himself to hospital because of suicidal impulses, 1918. Director of Carnegie Institute pursuaded Thayer to have one-man show, which he agreed to, 1919. Suffered several strokes and died on May 29, Monadnock, N.H.

BSK

Kenyon Cox

Born Warren, Oh., Oct. 7. Age fourteen, entered McMicken Art School in Cincinnati, studied 1870-73 under Frank Duveneck, classmate of Robert F. Blum. Traveled with Blum to see Philadelphia Centennial Exhibition and subsequently enrolled in Pennsylvania Academy of the Fine Arts, 1876. Moved to New York briefly where he and Blum shared studio. Traveled to Paris to study under Charles Emile Auguste Carolus-Duran, 1877. Enrolled at Ecole des Beaux-Arts in studios of Alexandre Cabanel and Jean Léon Gérôme, during day and evenings at Académie Julian, receiving criticism from Gustave Boulanger, Jules Joseph Lefèbvre and William Adolphe Bouguereau. Exhibited at Paris Salon, friendship established with Helleu, 1879-1882. Returned

to New York, 1883; exhibited at Society of American Artists, served on Board of Managers. Began teaching at Art Students' League, using teaching technique of Parisian ateliers, 1884-1909. Commissioned to do illustrations of French actors for *Century Magazine* and of Dante Gabriel Rossetti's poem "The Blessed Damozel," 1886. Married painter Louise Howland King, 1892. Painted murals for World's Columbian Exposition, Chicago, 1893. Collaborated on decorative projects with artists and architects involved in "American Renaissance," including Stanford White, Cass Gilbert, Will H. Low, Augustus Saint Gaudens, William Merritt Chase, Edwin Blashfield and Howard Pyle. From 1896, painted murals for Library of Congress; Walker Art Building, Bowdoin College; Minnesota State Capitol; Wisconsin State Capitol; Essex County Court House, N.J.; Appellate Court House, New York; also did designs for stained glass and seals, such as seal for Boston Public Library executed by Saint Gaudens. Published articles and books, including *French Modern Masters,* 1896; *The Nineteenth Century,* 1901; *Old Masters and New,* 1905; *Painters and Sculptors,* 1907; *The Classic Point of View,* 1911; *Artist and Public,* 1914; *Concerning Painting,* 1917. Lectured at National Academy of Design School on Art Schools of the Old World, 1900-17, and was instructor in composition. Appointed to committee of National Academy of Design and Society of American Artists to investigate merger of the two societies, 1905-06. Awarded Medal of Honor for mural painting by Architectural League of New York, 1910. Member American Academy of Arts and Letters. Died in New York, Mar. 17.

BSK

Maxfield Parrish

Born in Philadelphia, Pa., July 25. 1884-86, traveled with family to Europe; studied at Dr. Kornemann's school in Paris; contracted typhoid in Honfleur. Studied at Haverford College, Pa., 1888-1891. Parrish's father built home in artists' colony of Cornish, N.H. (where Abbott Handerson Thayer, George de Forest Brush, Thomas Dewing and others lived) 1893. Studied at Pennsylvania Academy of the Fine Arts under Robert Vonnoh and Thomas Pollock Anshutz and in Howard Pyle's class at Drexel Institute, 1892-94. 1895, first mural commission was for Mask and Wig Club, Phila., and first magazine cover commission was for *Harper's Bazaar.* Traveled to Brussels, Paris and London to see salon exhibits and museums, 1895. Exhibited with Society of American Artists and elected to membership, 1897. Built home and studio in Cornish, established permanent residence there, 1898. Exhibited and awarded honorable mention, Paris Exposition, 1900, and silver medal at Pan-American Exposition, Buffalo, N.Y. 1901. Traveled to Saranac Lake, N.Y. and Hot Springs, Ariz. (for *Century Magazine*) to paint and convalesce from tuberculosis. 1900-02. Commissioned to illustrate *Italian Villas and Their Gardens* by Edith Wharton for Century Company, traveled to Italy, refused commission to illustrate series on French châteaux, 1903. Designed covers for *Collier's Magazine,* 1904-1913. Honorary degree of LL.D. conferred by Haverford College, 1914. Awarded Medal of Honor for Painting by Architectural League of New York, 1917. Painted murals for hotels, private residences and theaters, 1906-1922. Did cover designs for *Life Magazine,* 1917-1925. Exhibition at Saint-Gaudens Memorial Museum, Cornish, N.H. 1950. Paintings commissioned by Brown-Bigelow Publishing Company, reproduced and distributed as calendars and greeting cards, 1934-1960. Completed last painting, 1961. Retrospective exhibitions at Bennington College, Vt. 1964, and George Walter Vincent Smith Art Museum, Springfield, Mass. 1966. Died in Cornish, N.H. Mar. 30.

BSK

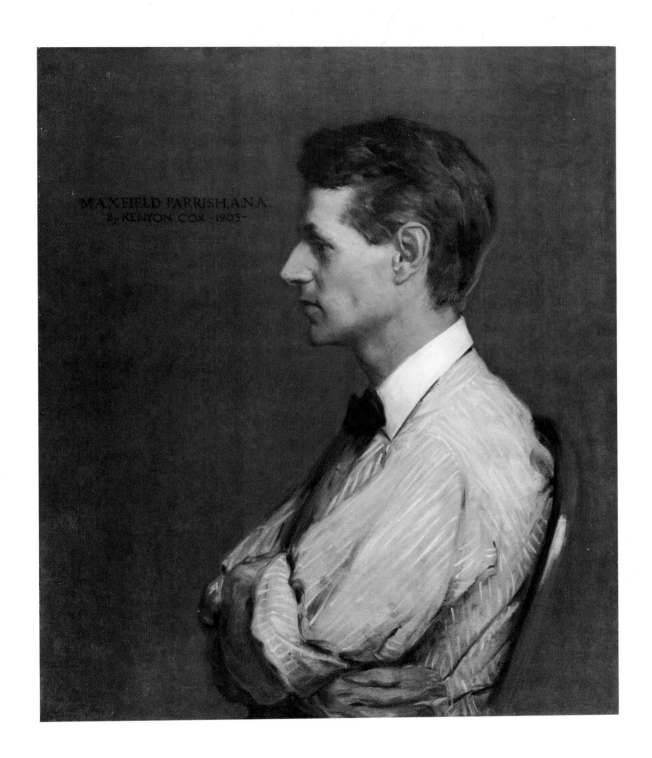

Kenyon Cox (1856-1919) A.N.A. 1900, N.A. 1903
PORTRAIT OF MAXFIELD PARRISH (1870-1966) A.N.A.
    1905, N.A. 1906
Oil on canvas
30 x 25
Signed upper left: MAXFIELD PARRISH, A.N.A. / BY
    KENYON COX - 1905 -

Cass Gilbert

Born Zaneville, Oh. on Nov. 24. Studied at Massachusetts Institute of Technology, was classmate of Arnold Brunner, 1879. Traveled to Europe, 1879-80. Returned to New York, worked as assistant to Stanford White at firm of McKim, Mead & White, 1880-82. Moved to St. Paul, Minnesota, designed Shingle and Queen Anne style architecture, 1883. Won competition for Minnesota State Capitol Building with his in Neoclassical design; commissioned John LaFarge, Kenyon Cox, Francis Millet, Howard Pyle and Edwin H. Blashfield to paint murals for buildings, 1893. Won commission for U.S. Customs House, N.Y., 1899. Designed Art Building for Louisiana Purchase Exposition, St. Louis, 1905. Designed Finney Memorial Chapel, Oberlin College, Ohio, 1907 (drawing in National Academy collection). Designed neo-Gothic Woolworth Building, 1911. 1913, received Medal of Honor from Architectural League (of which he was a founder) for Woolworth Building. Elected to National Institute of Arts and Letters, 1919. Won competition for Hudson River Bridge (known as George Washington Bridge), 1929, largest suspension bridge built at time. Served as first architect-president of National Academy, 1926-1930. Other commissions were Allen Memorial Art Museum, 1930-32, and U.S. Federal Court House, N.Y., 1935, both completed by his son. Elected to honorary membership in Royal Institute of British Architects; Royal Academy of Arts, London; Chevalier of the Legion of Honor, France; and Knight of the Order of King Albert of Belgium. Honorary Degrees of Doctor of Fine Arts conferred by New York University, LL.D. from University of Michigan, and Doctor of Letters from Columbia University. Died in Brockenhurst, England, May 17.

BSK

Elliott Daingerfield

Born in Harper's Ferry, Va., on March 26. 1880, Elliott moved to New York, briefly apprenticed to Walter Satterlee. Began to exhibit at National Academy of Design. 1884, worked in Holbein Studios, met George Inness. Married Roberta Strange French of Wilmington, N.C. 1891, won "point d'appui" in Holbein Studios, closely associating with other American artists there, including A. H. Wyant and Kenyon Cox. Wife died in childbirth. 1892, exhibited at Salmagundi Club, New York. Married Anna Grainger of Kentucky in 1895. 1896, exhibited sketches and studies of mountains of North Carolina at New York Watercolor Society; taught classes in composition at Philadelphia School of Design and Art Students' League, New York. Spent most summers in Blowing Rock, N.C.; traveled to Europe in summer 1897. 1902-07, worked on *The Epiphany* and *The Magnificat*, murals for Lady Chapel, Church of St. Mary the Virgin, New York. 1903, taught composition and painting from life and still life at Philadelphia School of Design for Women. 1908, moved from Holbein Studios to Gainsborough Studios on Central Park, New York. 1911, first public exhibition, Vose Galleries, Boston; completed his book about George Inness, *The Man and His Art.* Visited Grand Canyon at invitation of Santa Fe Railroad Company. 1913, again traveled West, staying with his family in Carmel, Cal., and touring Grand Canyon. 1914, exhibited Grand Canyon landscape with "Society of Men Who Paint the Far West" at Corcoran Gallery of Art, Washington, D.C. 1914 published monograph, *Ralph Albert Blakelock.* 1918, presented altarpiece to his church, St. Mary of the Hills, Blowing Rock. 1924, toured Europe for second time, painting Venetian scenes. Suffered physical breakdown the same year. Died in Gainsborough Studios of a heart attack on Oct. 22. Grand Central Art Galleries, New York, held memorial exhibition of paintings, April, 1934.

DA

Frederick Ballard Williams

Born in Brooklyn, N.Y., Oct. 21, son of John K. Williams and Jennie R. Conover Williams. First studied art in public schools of Bloomfield and Montclair, N.J. Later attended Cooper Union night school. Received a scholarship from John Ward Stimson's school, New York Institute of Artists Artisans and also studied at National Academy of Design under William Hamilton Gibson and C.Y. Turner. Spent a short time studying in England and France. Married Marian Gerry Duncan in October, 1900. Generally known for landscapes, some of which owe their inspiration to Grand Canyon trip of 1910, where he traveled as a guest of Santa Fe Railroad. Lived in Glen Ridge, N.J., from 1885, was an active contributor to several arts organizations. Elected a full member of National Academy of Design in 1909, was a member of its Council, 1910-11, and Assistant Treasurer, 1930-38. 1914-19, President of Salmagundi Club. At Montclair Art Museum, served on art committee which he chaired from 1913 to 1948; was president of museum, 1924-25. 1927, founder and national president of the American Artists Professional League, then largest arts organization in U.S. 1949, on retirement as chairman of art committee, given a one-man show at Montclair Art Museum. Recipient of many awards, among them Bronze Medal at Pan American Exhibition, Buffalo, and "Isidor Memorial Medal" for best figure composition, National Academy. Also awarded a gold medal of honor by American Artists Professional League for twenty-two years of service. Died in Glen Ridge, N.J., Dec. 11.

DA

Edith Mitchell Prellwitz

Born in South Orange, N.J., Jan. 28. Studied at Art Students' League under Kenyon Cox and George de Forest Brush; met Henry Prellwitz, student of Thomas Dewing. Traveled to Paris to study at Académie Julian in studios of William Adolphe Bouguereau, Tony Robert-Fleury and Gustave Claude Courtois. Exhibited at Paris Salon. Upon return to N.Y., established studio at Holbein Studio Building; Henry Prellwitz moved in across the hall 1892. Married him, 1894. Awarded Dodge Prize at Society of American Artists Exhibition, 1895. Used proceeds to build cottage in Cornish, N.H., where couple spent summers (other artists in Cornish/ Dublin area Maxfield Parrish, Augustus Saint Gaudens, Kenyon Cox, Charles Platt and George de Forest Brush. Awarded silver medal, Atlanta Exposition, 1895. Fire caused by lightening destroy studio and cottage; elected to Society of American Artists, 1898. Acquired studio and home in Peconic, Long Island, N.Y. 1899. (Became friends with painter Irving Wiles and his family who lived nearby.) Exhibited and received bronze medal, Pan-American Exposition, Buffalo, 1901. Traveled in Europe to Germany and Italy, and throughout United States. Became Associate of National Academy of Design when Society of American Artists merged with National Academy of Design, 1906. Continued to live and work in New York City and Peconic, Long Island. Died in Greenwich, R.I., Aug. 18.

BSK

Kenyon Cox (1856-1919) A.N.A. 1900, N.A. 1903
PORTRAIT OF CASS GILBERT (1859-1934) A.N.A. 1906,
  N.A. 1908, P.N.A. 1926-1933
Oil on canvas
30⅛ x 25⅛
Signed upper right: CASS GILBERT A.N.A. / BY KENYON COX, 1907

Elliott Daingerfield (1859-1932) A.N.A. 1902, N.A. 1906
PORTRAIT OF FREDERICK BALLARD WILLIAMS (1871-
    1959) A.N.A. 1907, N.A. 1909
Oil on canvas remounted on masonite
29¾ x 24⅞
Signed lower right: Fredk Ballard Williams / A.N.A. 1907- /
    by Elliott Daingerfield N.A. / 1907

Edith Mitchell Prellwitz (1865-1944) A.N.A. 1906
SELF-PORTRAIT
Oil on canvas
30⅛ x 25
Unsigned

Americans Abroad

Asher Brown Durand, who may be considered the most American of American artists in the middle of the nineteenth century, made a grand tour of Europe in 1840. In a letter quoted by his son, John, Durand recounted his admiration for the "great works of art," but he finally admitted:

> . . . when all this looking and studying and admiring shall have an end, I am free to confess I shall enjoy a sight of the signboards in the streets of New York more than all the pictures in Europe; and for real and unalloyed enjoyment of scenery, the rocks, trees and green meadows of Hoboken will have a charm that all Switzerland cannot boast.[1]

Durand's unabashed homesickness and less-than-overwhelmed regard for the European tradition[2] reflected the strength of the American tradition in the decades before the Civil War. The Hudson River School was then at the height of its significance and popularity, celebrating the native landscape in ways "thoroughly and minutely American in their character."[3]

The years just prior to and following the Civil War saw decided changes in the American attitude toward its European heritage. James Abbott McNeill Whistler departed for Paris in 1855. Promptly involving himself with the most advanced young artists of the Paris scene, he spent his life in Europe stirring controversy and spreading influence unprecedented for any American artist since Benjamin West. Following Whistler's notorious success, the American presence in Europe grew rapidly. Until around 1890 one would be hard pressed to discern any American schools of art unrelated to one or another concurrent European movement.

This conspicuous shift in perspective cannot be attributed to Whistler alone, of course. Rather, certain fundamental changes in America's outward view must be considered. The second half of the nineteenth century was a period of rapid technological expansion. Advances in transportation and communication reduced America's earlier isolation from the Old World. Increased awareness of European artistic trends was a natural outcome of these changes. The appearance of art journals published in Europe and the founding of equivalent American journals, coupled with the constantly improving technology of reproduction, made current European modes available to the American public at the moment of their discussion abroad.

A revolution in the patterns of collecting art, as well, began in the 1860s. The spectacularly successful import of the French school of landscape painting known as Barbizon provided new opportunities for profit for the young industry of art dealing. Among the most notable art dealers were

Durand-Ruel, who specialized in Barbizon painters and later promoted the Impressionists, and Goupil's, who were especially attached to the French Beaux-Arts painters. As early as 1873 an unidentified writer in *The New York Times* warned his readers to beware of "inferior works" painted for the American market by certain famous masters of the French Salon. He advised caution and the guidance of reputable dealers in the selection of their Gérômes, Meissoniers, Bouguereaus and Cabanels.[4]

American artists were being forced to compete in this new market. Hudson River paintings began to look narrow and naïve when compared to the dazzling technical mastery and sophisticated thematic material of the Europeans.[5] By the early 1880s few significant American artists could be found without some European training and experience. Many artists discovered, as Whistler and Mary Cassatt had, that the best of their work could be nurtured only by removing themselves more or less permanently to one of the major centers on the Continent or in England.

These expatriates, generally born between 1835 and 1860, seem to have been driven less by disillusionment—unlike the more famous "lost generation" of the 1920s—than by a longing for a larger, older context in which to grow and prosper. Of that group, five of the most interesting are represented in this show.

The oldest of the artists at hand was Elihu Vedder (1836–1923). Born on Varick Street in New York City, Vedder acquired his early training with popular genre painter Tompkins H. Matteson. He spent much of his youth shuttling between Havana, Cuba, where his father practiced dentistry, and Schenectady, New York, the home of his grandfather. By 1856 Vedder had resolved to become a painter, so he left for Paris, where he spent a short time drawing from casts in the studio of François Picot, the aging academic master. He seems to have been unimpressed by Picot and his academic method.[6] After a period of considerable experimentation, Vedder returned to a firm, linear style of figure design related to Beaux-Arts practice.

In April 1857 Vedder was on his way to Italy, to experiences that would considerably alter his life. He visited the major cities until August, when he settled in Florence, which at that time supported a considerable Anglo-American colony. Vedder later wrote, "They were all intellectual, highly cultured, literary and artistic—above all literary."[7]

While studying at the Florence Accademia under the plodding guidance of Raffaello Bonaiuti, Vedder came under the spell of the progressive group of artists known as "il Macchiaioli." Their *plein-air* sensibility shaped Vedder's early landscapes, which are among the most notable works in his *oeuvre*. In these paintings Vedder rendered distant craggy vistas in stark natural light (cf. *Volterra*, 1860, National Museum of American Art, Washington, D.C.). Already his romantic attraction to mystery was being expressed in these desolate images.

In 1860 Vedder's father demanded that he return from Europe in order to earn a living. With his funds depleted, the artist was forced to comply, going first to Cuba and then settling in New York City for the duration of the Civil War. Removed from his abiding inspiration—Italy and her countryside—Vedder began to work in the imaginative mode characteristic of his mature work.

During the first lean years in New York Vedder supported himself with commercial design and illustration work. Illustration at this time was beginning to attain status as art in America. It would eventually serve many notable artists on their way to success. Vedder, however, was already aware of "higher art," in the European manner, so he found the work demeaning.[8] In May 1862 he began showing at the National Academy of Design, first with paintings executed in Italy and then, in 1863, with new work. Later in the same year he was elected Associate of the Academy, testimony to the good impression he was making. One of Vedder's offerings in 1863 was the well-known *Questioner of the Sphinx* (Museum of Fine Arts, Boston). It contains images of longing, despair and dread that mark his New York painting.

In this phase of his work Vedder usually employed a barren landscape (cf. his *Volterra* series), richly painted with strong planes of light, with some mysterious image of foreboding. No more disturbing image could exist than his *Lair of the Sea Serpent* (1864, Museum of Fine Arts, Boston; smaller version, 1889, Metropolitan Museum of Art, New York), shown at the National Academy that year. A comparison of the two versions reveals much of Vedder's development. The Boston picture, slightly larger, is painted in a crusty, less meticulous manner than the later Metropolitan version. The body of the serpent is thrust more aggressively toward the frontal plane in the picture of 1864, and details such as clouds and grass are suppressed. The earlier work more effectively inspires primordial loathing.

Vedder's painting during the all-important New York period is represented here by his portrait (p. 117) of Andrew W. Warren (d. 1873). Vedder's work in portraiture was very limited, indeed. He was able to escape the necessity of painting portraits in order to live by virtue of his early success in other forms, so the portrait of Warren gives us a rare opportunity to see Vedder dealing with the special problem of making a living likeness. Not surprisingly, the artist portrayed his friend in a conventionally romantic manner, turned in profile, looking dreamily toward an unknown vista. Nevertheless, the faraway look and the placement of the figure high in the picture plane give the portrayal a marked tension and a notable restlessness, quite different from the axial stability and cameo-like clarity of Vedder's portrait of Kate Field, painted in Florence around 1856–57. In the Warren portrait, Vedder may be demonstrating his own restlessness at having to remain in America, but more probably it shows Vedder's then current interest in the psychologically tense moment and in mysterious states of mind.

Vedder managed to establish himself in New York as a unique talent on the American scene. He was applauded by critics as diverse as James Jackson Jarves and the Ruskinians of the New Path group. While Jarves saw the *Lair of the Sea Serpent* as an illustration of "phases of mind and feelings," using "nature's forms simply as language to express thought,"[9] the New Path critics were able to praise its technical merit and literalness.[10] Thus, by 1865 Vedder was able to return to Italy with prospects for a secure future. He established a pattern of expatriatism that would be the model for the next generation. Trained in Europe, he established a reputation in America that served him for the rest of his life abroad.

Vedder's work from 1865 onward evolved quickly toward its mature style. His paintings were variously landscapes in the severe manner of his Italian oeuvre, allegorical figures rendered in a dry, linear style and costume pieces. The latter two types were those upon which his reputation would continue to be upheld. The figures ranged from simple renditions of the model, draped or undraped, alone or in groups (cf. *Greek Girls Bathing,* 1877, Metropolitan Museum of Art, New York) to complex and imaginative allegories, such as his illustrations for the *Rubaiyat of Omar Khayyam* (Boston: Houghton Mifflin, 1883–84). The *Rubaiyat* illustrations brought Vedder to the height of his fame. They also initiated a new direction for American book illustration, away from Edwin Austin Abbey (q.v.) and his delicate but painstakingly tonal and particularist mode, toward the sinuous exoticism of Art Nouveau.

A significant aspect of Vedder's contribution to American art was his extensive excursion into the field of decorative art. From the 1880s Vedder designed for every medium from greeting cards for L. Prang & Co. to stained glass for Tiffany and major mural projects, both private and public. All of Vedder's decorative work, including his murals for the World's Columbian Exposition in Chicago of 1893, pulls together medievalizing detail derived from the Pre-Raphaelites and William Morris and Beaux-Arts figurative design. In so doing, Vedder delineated the taste of his time with an acuity rivalled only by artists twenty years his junior.

Among Vedder's younger compatriots were Edwin Austin Abbey (1852–1911) and John Singer Sargent (1856–1925). Abbey has already been mentioned in relation to the art of book illustration, the medium in which he began his career when his illustrations were published by *Harper's* in 1870. The artist had earlier studied at the Pennsylvania Academy of the Fine Arts, while apprenticing to a Philadelphia publishing house. By 1871 Abbey had been hired by *Harper's Weekly* as its house illustrator. Abbey's early involvement with illustration marked the direction of his entire career. From the beginning he was known for the finesse of his drawing. He quickly developed a manner, later much imitated, that translated without loss of detail or emphasis into wood engraving.[11] He was also particularly well-suited to rendering historic drama, in which he exhaustively searched out telling detail and situated it firmly in a tonal scale that emphasized formal organization. This training uniquely equipped Abbey for painting the large history subjects that he would undertake in 1889.

In 1879 Abbey was sent by *Harper's* to England to research a series of illustrations for Robert Herrick's poetry. Abbey was so enchanted with England that he remained there until his death. He had been predisposed to like England for some time before his actual departure, however. During his student days Abbey had been attracted to the Pre-Raphaelites, and he, unlike the older Vedder, openly acknowledged his allegiance to the Brotherhood. As a student with Christian Schuessele at the Pennsylvania Academy, Abbey had been deeply affected by Rossetti's writings.

> To a large degree the romantic element in [Rossetti's] writings had a deep influence [on Abbey], and nearly everything that Rossetti wrote he accepted without reservation.[12]

Abbey's Pre-Raphaelitism is best characterized in his own words:

> What I'd like to do is the representation of events not as they might be supposed poetically to have happened, but as they really might have happened.[13]

In 1889 Abbey began to paint in earnest. He had already been elected to the Royal Institute of Painters in Watercolor in 1883, and he had exhibited drawings successfully at the Royal Academy in 1885. He must have felt compelled to paint in oil through his associations with painters, especially Sargent, and his activity in the orbit of the Royal Academy. His first major work, *May Day Morning* (Yale University Art Gallery, New Haven), was exhibited at the Royal Academy in 1890. It was such a success that he and Sargent soon received an important commission for mural decorations in the Boston Public Library.

Abbey and Sargent had shared a great deal since 1885, when Sargent had begun summering with the Abbeys at their country home in Broadway. In addition to their joint Boston Public Library commission, Sargent and Abbey had even worked together in Abbey's huge studio.

Sargent's international reputation as a portraitist grew steadily from the beginning of his professional career in 1879. At the Salon of that year, Sargent had shown the lithely painted portrait of his master, Carolus-Duran (Sterling and Francine Clark Art Institute, Williamstown, Mass.), with much success. In 1884 Sargent's modernist sympathies and bold manner reached a crescendo of notoriety with his portrait of Mme. Gautreau known as *Madame X* (Metropolitan Museum of Art, New York). The public and critics alike were so shocked by the lady's *décolletage* and the indecent lavender-powdering of her skin that Sargent felt compelled to retreat to England.

The years from 1885 to 1890 were important for Sargent, for he worked on figure and landscape studies more and more under the influence of Monet and Impressionism. He had spent some time with Monet at Giverny, in the summer of 1887,[14] when the profile portrait of Monet in the collection of the National Academy probably was executed.

In 1889 Sargent visited New York City to complete a series of portrait commissions that helped revive his American reputation. His career in portraiture was again on the ascendant. He was elected Associate of the National Academy in 1891, from which time dates his *Self-Portrait* (p. 39). But his election to the Academy was as much a reflection of Sargent's international repute as it was of the liberalizing tendency of the Academy at this time. This painting demonstrates little of the stylish verve or bravura handling associated with Sargent's well-known society portraits. It is a simple, directly observed image rendered in an equally simple and direct manner. One might take it for a life study in preparation for a portrait rather than a formal presentation piece. It does, however, reveal that Sargent was an eminently capable and dispassionate observer when he was free of the demands of commissioned portraiture.

The success of Sargent and Abbey was virtually unlimited. Both had been accorded almost every honor Europe and America could bestow. Sargent became the official portraitist of English aristocracy, and Abbey, being especially suited to large-scale history painting, was commissioned in 1901 to commemorate the coronation of Edward VII. No such honor had been awarded to an American since the era of West's presidency of the Royal Academy. Both Sargent and Abbey epitomized the Edwardian age: elegant, dashing, nostalgic—ideals to which Abbey subscribed until his death in 1911. Sargent—success and fame firmly in hand—withdrew during the last twenty years of his life from the world of society in favor of more personal expressions. His late landscapes, especially those painted in the Austrian Tyrol prior to World War I (cf. *Alpine Pool*, Metropolitan Museum of Art, New York) are remarkable for their richly pigmented surfaces and abstract light, reminiscent of the late works of Monet. These paintings were the salvation of Sargent's reputation during the years immediately following his death in 1925, while Abbey's reputation suffered for his lack of redeeming "modernist" works.

John White Alexander (1856–1915) also belonged to *La Belle Epoque*, but he must be related to Paris of the 1890s, where he lived from 1890 to 1901. Alexander was born in Pennsylvania, but he had established himself in New York City by 1875. Alexander's friendship with Abbey dates from this time. They were both illustrators for *Harper's Weekly*, but Alexander did not stay long at that post. By 1877 he was in Munich, studying at the Academy of Fine Arts under the strict eye of Carl von Piloty. During the summer of 1878 Alexander joined several other Americans who were studying in Munich and traveled to the Bavarian town of Polling, to the summer retreat of the "Duveneck Boys," among them J. Frank Currier, Walter Shirlaw and Duveneck himself. Alexander easily came under the spell of Duveneck's dark, closely observed, but freshly brushed manner. Later that year the entire group proceeded to Italy where, in Venice, Alexander met Whistler and Henry James, who were to become so significant to Alexander later in his career.

In 1881 Alexander returned to New York to begin a career of teaching, illustration and portrait painting. He distinguished himself in all of these pursuits. Alexander's 1881–82 *Portrait of Thurlo Weed* (National Academy of Design, New York) is a notable example of his early Munich manner. In it, the dark figure of Weed emerges from a murky background and is thrust back in brilliant light, while paint and drawing disintegrate toward the edges of the picture. Already Whistler's manner of broken line and diminishing edges, seen especially in the etchings, informs Alexander's style.

The decade of the 1880s was a productive one for Alexander, but his career did not attain particular note until he moved his family to Paris in 1891. Paris in the 1890s was seething with artistic activity. Alexander and his wife, Elizabeth, moved quickly into the circle of esthetes and *literaires* who animated the heart of that artistic life. Their group included Octave Mirbeau, critic and defender of the vanguard, Oscar Wilde, Henry James and, of course, Whistler. Through these men they met Mallarmé, Arsène Alexandre and André Gide.[17] Elizabeth Alexander recalled meeting Rodin, Cazin and Puvis de Chavannes[18] at their first visit to the new Salon of the Société Nationale des Beaux-Arts. Alexander associated himself with the new Salon, the so-called Champs-de-Mars, formed when Meissonier and Puvis quarreled with William Adolphe Bouguereau over the conduct of the *hors concours* at the old Salon.[19] Showing with the Champs-de-Mars for the first time in 1893, Alexander aligned himself with the esthetes surrounding Whistler. He showed three portraits, titled simply by color—in the Whistlerian manner—*Portrait Gris*. In 1895 Alexander submitted five works entitled *Repose*, one of which may be a portrait of Loie Fuller, the American dancer (Metropolitan Museum of Art, New York). In this painting, sinuous line—not the effulgent embankments of Vedder, but pure line—traces the surface. The sitter's half-seen head seems almost an interruption of the elegant design.

In 1901, the year of his election to the National Academy of Design, Alexander returned to New York. In the same year he completed the two portraits in this exhibition, *Self-Portrait* (p. 119) and *Portrait of Edwin Austin Abbey* (p. 121). It is noteworthy that, after the great success he had enjoyed in Paris during the previous decade, he should revert, as Sargent had, to an earlier manner for his works for the Academy. Both are painted in the dark, dry manner of the *Portrait of Thurlo Weed*; they are, in fact, even less finished. Only the faces are really painted; the remainder of the coarse canvas that he habitually used was hardly more than stained. He abandoned the luminously tonal coloration of the Paris years, as well as the linear, abstract design he had previously exploited so well. In any event, we are presented with images of turn-of-the-century worldliness, more strikingly *bon vivant* in his own portrait than in the more conventional portrait of Abbey.

From the moment of his return to New York, Alexander was included in the hierarchy of American art, along with Vedder, Abbey and Sargent before him. His career as a portraitist also peaked after his return to this country. This was chiefly due to the progressive and fashionable style in which he worked, as well as to Sargent's distance from competition. Alexander's career was further buoyed by Sargent's withdrawal from the portrait market later in the first decade of this century. Like Vedder and Abbey—and, to some extent, Sargent—Alexander's reputation was inundated by French modernism during the first three decades of the twentieth century. Alexander's less progressive style could not be again appreciated until the strictness of the modernist aesthetic had begun to loosen, as it did in the early 1960s.

Another artist, immensely honored in his lifetime, was Gari Melchers (1860–1932), although no artist further from the estheticisms of Vedder, Abbey, Sargent and Alexander could be imaged. Melchers was born in Detroit, Michigan. His father, who came from Westphalia, had studied with Carpeaux and Etex in Paris, and he became a sculptor of slight distinction. When his eldest son expressed an interest in art, he was sent not to Paris but to the more staid Düsseldorf Academy. The training Melchers received was conventional, and he seems not to have attempted to associate with more advanced ideas. By 1880 he was in Paris at the Académie Julian, that haven of relative freedom for foreigners, especially Americans, and at the Ecole des Beaux-Arts. He studied with the fairly young academic master Jules Joseph Lefèbvre and the older, more conservative Gustave Boulanger. As early as 1882 Melchers was showing at the Salon, and he received an Honorable Mention there in 1886.

From this point on, Melchers's career was one of unprecedented honors, their quantity outstripping the recognition received by his more famous contemporaries. Working in a studio in Egmond-aan-Zee, The Netherlands, at which he had established himself in 1884, Melchers conquered the official art world of two continents. He did so with a sureness that belies the humility seen in his *Self-Portrait* (p. 122), which, of all the portraits in this group, demonstrates the greatest alignment with the mainstream of the artist's work. In the *Self-Portrait*, Melchers presents himself in an attitude that at once advances and retreats. He steps forward, but his bowed head suggests a retiring nature, and is perhaps somewhat studied in its effect. The cool, light palette, as well as the sturdy execution, all accurately reflect his genre painting of this period.

Melchers accomplished his vast success not with complex allegories, grand-manner history painting or elegantly stylized portraiture, but with soundly structured, unassuming genre paintings chiefly of Dutch subjects. His painting has a strength that demonstrates some affinity with Courbet, although the more sentimental tone of his pictures aligns him with Millet and the genre school around Josef Israels, Melchers's Dutch contemporary.

Daniel S. Hodgson

Notes

1. John Durand, *The Life and Times of Asher B. Durand* (New York: Scribner's, 1894), p. 165
2. Barbara Novak, *American Painting in the Nineteenth Century* (New York: Praeger, 1969), p. 83
3. H. T. Tuckerman, *Book of the Artists*, (1867: Repr., New York: James F. Carr, 1966) p. 189
4. "Some Views of the Paris Salon," *The New York Times*, Oct. 23, 1873, sec. 2, p. 1
5. Mariana Van Rensselaer, "Frederick Arthur Bridgeman," *American Art and American Art Collections*, 1 (1889), p. 177
6. Joshua C. Taylor, "Perceptions and Digressions," *Perceptions and Digressions: The Art of Elihu Vedder* (Washington: Smithsonian Institution Press, 1979), p. 33
7. E. Vedder, *Digressions of V.* (Boston and New York: Houghton Mifflin, 1910), p. 146
8. *Ibid.*, p. 55
9. James Jackson Jarves, *The Art-Idea*, (1864: Repr., Cambridge: Harvard University Press, 1960), p. 202
10. Taylor, *op. cit.*, p. 69
11. Michael Quick, "Abbey as Illustrator," *Edwin Austin Abbey* (exh. cat., Yale University Art Gallery, 1973/74), p. 24
12. L. V. Lucas, *The Life and Work of E. A. Abbey, R.A.* (London: Metheun, 1921), p. 14
13. *Ibid.*, p. 189
14. Richard Ormond, *John Singer Sargent* (New York: Harper and Row, 1970), p. 42
15. *Ibid.*, p. 66
16. *Ibid.*, p. 43
17. Mary Anne Goley, *John White Alexander* (exh. cat., National Collection of Fine Arts, 1976/77), n.p.
18. *Ibid.*
19. For a description of the break that led to the foundation of the Société Nationale des Beaux-Arts, see Philippe Guilloux, *Meissonier, Trois Siècles d'Histoire* (Paris: Editions Coperic, 1980) p. 167

Elihu Vedder (1836-1923) A.N.A. 1863, N.A. 1865
PORTRAIT OF ANDREW W. WARREN (?-1873) A.N.A. 1863
Oil on canvas remounted masonite
30 x 25
Signed lower right: AW. Warren / by Elihu Vedder/ April 25th

Elihu Vedder

Born in New York City, Feb. 26. Lived in Schenectady, N.Y. and Cuba as a child. Received first art education from Tomkins H. Matteson in Shelbourne, N.Y. Traveled to Paris to study under François-Edward Picot, 1856. Moved to Florence, studied with Raffaello Bonaiuti; became friendly with the young *plein-air* painters called *Il Macchiaioli* who frequented the Caffé Michelangiolo. Returned to U.S. via Cuba, 1860. Lived in New York and Boston, supporting his painting through magazine illustrations; painted on New England Coast. A member of artistic and literary circle including Walt Whitman, John LaFarge, Winslow Homer, William Morris Hunt. 1863, elected Associate of National Academy (same year as Homer and LaFarge). Member of Century Club and Tile Club, 1861-65. 1866, traveled to Brittany with Charles C. Coleman and William Morris Hunt, met Elizabeth Caroline Rose Krans (Carrie), whom he married in 1869. Represented at Second Biennale in Venice, 1867. Settled permanently in Rome; traveled to England, became acquainted with Pre-Raphaelites through English artists met in Rome, 1869. Became involved in decorative arts, beginning in 1880's; commissioned to paint murals by Stanford White, William Rutherford Mead and Charles F. McKim. Illustrations for *Rubaiyat of Omar Khayyam* published in 1884. Settled permanently in Rome 1889; kept close contact with American scholars and artists there. Completed murals for Bowdoin College, 1892; mosaics for Library of Congress, 1896. Last trip to U.S. 1901. Began to write poetry after death of wife, 1909. Published autobiography *Digressions of V.*, 1910. Books of poetry with his own illustrations, *Miscellaneous Moods in Verse*, published 1914; and *Doubt and Other Things* published 1923. Died in Rome, Jan. 29.

BSK

Andrew W. Warren

Born and lived in Coventry, N.Y. Began exhibiting landscapes in annual exhibitions National Academy of Design in 1854. Apparently traveled to South and Central America, 1859. Had a studio in New York City, 1860. Traveled through New England and Canada, 1860-62. Did illustrations of Civil War scenes for *Harper's Magazine*, 1864. Possibly met Elihu Vedder at this time, or through the National Academy, elected the same year. May have known Sanford Robinson Gifford, who owned one of his paintings. Exhibited regularly at National Academy until 1872. Died in Waterville, N.Y., June 15.

BSK

John Singer Sargent

Born in Florence, Italy, Jan. 10 or 12 to expatriate American parents. In youth moved throughout Europe: Italy, France, England. Began drawing animals in Paris zoo, 1865. Took classes with German-American painter Carl Welsch in Rome, 1868. Study at Accademia delle Belle Arti, Florence, 1870. Began studying at Ecole des Beaux-Arts, Paris, under Charles Emile Auguste Carolus-Duran, fellow students in atelier were Will H. Low, J. Carroll Beckwith, Julian Alden Weir, Paul Helleu, 1874. Beckwith and Sargent shared a studio, 1875. Sargent met Claude Monet in Paris, Sargent and family traveled to America to see Philadelphia Centennial Exhibition and throughout New England and Canada, 1876. To Cancale, Brittany and Lyons in summer with Eugene Lachaise and Beckwith, 1877. Worked with Carolus-Duran on murals in Louvre, incorporated portraits of each other into composition. Sargent and Whistler exhibit with Society of American Artists, 1878. Traveled to Spain, studied Velázquez and incorporated his silver tonalities into paintings, 1879. Traveled to Morocco and Spain, to Holland to study Frans Hals, established studio in Venice, 1880. Traveled back and forth between Italy and France, 1881-83. Rented new studio in Paris, new neighbors included Giovanni Boldini, Carrier-Belleuse. Scandal caused by exhibition of his portrait known as *Madame X* at Paris Salon, 1884. Moved to London to summer with Vickers family, his first English patrons; painted Robert Louis Stevenson. Rented studio next to Whistler's. Friend Edwin Austin Abbey introduced him to Henry James; painted second portrait of Stevenson, 1884-85. James introduced Mrs. Jack Gardiner to Sargent, 1886. In Boston, painted her portrait among many other commissions; exhibited 20 paintings at St. Botolph Club, 1887-88. Served on jury on Salon exhibition, Paris; visited Monet at Giverny, 1889; returned to U.S., 1889. Organized party at William Merritt Chase's 10th Street studio with Mrs. Gardiner. Spanish dancer Carmencita entertained, and Chase and Sargent painted her. Exhibited at Society of American Artists; commissioned to paint Boston Public Library murals, 1890. Exhibited at World's Columbian Exposition, Chicago, 1893. Elected Associate of the Royal Academy of Arts, 1894. Shared studio with Abbey while both worked on Boston Public Library murals. Installed part of murals, 1891-95. Elected both National and Royal Academician; made Officer of the Legion d'Honneur, France, 1897. Honorary degree of LL.D. conferred by University of Pennsylvania, 1903; honorary degree of D.C.L. by Oxford University, 1904. Given Ordre pour le Merite and Order of Leopold of Belgium; honorary degree of LL.D. conferred by Cambridge University, 1909. Exhibited at Panama-Pacific Exposition, 1915. 1916, installed murals at Boston Public Library. Commissioned to decorate rotunda of Museum of Fine Arts, Boston. Honorary degree of LL.D. conferred by Yale University; honorary degree of Art D. by Harvard University, 1916. Carnegie Institute, Pittsburgh, exhibited his watercolors and Winslow Homer's, 1917. Designed and installed Library murals for Harvard, 1922. On eve of sailing for installation of murals at Museum of Fine Arts, Boston, died in London, Apr. 15. Murals subsequently unveiled at opening of Sargent Memorial Exhibition, 1925. *See color, page 39.*

BSK

John White Alexander (1856-1915) A.N.A. 1901, N.A.
1902, P.N.A. 1909-1915
SELF-PORTRAIT
Oil on canvas
30¼ x 25
Signed lower left: John W Alexander

John White Alexander

Born Allegheny, Pa., Oct. 7. Orphaned at age five, lived with grandparents. Began working for Western Telegraph as messenger, did crayon portraits for photographer, 1868. Came to New York, worked in art department of *Harper's Magazine* as office boy and eventually as illustrator, 1874-77. (Edwin Austin Abbey also at *Harper's* at this time.) Left for Europe, stopping in Paris and continued on to Munich where he studied at Royal Academy under a Professor Benczur for three months. Left Munich for Polling, an artists' colony headed by Frank Duveneck, 1878. Traveled with the "Duveneck Boys"—including William Merritt Chase, Walter Shirlaw and Thomas Dewing—to Florence and Venice, 1879. In Venice established friendship with James Abbott McNeill Whistler. Shared studio with Duveneck in Florence, taught some of Duveneck's classes, then returned to New York, 1881. Painted portraits and illustrated as means of support. Drawing instructor at Princeton University, 1881-84. Traveled to Spain where he saw Velázquez's paintings, also to Holland, France, England and North Africa. Commissioned by the *Century Magazine* to do charcoal portraits of literary figures and famous expatriates, and through such a commission of 1884 established friendship with Robert Lewis Stevenson. Pursued portraiture, 1881-1891. Married Elizabeth Alexander, 1888; birth of only child, 1889. Suffered from weakened health, 1889. Upon medical advice moved to Paris, 1890. Alexander becomes involved in Symbolist movement, met important artistic and literary figures such as André Gide, Auguste Rodin, Oscar Wilde, Claude Debussy, John Singer Sargent and American patron Mrs. Jack Gardiner. Symbolist movement and Art Nouveau exert important influence on his work. Summered in Brittany and resumed painting, 1891. Exhibited at Salon du Champs-de-Mars, elected Associate of Société Nationale des Beaux-Arts, 1893. Elected full member, 1894. Commissioned to paint mural in Library of Congress, 1896. Invited to exhibit with avant-garde groups in Brussels, Munich and Vienna. Secured loans of paintings by contemporary Europeans and expatriate Americans for Carnegie Internationals, 1895-98. Returned to New York, 1901. Given commission to paint forty-eight murals in Carnegie Institute, Pittsburgh; Alexander and wife collaborated with actress Maude Adams on designing all aspects of her productions, 1905. Founded School Art League whose purpose was to establish education programs in museums for children. 1909, elected President of National Academy, served until his death in New York on May 31.

BSK

Edwin Austin Abbey

Born Philadelphia, Apr. 1. Attended classes at Pennsylvania Academy of the Fine Arts under Christian Schuessle, 1868. Published his first drawings, 1866. Went to New York and joined *Harper's Magazine*, working as illustrator, 1871-78. Sent to London by *Harper's* to gather material for illustration of poetry by Robert Herrick, 1878. Settled permanently in England early 1880's. Worked mostly in black and white until friend Francis Millet influenced him to begin to paint, 1889. Married an American also living in England, Gertrude Mead, 1890. Commissioned by Charles Follen McKim to paint murals for Boston Public Library, 1895. Elected Associate of Royal Academy of Arts and Royal Academician, 1898. Appointed official court painter, commissioned to paint coronation of King Edward VII (study in collection of National Academy of Design). Invited to paint coronation of George V, but declined because of difficulty obtaining portraits for previous work. Commissioned to paint three panels for Pennsylvania State Capitol in Harrisburg. Refused knighthood in order to retain American citizenship. Died in London, 1911. Upon wife's death, 1943, their joint bequest established Edwin Austin Abbey Mural Scholarship to encourage study of mural painting both at National Academy and Royal Academy.

BSK

Gari Melchers

Born in Detroit, Mich., Aug. 11. Traveled to Germany to study at Royal Academy in Düsseldorf under Karl von Gebhardt and Peter Janssen. Enrolled at Académie Julian, Paris, under Jules Joseph Lefèbvre and Gustave Boulanger, 1881; spent summer in Brittany, exhibited at the Paris Salon, 1882. Met Puvis de Chavannes; close friendship continued throughout lifetime. Established a studio in the Netherlands, coastal town of Egmond-aan-Zee, 1884. Exhibited and commissioned to paint murals for the Manufactures and Liberal Arts Building of the World's Columbian Exposition, Chicago, 1893, as well as decorations for the Library of Congress, 1896. Won First Class Gold Medal in Munich (James Abbott McNeill Whistler took Second Medal), 1888. Became Chevalier of the Legion of Honor in France, 1895. Married Corinne L. MacKale, artist, 1903. Commissioned to paint full-length portraits for Rhode Island State Capitol, 1908, by William Rutherford Mead. In 1907 became Knight of Order of St. Michael of Bavaria. Invited by Grand Duke of Saxe-Weimar to take post of professor of painting at Weimar Academy, which he accepted and held 1909-1914. Returned permanently to U.S. in 1914, lived in New York. Awarded honorary LL.D. from University of Michigan, 1913. Elected to American Academy of Arts and Letters and to Century Club; moved to Falmouth, Va. 1916. Commissioned by Cass Gilbert to decorate interiors of several of his buildings; e.g., and murals in Detroit Public Library, 1920. Served as president of Century Club, 1930-32. Died in Falmouth, Va., Nov. 30.

BSK

John White Alexander (1856-1915) A.N.A 1901, N.A. 1902,
  P.N.A. 1909-1915
PORTRAIT OF EDWIN AUSTIN ABBEY (1852-1911)
  A.N.A. 1901, N.A. 1902
Oil on canvas remounted on masonite
30 x 25
Signed lower left: John W Alexander

Gari Melchers (1860-1932) A.N.A. 1904, N.A. 1906
SELF-PORTRAIT
Oil on canvas
31¼ x 25½
Signed lower right: Gari Melchers / 1905

The American Impressionists

AMERICAN IMPRESSIONISM, THE SUBJECT OF SEVERAL MAJOR BOOKS AND NUMEROUS EXHIBITIONS in the last decade, is no longer considered to be merely a pale reflection of the movement that originated in France in the 1860s.[1] Certainly many of the young artists who sought academic training in Paris in the 1880s and 1890s brought French Impressionist methods and motifs back to America, but their approach to the style was eclectic rather than doctrinaire. These young Americans were in France at a time when Impressionism was beginning to be accepted as a vital, contemporary esthetic. They interpreted it as a culmination of the *plein-air* work of the Barbizon painters—and of younger men like Jules Bastien-Lepage—a movement toward greater luminosity and truth to appearance. Even Theodore Robinson, the closest of the American artists to Claude Monet, viewed Monet's Impressionism as a tremendous step forward in realist painting, rather than as a radical break with traditional practice. He wrote that Monet had no desire to shock and was not rebelling against "what has always been and always will be necessary, drawing, search for form—values."[2]

For American painters of the late nineteenth century, adoption of the Impressionist palette, brushwork and motifs did not necessarily imply abandonment of their hard-won academic skills: the superb draftsmanship and the assured building of form through carefully studied value relations. Rather, the use of high-key, saturated color was seen as the best method for rendering brilliant sunlight effects, and the application of paint in small touches was viewed as useful for conveying precise color values, as well as for indicating the vibration of atmosphere.

The Impressionism revealed by these artists in a number of exhibitions mounted on their return to the United States ranged from the experiments in unmixed color of Robert Vonnoh and John Leslie Breck, through the more orthodox styles of Theodore Wendel, Childe Hassam, Willard Metcalf and Theodore Robinson, to the modernist tendencies of John Henry Twachtman, to name only a few.[3] American critical opinion was surprisingly receptive to this new esthetic, having been prepared for it by several exhibitions of French Impressionist paintings brought to this country in the 1880s by the Paris-based art dealer Paul Durand-Ruel.[4] By the time of the Chicago World's Columbian Exposition in 1893, various forms of Impressionism had entered the mainstream of American art. It became as difficult for a progressive artist working in the 1890s to avoid Impressionism as for one in the 1950s to escape the influence of Abstract Expressionism.

The four artists grouped here as Impressionists represent the parameters of the style in America. Julian Alden Weir was one of the older generation who came late to Impressionism after painting in a more academic manner; Edmund Tarbell and Robert Reid were among those younger artists who absorbed the esthetic in their student years; and Lawton Parker was one of the Giverny Group who practiced a variant of the style in the first years of this century. All but Parker were members of The Ten, a predominately Impressionist organization, formed in 1897 as a protest against the exhibitions of the Society of American Artists. Their quarrel did not extend to the National Academy of Design, however. Weir was elected an academician in 1885, Tarbell and Reid in 1906, and all were awarded numerous prizes in the Academy's exhibitions.[5]

Julian Alden Weir (1852–1919) was born in West Point, New York. He studied first with his father Robert, who was a professor of drawing at the United States Military Academy, before enrolling in the National Academy school in 1870.[6] In the fall of 1873 he traveled to Paris and entered Jean Léon Gérôme's studio at the Ecole des Beaux-Arts. Weir soon became a friend and ardent partisan of Bastien-Lepage, whose *plein-air* paintings were among the most progressive of that era outside the Impressionist group. Before leaving France in 1877 Weir saw the third Impressionist exhibition. In an oft-quoted letter to his parents, he wrote, "I never in my life saw such horrible things. . . . They do not observe drawing or form but give you an impression of what they call nature."[7] Similar comments could be read in newspapers at the time, but this criticism probably reflected Weir's training with Gérôme, who emphasized conscientious draftsmanship and careful finish at the expense of color.

The still lifes and figure paintings Weir executed after his return to New York in 1877 were strongly modeled and rich and dark in tone, and were seen to exemplify the academic ideal of *"le bon peinture, the intrinsic beauty of surface obtainable in oil painting, which ought to be cherished for its own sake."*[8] Characteristically, Weir was open to change and sympathetic to new ideas. His interest in the Impressionist esthetic grew during the 1880s, and by the end of the decade he was painting landscapes in a high key with broken brushwork. Rural landscapes continued to occupy Weir well into the twentieth century, and although more advanced in style than figure paintings of the same period, they evidenced Weir's continuing concern with value relations and tonal harmonies.

The two paintings by Weir included in the present exhibition—the diploma *Portrait of George Willoughby Maynard*, accepted by the Academy in 1882, and Weir's own qualifying portrait of 1886— belong to the earlier period, when light was important chiefly as it modeled form. In the Maynard portrait, the dramatic studio lighting reveals the face and hand, leaving irrelevant details in shadow. A sequence of curves, extending from the chair back through the hand and arm to the pronounced oval of the head, unifies the composition. The brushwork is delicate and unobtrusive; the flesh tones are luminous and carefully blended. The prevailing gray-green tonality suggests an appreciation of Whistler's monochromatic harmonies. Characteristic of Weir's portraits is the depiction of the inherent distinction of the sitter, as well of his palpable presence.

The image of the sitter in Weir's *Self-Portrait* is no less serious than that of Maynard, but the paint application is freer and the composition less conventional. The face is strongly modeled in planes of parallel brushstrokes. There is a play on highlights and rounded contours of both the face and the background objects. These objects, carefully placed in relation to the silhouette formed by the figure, serve as references to Weir's profession and interests.

The experience of painters such as Edmund Tarbell and Robert Reid, who studied in Paris in the 1880s, was different from those there a decade earlier. But for them, also, the *plein-air* style of Bastien-Lepage continued to be the most easily assimilated until direct contact with Monet was made by Robinson and others after 1887.

Edmund Charles Tarbell (1862–1938), who was born in West Groton, Massachusetts, entered the Boston Museum School in 1879, preceding Robert Reid and Frank Benson. The three men were students of Otto Grundmann, an exponent of the painterly, academic style practiced by Weir at that time. In 1883 Tarbell left for Paris, where he studied for two years at the Académie Julian in the atelier of Gustave Boulanger and Jules Joseph Lefèbvre, who were much favored by American students. After his return to America Tarbell began teaching in 1889 at the Boston Museum School, where he influenced many of the artists of the next generation.[9]

Although a contemporary critic wrote of Tarbell, "no young painter, it is safe to say, ever brought back to this country a better appreciation of the artistic possibilities of impression,"[10] his assimilation of Impressionist methods was neither immediate nor complete. Tarbell first made full use of brilliant saturated color and broken brushwork in a group of paintings of sunlit figures in the early 1890s. Even in these paintings, the figures receive the most attention (they are, in fact, portraits), for they detach themselves from their backgrounds in a fashion more characteristic of traditional academic practice than of French Impressionism. By the end of the decade Tarbell's palette had darkened, and he began to concentrate on interior scenes, where the light could be carefully controlled. Although he retained the vigorous Impressionist brushwork and continued to paint more informal outdoor scenes well past 1900, Tarbell's late interiors and portraits were more tightly painted, in an effort to achieve the timeless quality of a painting by Jan Vermeer, rather than immediacy of impression.

Tarbell's *Self-Portrait* in the present exhibition was given to the Academy in 1945 by the family of Samuel T. Shaw, the noted collector of American art and the donor of the annual Shaw prize at the Society of American Artists' exhibitions.[11] Judging from a letter to Shaw from Frank Benson in 1899, it would seem that Shaw intended to commission self-portraits from those artists whose works he owned.

> It would be difficult ever to get Tarbell to paint a head for you as he is always so busy with his pictures. He is doing some fine things. I will find time to paint you a head of myself sometime this winter. I think your scheme is a fine one.[12]

The Tarbell *Self-Portrait* was probably acquired about 1900, a date that would agree both with Tarbell's age and with the dark tonality and vigorous painterly style. The controlled studio light, which allows the face to emerge dramatically from shadow, is similar to that in interiors of the same date. The pigment is thickly applied, and the face is modeled through careful gradations of color in fluid brushstrokes. Unlike Tarbell's more conventional diploma *Self-Portrait* (1905) in the Academy collection, this one is noteworthy for its immediacy and unity of effect, as though it were painted all at once.

Robert Reid (1862–1929), born in Stockbridge, Massachusetts, was a fellow student of Tarbell's at the Boston Museum School. Reid then spent a year at the Art Students' League in New York City before following Tarbell to Paris and the Académie Julian in 1885. When he returned to America in 1889, Reid settled in New York, rather than in Boston.[13] At this time he concentrated on paintings of single figures in brilliant outdoor sunlight. Their saturated colors and vigorous all-over brushwork unite figure and background, resulting in Reid's closest approach to orthodox Impressionism. In 1892 Reid, Weir and six other artists were commissioned to paint one of the murals in the dome of the Liberal Arts Building of the Chicago World's Columbian Exposition. Unlike Weir, Reid found the work congenial. Subsequent mural commissions occupied him, to the exclusion of easel pictures, until the turn of the century.

Reid's experience with large-scale architectural decoration had an inevitable effect on the later compositions of attractive young women and flowers for which he is best known. Unlike the paintings of the early 1890s, these were not so much impressions as pretexts for the decorative arrangement of masses of brilliant color within sinuous Art Nouveau line. Reid's brushwork, always vigorous, became more linear in these paintings, following the contours of the objects. These later works are Impressionist only in their light tonality, their subjectlessness and deliberate contemporaneity. Reid wrote of them that "the subject and treatment are all of my time, beauty of course first, but its expression is through the people and scenes by which the painter himself is surrounded."[14]

Later in his life Reid depended on portrait commissions for a livelihood. He developed a rapid technique for their execution, using unmixed pigments thinly applied on coarse canvas to suggest, rather than construct, the forms. These "portrait impressions," as Reid termed them, have the appearance of drawings in color. Something of the same quality is evident in Reid's diploma *Self-Portrait* of 1904. The face is defined by successive strokes of dry pigment that outline the features, rather than model them. Even so, the face is more consciously finished than the background, which is a thin wash of pale color that serves to silhouette the head. The effect is that of a flat design, rather than a solid figure. But the suggestion of genial personality is vivid, and one feels that the likeness was an accurate one.

Lawton Parker (1868–1954) was born in Fairfield, Michigan, and although he was not much younger than Tarbell and Reid, his early career parallels that of Frederick Frieseke, six years his junior.[15] After training at the Chicago Art Institute school from 1886 to 1888, Parker made his first trip to Paris, studying briefly at the Académie Julian before enrolling at the Ecole des Beaux-Arts in March 1889. He returned to the Midwest, apparently around 1890, where he supported himself for several years painting portraits before he went to study at the Art Students' League in New York. Two years later, in October 1896, Parker was awarded the John Armstrong Chaloner Paris Prize, a five-year fellowship of $4,000, which enabled him to return to France for work under Gérôme at the Ecole des Beaux-Arts.[16] With such a background, it is not surprising that his first entry in the old Salon in 1900—an academic nude, painted with assurance and dash—was given an honorable mention.

During the next ten years Parker continued to paint portraits, but sometime before 1910 he began to paint figures outdoors during summers spent at Giverny. He was probably attracted to Giverny by Frieseke, who had settled there in 1906. Frieseke's *plein-air* canvases, with their scintillating sunlit colors, broken brushwork and decorative patterning, set the precedent for paintings by the new colony of American artists recognized by the end of the decade as a distinct Giverny Group.[17] Paintings by four of the group, Frieseke, Parker, Richard Miller and Guy Rose, were shown in a 1910 New York exhibition. They were hailed as evidence of a new development in Impressionism and were compared favorably with contemporary works by Monet. Certain stylistic divergencies were noted, however: colors, though brilliant, were carefully mixed beforehand, and the modeling was quite solid, with little dissolution of form. Indeed, one critic remarked of the paintings that although they appeared impressionistic, they displayed "the drawing that is a season ticket to official exhibitions hidden a little, made to seem rebellious by color borrowed from the ranks of the anarchists."[18]

Something of this ambiguity may be seen in Parker's diploma portrait of Frieseke, accepted by the Academy in 1913.[19] Frieseke is shown reading on the yellow sun porch of his house in Giverny. The sunlight, pouring through the window behind him, suffuses the canvas, silhouetting his profile and flattening his body into a two-dimensional shape. This painting, seemingly the most Impressionist of the portraits discussed, reveals certain anomalies on second glance: brushwork is used to indicate the texture of individual objects, rather than enveloping light; colors are mixed before application and limited to shades of blue-green and yellow; and the face is consciously modeled, in contrast to the summary background. Parker's *plein-air* paintings of this period more successfully integrate figure and background, but he was to abandon them for more conventional work when, in 1913, a nude painted indoors (in ordinary daylight, which was Frieseke's practice) won for him the first gold medal ever awarded to an American in the old Salon.[20]

Perhaps concentration on a specific likeness precluded the possibility of an "Impressionist portrait," although such a thing was attempted by Vonnoh and others in the 1890s. For the four painters just discussed, the reality of the natural world was more compelling than that of the two-dimensional canvas. They were not willing to sacrifice substance to the light that revealed it or to the paint that recreated it. They attempted the more difficult, if not impossible, task of combining academic techniques that suggest palpable reality with the latest methods for achieving luminosity and pictorial unity.

May Brawley Hill

Notes

1. Among the books are Donelson F. Hoopes, *The American Impressionists* (New York: 1972); Richard J. Boyle, *American Impressionism* (Boston: 1974); and the most comprehensive, William H. Gerdts, *American Impressionism* (Seattle: 1980). The latter, published in conjunction with an exhibition organized by the Henry Art Gallery, University of Washington, contains an extensive bibliography and is a necessary first reference for anyone wishing to study the subject in depth. Several recent exhibitions, with accompanying catalogues, should be mentioned: Harold Spencer, *et al.*, *Connecticut and American Impressionism*, William Benton Museum of Art, University of Connecticut (Storrs), Hurlbutt Gallery (Greenwich) and Lyme Historical Society, 1980; Harvey L. Jones, *Impressionism: The California View*, The Oakland Museum of Art, California, 1981; David Sellin, *Americans in Brittany and Normandy 1860–1910*, Phoenix Art Museum, 1982; and Laura L. Meixner, *An International Episode; Millet, Monet and Their North American Counterparts*, Dixon Gallery, Memphis, 1982.

2. Theodore Robinson, unpublished diaries, 1892–1896, Frick Art Reference Library, New York, entry for October 3, 1892. Robinson said much the same thing in his article "Claude Monet," *Century Magazine*, **44** (1892), pp. 696–701. A critic of the Boston *Evening Transcript* wrote of Monet the same year, "he is no isolated phenomenon, but part and parcel of the French landscape movement of the century." (Quoted in Meixner, *op. cit.*, p. 140)

3. Breck's paintings from the summer of 1887—spent with Metcalf, Wendel and Robinson in Giverny—were shown privately in Boston that fall. (See "Boston Art and Artists," *Art Amateur*, 17 [1887], p. 93.) Metcalf

had a one-man show at the St. Botolph Club, Boston, in 1889 and Breck in 1890. Weir and Twachtman held a joint exhibition at Ortigies Gallery, New York, in 1889. But 1891 was a banner year for exhibitions by the American Impressionists: in Boston, Wendel in his studio, Tarbell and Benson at the Chase Gallery and Vonnoh at the Williams and Everett Gallery; in New York, Weir at Blakeslee Gallery and Twachtman at Wunderlich Gallery.

4. For a discussion of the introduction of Impressionism to the American public, see Gerdts, *op. cit.*, pp. 27–31.

5. Weir was awarded the Inness gold medal in 1906, and he served as president of the Academy from 1915 to 1917. Tarbell won the Clarke prize in 1892, the Hallgarten first prize in 1894, the Saltus medal in 1908, and the Isidor medal in 1929. Reid won the Clarke prize in 1892 and the Hallgarten first prize in 1898. Parker, elected an Associate in 1916, won the Altman prize in the same year.

6. For a discussion of Weir's relationship with the National Academy, see Doreen B. Burke, *Julian Alden Weir and the National Academy of Design* (New York: 1981). Weir is the subject of a major exhibition organized by Burke for the Metropolitan Museum of Art, New York.

7. Julian Alden Weir Papers, Archives of American Art, New York, letter of April 15, 1877 (71:902). Weir was able to appreciate a different sort of painting and had written earlier, "Corot and Daubigny have such a feeling of nature with apparently no finish that it is a great pleasure to see them." (letter of May 13, 1874, 71:211) As a student in Paris, Weir did not think highly of Manet, but only a few years later he was instrumental in the purchase of two Manet paintings by the American collector Erwin Davis.

8. Duncan Phillips, "J. Alden Weir," *The Art Bulletin*, 2 (1920), p. 199.

9. See Patricia Jobe Pierce, *Edmund C. Tarbell and the Boston School of Painting (1889–1980)* (Hingham, Mass.: 1980). Many of these young artists taught in American art schools on their return. The date of 1879 for Tarbell's entry into the Museum School is taken from Bernice Kramer Leader, "The Boston School and Vermeer," *Arts Magazine*, 55 (Nov. 1980), p. 176.

10. Frederick W. Coburn, "Edmund C. Tarbell," *International Studio*, 32 (Sept. 1907), p. lxxx.

11. Samuel T. Shaw purchased a figure painting in each exhibition of the Society of American Artists from 1892 until its merger with the Academy in 1906. Tarbell won the prize in 1893.

12. Samuel T. Shaw Papers, National Academy of Design Archives, letter dated December 10, [1899]. Included in the Shaw gift to the Academy was a study for the Tarbell portrait and a self-portrait by Irving Wiles. A self-portrait by William Merritt Chase appeared in the sale of the Shaw collection, American Art Association, January 21–22, 1926, New York. Evidently Shaw had known Tarbell since his student days in France (where Shaw had gone to study political economy), for the painting is twice inscribed, "we studied together at Bois-le-Roi Fontainbleau. . . ."

13. Other Boston-area artists chose not to settle there, among them Hassam, Vonnoh, Breck and Metcalf. For a study of Reid's student days and early work, see H. Barbara Weinberg, "Robert Reid, Academic Impressionist," *Archives of American Art Journal*, 15 (1975), pp. 2–11.

14. James William Pattison, "Robert Reid Painter," *House Beautiful*, 20 (July 1906), p. 20.

15. Frederick Frieseke (1874–1939) was born in Owosso, Michigan. Like Parker, he studied at the Art Institute of Chicago and the Art Students' League, New York, before going to Paris in 1898.

16. For a description of this prize, established by John Armstrong Chaloner, a grandson of John Jacob Astor, see "The Fine Arts," *The Critic*, 18 (Feb. 18, 1891), p. 88. The requirements were eased somewhat by the time of the second award to Parker in 1896; see "Won Chalner [sic] Scholarship," *The New York Times*, Oct. 16, 1896, p. 17. Chaloner was declared insane in 1898. After much litigation, he had himself pronounced sane and capable of managing his own affairs in 1919. The third Paris Prize was made in 1921, when Lawton Parker served as one of three trustees for the Paris Prize Foundation. (I am indebted to Abigail Gerdts for this information from the Archives of the Academy.)

17. "At the Madison Art Gallery, 305 Madison Avenue, a group of Americans living abroad (who call themselves the Giverny Group) are having an exhibition. There were originally six of these men, but now that Edmund Greacen and Karl Anderson are living and painting at home, there are only four." The New York *Telegraph*, Dec. 21, 1910, quoted in *Paintings by Lawton Parker*, Art Institute of Chicago, 1912, n.p. These artists are grouped together in Mildred Giddings Burrage, "Art and Artists at Giverny," *The World To-Day*, 20 (March 1911), pp. 344–51, and in Thomas Wilson, "Carnegie Institute Exhibition," *Fine Arts Journal*, 25 (1911), p. 145.

    It is difficult to know which of these artists, mostly from the Midwest, settled first in Giverny. Guy Rose owned a house there from about 1904 to 1912; see his letter of November 6, 1912, to William Macbeth, Archives of American Art (NMc10:1182). According to information in the Edmund Greacen Papers, Archives of American Art (99:131), Greacen lived in Giverny from 1905 to 1909. Karl Anderson painted there in the summer of 1909. Richard Miller spent many summers in Giverny, often bringing pupils there. Frieseke remained there during the war years, while Parker returned to America in 1913.

18. The New York *American*, quoted in *Paintings by Lawton Parker*, *op. cit.* (no date given for the article). The exhibition was reviewed by *The New York Times* on December 25, 1910, p. 15, "News and Notes of the Art World."

19. This portrait was first mentioned in the Minutes of the Academy Council on April 21, 1913: "it had been understood that Mr. Lawton Parker had brought Mr. Frieseke's portrait from Europe but that the whereabouts of this portrait could not be ascertained." In the Council Minutes for November 3, 1913, the painting was accepted. A portrait of Frieseke painting a nude *en plein air* by Karl Anderson was included in the *Americans in Brittany and Normandy* exhibition. Parker's own diploma portrait was painted by Irving Wiles in 1918.

20. This painting, a modern Danaë entitled *Paresse*, or *Idleness*, achieved great notoriety when exhibited in this country; see Evelyn Marie Stuart, "Inconsistency of Censors," *Fine Arts Journal*, 29 (July 1914), pp. 347–50. It seems to have influenced the composition of Frieseke's *Sleep*, awarded the grand prize in the 1915 Panama-Pacific Exposition, San Francisco.

Julian Alden Weir

Born in West Point, N.Y., Aug. 30, son of painter Robert Weir. Studied with father and half-brother, John Fergeson Weir at West Point; at National Academy School under Lemuel E. Wilmarth, 1870-73. Other students with whom he established friendships were Albert P. Ryder, George de Forest Brush, William Merritt Chase and Abbott Handerson Thayer. Traveled to Europe, enrolled at Ecole des Beaux-Arts, Paris, under Jean Léon Gérôme. Met Jules Bastien-Lepage, 1873. Traveled to Belgium and Netherlands, 1874-75. In Spain met Sir Henry Thompson who later introduced him to Whistler. Painted summer, 1874, in Pont Aven with Edgar M. Ward. On return to U.S., stopped in London and met Whistler, 1877. Elected member of Society of American Artists, 1877. Responsible for securing loans of American expatriate and European artists to Society of American Artists exhibitions, 1878. Established studio at Benedict Building; neighbors included Albert Ryder, George Maynard, Wyatt Eaton and Olin Warner. Exhibited at National Academy of Design and Society of American Artists, 1880. Held various offices in Society of American Artists, 1880; elected President, 1882. Returned to Europe, 1881; with brother and John Twachtman, worked as consultant to important collectors while there. 1883, back in U.S. married and bought home in Branchville, Conn., which became informal meeting place for artists, including Albert P. Ryder and Theodore Robinson. Taught at Art Students' League and Cooper Union. Member of Tile Club with John Twachtman, William Merritt Chase, Edwin Austin Abbey, Stanford White and others, 1877-87. Exhibited with Twachtman at Blakeslee Gallery, 1891, again with him in comparative exhibition with Claude Monet and Paul Besnard at American Art Galleries, 1893. Commissioned to paint murals at World's Columbian Exposition, Chicago, 1893. Resigned from Society of American Artists to join The Ten American Impressionists along with Childe Hassam, Frank Benson, Joseph DeCamp, Thomas Dewing, Willard Metcalf, Robert Reid, Edward Simmons, Edmund Tarbell and John Twachtman (Chase took vacancy after Twachtman's death in 1902). Served as member of National Academy of Design Council, 1907-1914. Elected Officer of Association of American Painters and Sculptors, 1913, which organized Armory Show. Resigned presidency when organization published its opposition to National Academy of Design, 1914. President of National Academy, 1915-17. Resigned owing to failing health. Died in New York City, Dec. 8.
See color, page 40. BSK

George Willoughby Maynard

Born in Washington, D.C., Mar. 5. Studied at National Academy of Design; in Belgium, at Royal Academy of Fine Arts, Antwerp, 1869-73. First exhibited at National Academy, 1875. Maintained studio in Paris, 1878. Studied in Rome and under Edwin White in Florence. Returned to New York, establishing studio at 80 East Washington Square (Benedict Building). Became member of Society of American Artists, 1880. Neighbors and friends as well as members of Society of American Artists include Julian Alden Weir, Wyatt Eaton, Albert P. Ryder and Olin Warner. Awarded Temple Gold Medal from Pennsylvania Academy of the Fine Arts, 1884. Commissioned to paint murals for ceiling of auditorium of Metropolitan Opera House, New York; Bijou Theatre, Boston; and St. John's Church, Jamaica Plains, Mass., early 1880's. Received Gold Medal from American Art Association, 1888. Exhibited and won award at American Watercolor Society, 1889. Awarded Designers Medal for murals in World's Columbian Exposition buildings, Chicago, 1892. As prominent designer of murals and decorations, served on International Jury of Awards for Columbian Exposition, 1893. Received commissions for designs of brass inlays for floor of Boston Public Library, 1895 (John Singer Sargent and Edwin Austin Abbey also contributed decorations). Eight designs in Pompiian style for Library of Congress, 1896. One of five Directors of Fine Arts Federation, founded 1897, in addition to other artist J.Q.A. Ward; and architects John M. Carrere, and George B. Post, and businessman E.H. Bell. Exhibited at Pan-American Exposition, Buffalo, 1901. Member of Century Association and instructor at National Academy of Design school, 1889-1917; also served as keeper of Academy's permanent collection. Married Louise Brownell, 1907, Academy librarian during 1920s and 30s. Died in New York, Apr. 5.
BSK

Edmund Charles Tarbell

Born in Groton, Mass., Apr. 26. Decided to become an artist at age ten, 1872. Took evening drawing classes at Normal Art School. Worked as apprentice in lithographic company, 1877-79. On advice of co-worker Horace J. Burdick, enrolled in School of Museum of Fine Arts, Boston. Studied under Otto Grundmann (who was trained at Antwerp Academy) and Frederic Crowninshield. Became a friend of Frank Benson, 1879. 1881-85, traveled with him to Paris. Both enrolled at Académie Julian under Gustave Boulanger and Jules Joseph Lefèbvre. Traveled through England, Italy, and Germany. Returned to Boston, 1885. Became influential teacher at Museum of Fine Arts, 1889-1912. Lilian Westcott Hale, a student of his. Taught and painted with friends Frank Benson, Childe Hassam, Willard Metcalf, Joseph De Camp, Philip Hale and William Paxton. Began accepting portrait commissions, 1890's; influenced by Dennis Bunker and John Singer Sargent at this time. Invited to join The Ten American Impressionists along with New York artists J. Alden Weir, Robert Reid and John Twachtman, 1898. Held one-man show at the St. Botolph Club, 1898. Exhibited regularly with The Ten. Reelected Associate of National Academy of Design, 1904. Died in New Castle, N.H., Aug. 1.
BSK

Lawton S. Parker

Born in Fairfield, Mich. Aug. 7. Studied in Paris at the Académie Julian under William Adolphe Bouguereau and Tony Robert-Fleury, 1889. Returned to U.S., studied at Art Students' League under Henry Siddons Mowbray and William Merritt Chase, 1897. Traveled back to Paris to study mural painting with Paul Besnard and enrolled at Ecole des Beaux-Arts in studios of Jean Léon Gérôme and Jean Paul Laurens. At that time knew Richard Miller, Frederick W. MacMonnies and Frederick Frieseke. Went to Giverny to paint figures in sunlight, 1902. Became non-resident professor of painting at Art Institute of Chicago and president of Chicago Academy of Fine Arts, 1903. Received Gold Medal at International Exhibition in Munich, 1905. Exhibited with "Giverny Group" at Madison Art Gallery, New York, along with Frieseke, Miller, Karl Anderson, Edmund Greacen and Guy Rose, favorably received in 1910. Lived and painted in France until 1942 when he fled Occupation and returned to U.S. Exhibited in Europe and U.S. throughout career. Died in Pasadena, Cal. Sept. 25.
See color, page 41. BSK

Julian Alden Weir (1852-1919) A.N.A. 1885, N.A. 1886,
   P.N.A. 1915-1917
PORTRAIT OF GEORGE WILLOUGHBY MAYNARD
   (1843-1923) A.N.A. 1881, N.A. 1885
Oil on canvas
30¼ x 24¼
Unsigned

Frederick Carl Frieseke

Born Owosso, Mich., Apr. 7. Studied at Art Institute of Chicago, 1893-96. Then moved to New York to study at Art Students' League, 1897. Left New York for Paris to study at Académie Julian under Benjamin Constant and Jean Paul Laurens, 1898. Began spending summers at Giverny, winters in Paris, 1900. Lived in house next to Claude Monet, previously owned by Theodore Robinson, 1906. Elected Associate of Société Nationale des Beaux-Arts, 1908. Exhibited widely in Europe and U.S. including Venice Biennale and inaugural exhibition at Baltimore Museum of Art. A permanent resident of France by 1898, visited U.S. infrequently, represented by Macbeth Galleries, New York, 1912-1939. Made Chevalier of the French Legion of Honor; bought house in Mesnil-sur-Blangy, Normandy, 1920. Exhibited at Jeu de Paume, Paris, 1922. Died at Mesnil-sur-Blangy, Aug. 28.

BSK

Robert Reid

Born in Stockbridge, Mass., July 29. Studied in private schools in Stockbridge and Phillips Academy in Andover. Enrolled for four years at school of Museum of Fine Arts, Boston, classmate of Edmund C. Tarbell and Frank Benson. Moved to New York to study at Art Students' League, 1885. 1885-89, in Paris, studied at Académie Julian under Gustave Boulanger and Jules Joseph Lefèbvre. Fellow students were John Twachtman, Frank Benson, Edmund Tarbell, Childe Hassam and Willard Metcalf (later to be the core of The Ten American Impressionists). Exhibited annually at Paris Salon, 1886-89, and Paris Exposition, 1889. Returned to New York, became member of Society of American Artists. Taught painting at Art Students' League and Cooper Union in New York, also at Broadmoor Art Academy, Colorado Springs. Showed work in last exhibition of Society of Painters in Pastel, 1890. Commissioned to paint eight domes for Liberal Arts Building at World's Columbian Exposition, Chicago, 1893, which established him as a mural painter. Painted decorations for Library of Congress, Washington, 1896. First New York mural commission was Fifth Avenue Hotel, followed by murals for Appellate Courthouse and Massachusetts State House, Boston, 1897-98. 1898, helped The Ten American Impressionists and exhibited with them; same year won first Hallgarten Prize at National Academy of Design. Exhibited and painted murals for Paris Exposition Universelle, 1900. Designed stained glass for Memorial Church, Fairhaven, Mass. 1901-05. Exhibited at Corcoran Gallery of Art, Washington D.C., 1908. Awarded Gold Medal at Panama-Pacific Exposition, San Francisco, 1915. Later mural commissions include Palace of Legion of Honor, San Francisco. Died in New York, Dec. 2.

BSK

Dines Carlsen

Born New York City, Mar. 8. Studied painting with father Emil Carlsen. Received no formal education, was tutored at home by mother who was teacher and a journalist for New York *Herald*. First exhibited painting at National Academy of Design, 1915. Exhibited regularly at Pennsylvania Academy of the Fine Arts from 1917. Exhibited widely in U.S. at important juried shows, such as Corcoran Gallery of Art, Washington; Carnegie Institute, Pittsburgh; Art Institute of Chicago; City Art Museum, St. Louis; Detroit Institute of Arts. At time of election was youngest artist to became Associate of National Academy of Design, 1922. Two-man shows with father at Grand Central Art Galleries and Macbeth Galleries, 1929. Served in army during World War II as mechanical draftsman. Lived at family home in Falls Village, Conn. Became interested in music and astronomy, through these interests met and married Florence Gulick Shaw, 1951. Taught students privately in his home. Served as President of Board of Managers of Mountain Music, an organization devoted to preservation of chamber music in America. One-man show at Grand Central Art Galleries, 1954. Spent summers in Summerville, S.C. Died in Falls Village, Conn. Oct. 1. *See color, page 42.*

BSK

Emil Carlsen

Born Copenhagen, Denmark, Oct. 19. Studied architecture at Danish Royal Academy, 1868-1872. Emigrated to United States, settled in Chicago, 1872. Apprenticed to architect, then Danish artist Laurits Bernard Holst. Taught at Art Institute of Chicago, 1872-74. Travel to Europe, Denmark, then to France for six months, returned to establish studio in New York, 1875. Moved to Boston, painted background details of paintings by Alexander Pope; became member of St. Botolph Club, 1876. First exhibit at Pennsylvania Academy of the Fine Arts, 1883. Commissioned by New York dealer T.J. Blakeslee to travel to Paris and paint still lifes, 1884-86. Returned to New York, rented studio on 23rd Street adjacent to that of artist J. Francis Murphy (friend from Chicago and Paris), then rented studio on 55th Street, which he later passed on to Julian Alden Weir, 1886. Accepted directorship of San Francisco Art Association School; taught for two years while director, 1887-89. Returned to New York permanently, began teaching at National Academy of Design and Pennsylvania Academy, 1891. Married Luella May Ruby, 1896. Birth of son, Dines, 1901. Elected to Society of American Artists, 1902. Traveled to Europe with family, 1908. Exhibit at Internacional de Arte Buenos Aires, won bronze medal, 1910. Exhibited in important galleries, and juried exhibitions including one-man and small group shows at Macbeth Gallery with J. Alden Weir, Childe Hassam, Helen Turner and Kenneth Hayes Miller, 1910-19. 1923, wrote essay for Duncan Phillips's book on Weir; exhibition at Macbeth Gallery with Weir and Theodore Robinson; one-man show at Macbeth, included in Special Exhibition of Painting at Corcoran Gallery, Washington. Exhibited in and juried first members' exhibition at Grand Central Art Galleries, 1928. Exhibited there and at Macbeth with son, Dines, 1929. Died in New York, Jan. 2. *See color, page 42.*

BSK

Edmund Charles Tarbell (1862-1938) A.N.A. 1904, N.A. 1906
SELF-PORTRAIT
Oil on canvas
21 x 17⅛
Signed lower edge: 1889 Self-Portrait Edmund C. Tarbell / we
    studied together at Bois-le-Roi-Fontainebleau
Gift of the family of James E. Shaw

Robert Reid (1862-1929) A.N.A. 1902, N.A. 1906
SELF-PORTRAIT
Oil on canvas
27⅝ x 24¾
Signed lower left: Robert Reid 1904

The Ashcan School

As a teacher and theorist, Philadelphia- and French-trained Robert Henri had a powerful influence upon a generation of art students. His own style was a strong and dramatic Caravaggism influenced by Edouard Manet and the Spanish Baroque. He encouraged in his students and friends both a bold technique and an interest in the subject matter to be found in their urban environment. Against the background of emerging abstract styles in Europe, such late nineteenth-century approaches can hardly be considered avant-garde, but Henri cast himself in the role of innovator and readily took issue when his more conservative fellow jurors at the National Academy declined to accept works by his friends and students for annual exhibitions. After such a disagreement in 1907, Henri led seven of his friends in forming a separate exhibiting group, whose single show opened at the Macbeth Gallery in New York on February 3, 1908, before touring to eight museums across the country. The group, dubbed "The Eight," consisted of Henri's longtime associates and fellow students John Sloan, William Glackens, Everett Shinn and George Luks, and his more recent friends, Arthur B. Davies, Maurice Prendergast and Ernest Lawson. Although the latter three artists brought quite dissimilar styles to the group, his old friends from Henri's Philadelphia student days shared a background in newspaper illustrations that prepared them to paint lower-class life on the city's streets. Together with Henri students like George Bellows, who also painted the urban scene, these artists close to Henri received the disapproving label "The Ashcan School."

The portraiture of Henri's prime, as seen in his *Portrait of George Bellows* (p. 135), recalls that of the Munich-school artists (p. 36 and p. 79) in its dark background and dramatic lighting. Like them, Henri drew upon the Old Masters to achieve a forceful presentation, and the portrait's blocky brushwork recalls their boldest experimental work.

Much of the "virility" that Henri encouraged in the direct technique of his students can be found, in turn, in Bellows's *Portrait of Paul Manship* (p.43), which also draws strength from the bold contrasts in Henri's method. A closer look, however, reveals that color has replaced Old Master tone in the student's portrait: the background is now in greens and the sculptor's face is enlivened by tints of a forced brightness. Bellows's portrait of 1915 reflects a sea change in the styles of several of his group, including Henri and Sloan, who were also strongly influenced in the period after 1910 by the color theories of Hardesty Maratta and Denman Ross and adopted a much more vivid palette. Around this time, William Glackens also moved away from the brownish tones of his earlier work toward a manner influenced by the French Impressionists and by Auguste Renoir in particular. Glackens's *Portrait of Ernest Lawson* (p.44) is interpreted entirely in terms of flickering pastel colors that envelope the forms in a soft caress.

Michael Quick

Robert Henri

Born Robert Henry Cozad in Cincinnati, Ohio on June 24. 1882, his father shot a man in self-defense; fearing reprisals, family fled Cincinnati, traveling first to Denver, then Atlantic City; they assumed various names, Robert dropping last and modifying middle name, a choice he did not reverse after father's vindication. 1886-88, attended Pennsylvania Academy of the Fine Arts, studying with Thomas Anshutz, James B. Kelly and Thomas Hovenden. 1888, left Philadelphia with friends to study in Paris at the Académie Julian under William Adolphe Bouguereau and Tony Robert-Fleury and, for a brief time, at Ecole des Beaux-Arts. Remained in France until 1891, summering at Concarneau in 1889 and St. Nazaire in 1890, visiting Italy that fall. Returned to Philadelphia in 1891 to study again at Pennsylvania Academy of the Fine Arts, this time as a student of Robert Vonnoh. 1892-95, taught at Philadelphia School of Design for Women; also opened his studio for informal gatherings with younger artists, John Sloan and William Glackens among them. Later shared a studio with Glackens before traveling with him to Paris in 1895. Toured Holland and Belgium with Glackens and Elmer Schofield. First acceptance in Paris Salon. 1897, returned to Philadelphia where he organized his first one-man show, at Pennsylvania Academy. Following year married gifted pupil, Linda Craige, and left Philadelphia for another two years in Paris. 1899, achieved recognition when French government bought *La Neige*, a painting of that year. Returned to U.S. in 1900, settling in New York, his home for rest of life. Resumed teaching and turned attention to portraiture. 1902, one-man show at Macbeth Galleries, New York; accepted teaching position at William Merritt Chase's New York School of Art. Elected to Society of American Artists in 1903. 1904, exhibited with Glackens, Sloan and Luks at National Arts Club. Henri loyally defended his students' work against criticism at jury sessions of National Academy 1907; withdrew his entry from National Academy's spring exhibition following rejection of works by Glackens, Luks, Shinn, Rockwell Kent and Carl Sprinchorn. Organized controversial exhibition of The Eight (Henri, Glackens, Sloan, Luks, Shinn, Davies, Lawson and Prendergast) at Macbeth Galleries, February 3-15, 1908. First wife died in 1905; 1908, he married Marjorie Organ of New York. 1908, resigned from New York School of Art; 1909, opened Henri School of Art where he taught George Bellows, Edward Hopper, Rockwell Kent and Stuart Davis, among others. 1910, helped organize the Exhibition of Independent Artists, the first non-juried exhibition in U.S.; it opened to coincide with National Academy's spring exhibition. Taught at the Modern School, 1911-18. His success assured, traveled widely in U.S. and Europe. 1915, invited to teach at Art Students' League, continued to teach and lecture there almost every year through 1928. *The Art Spirit*, his philosophy and ideas about art as compiled and . transcribed by his student Margery Ryerson, published in 1923. Died July 12, 1929, in New York. Metropolitan Museum of Art held memorial exhibition, 1931.

DA

George Bellows

Born in Columbus, Ohio on August 12. Showed early interest in drawing. 1901–04, Ohio State University. 1904, moved to New York to study at New York School of Art under Robert Henri. 1906, set up own studio in Lincoln Arcade Building, exhibited for first time later that year. 1907, showed at spring exhibition of National Academy of Design. 1908, Second Hallgarten Prize, his first award from National Academy. 1909, Pennsylvania Academy of the Fine Arts purchased *North River*, his first sale to a museum; elected an Associate of the National Academy of Design, the youngest member in its history. 1910, taught life class at Art Students' League, New York; married Emma Louise Story of Upper Montclair, N.J.; bought a home in New York City where he set up his studio and lived until his death. 1911, first one-man show at Madison Gallery, New York. Spent summer of 1911 with Robert Henri, Monhegan Island, Me., returning there in 1913 and 1914. 1912, joined staff of *The Masses*, the radical monthly, as an illustrator. 1913, exhibited in Armory Show which he helped organize. Took up lithography in 1916, with George C. Miller as printer.1918, helped form the New Society of American Artists; also became interested in "Dynamic Symmetry," a system of geometrical and proportional relationships in composition. Continued an active teaching career both at Art Students' League and, in 1919, at Art Institute of Chicago. Purchased land in Woodstock, N.Y., in 1921 and there designed and built his own house the following year. Increasingly interested in lithography, produced fifty-nine lithographs in 1921, with Bolton Brown as printer; 1923–24, produced another sixty-four lithographs. Died in New York, following an appendectomy; January 8. Metropolitan Museum of Art held memorial exhibition October–November. *See color, page 43.*

DA

Paul Manship

Born in St. Paul, Minn. on Dec. 25. Attended the Mechanical Arts High School and St. Paul Institute of Art before traveling to New York in 1905 to further artistic training at Art Students' League. Career as sculptor began while working as summertime assistant to Solon Borghum. Studied at Pennsylvania Academy of the Fine Arts in 1906 under Charles Grafly. Traveled to Spain the following summer with Hunt Diedrich. Worked as assistant to Isidor Konti, improving modeling technique. Won the Prix de Rome for sculpture in 1909 and spent next three years at American Academy in Rome. Soon after return to America, married Isabel McIlwaine in New York. Received many commissions for garden sculpture from New York architects Charles Platt and Welles Bosworth. Spent much time designing and modeling life-size figures and monumental sculpture for estates of Harold McCormack, Charles Schwab and Herbert Pratt. Designed decorative reliefs for American Telephone and Telegraph Company Building, New York. Along with commissions for large-scale sculpture, created numerous bronze figurines and small group compositions which established his reputation in museums throughout U.S. Entries in 1914 exhibition at National Academy of Design were especially praised. Received early recognition from National Academy, elected to full membership in 1916. Elected to National Sculpture Society and Architectural League of New York soon afterwards. Memberships in other distinguished organizations followed. Manship actively supported arts organizations, serving as president of National Sculpture Society, 1939-1942, and Vice-president of National Academy 1942-48. 1937, Corcoran Gallery of Art, Washington, D.C., one-man show of 54 bronze statues; portraits in bronze, marble and terracotta; and several medals and portrait medals. *Prometheus Fountain* (1933) in New York's Rockefeller Plaza and *Woodrow Wilson Memorial* (1939) in Geneva, Switzerland, gave him wide recognition. Served as a member of Smithsonian Arts Commission continuously for twenty-five years, fourteen as chairman. Also participated as sculptor member of the Fine Arts Commission, Washington, D.C., 1937-1941. Retrospective exhibition of sculpture at Smithsonian Institution, 1958. Died in New York on Jan. 31. *See color, page 43.*

DA

Robert Henri (1865-1929) A.N.A. 1905, N.A. 1906
PORTRAIT OF GEORGE W. BELLOWS (1882-1925)
  A.N.A. 1909, N.A. 1913
Oil on canvas
32 x 26
Signed lower right: George W Bellows ANA / Robert Henri

William Glackens

Born in Philadelphia, on March 13. Attended Central High School, where John Sloan and Albert Barnes were fellow students. 1891-95, artist-reporter for various Philadelphia papers, including the *Record, Press* and *Ledger*. John Sloan, George B. Luks and Everett Shinn also on staff of *Press*. Beginning 1892, attended night classes at Pennsylvania Academy of the Fine Arts, studying irregularly with Thomas Anshutz, a former Eakins pupil. 1894, shared studio with Robert Henri on Chestnut Street, Philadelphia. 1895, worked his way to Europe on cattle boat, visiting Holland with Henri and Elmer Schofield. Painted scenery around Paris and forest of Fontainebleau with Henri and Canadian painter James Wilson Morrice. 1896, returned to America and settled in New York where George Luks helped him get a job with *New York World*. Also worked for *New York Herald* and various magazines. Sent to Cuba in 1898 as correspondent for *McClure's Magazine* to illustrate Cuban campaign of Spanish-American War. 1901, exhibited at Allen Gallery, New York City, with Alfred Maurer, Robert Henri, John Sloan and others. Glackens's entries in exhibition won critical acclaim. Continued illustrating for *Scribner's, Putnam's, Saturday Evening Post* and other magazines to earn livelihood despite his dislike for illustrating. 1904, married artist Edith Dimock in Hartford, Conn.; Henri painted pendant full-length portraits of pair in formal attire. 1904-08, lived at Washington Square, New York; exhibited at National Arts Club with Luks, Henri, Maurice Prendergast and Arthur B. Davies. 1905, *Chéz Mouquin* won Honorable Mention at annual exhibition of Carnegie Institute, Pittsburgh, juried by Thomas Eakins and Julian Alden Weir, among others. 1907, paintings by Luks and Glackens rejected by National Academy of Design for spring exhibition. Glackens represented in exhibition of The Eight, Macbeth Galleries, New York, 1908. Two years later, helped arrange exhibition of Independents, a show organized in defiance of academic selection process. Traveled to Europe to buy paintings for Dr. Albert Barnes, returning with canvases by Manet, Degas, Cézanne, Matisse and others. 1913, helped organize Armory Show, chairing committee selecting American entries; illustrated Theodore Dreiser's *A Traveler At Forty* and then gave up illustration to concentrate entirely on painting. 1917, elected first president of newly formed Society of Independent Artists. Received Temple Gold Medal in 1924 for a painting subsequently known as the *Temple Gold Medal Nude*. 1925-1932, periodically returned to France, painting in Paris, its suburbs and south of France. 1937, received Grand Prix for Painting, Paris Exposition. May 22, 1938, died suddenly while visiting his friend Charles Prendergast in Westport, Conn. December, 1938, Whitney Museum of American Art held memorial exhibition selected by friends, Guy Pène du Bois, Eugene Speicher and Leon Kroll. American Federation of the Arts then toured a selection of these paintings to several American museums. *See color, page 44.*

DA

Ernest Lawson

Born in San Francisco, Cal., on March 22. Interested in drawing at a young age, despite family's disapproval. 1888, with family in Kansas City, apprenticed to F. Jennings Warrington, a traveling salesman who taught textile design methods. Studied briefly with Ella Holman, teacher at Kansas City Art Institute who later became his wife. 1889, to Mexico City with family; work as draftsman for firm of English engineers, evening study at San Carlos Art School. Moved to New York in 1890 to study art, first at Art Students' League under John Twachtman and later at art school founded by Twachtman and Julian Alden Weir in Cos Cob, Conn. 1893, to France to study at Académie Julian under Jean-Paul Laurens and Benjamin Constant; that summer in Martigues, a fishing village in southern France, followed by visit to Moret-sur-Loring, near Fontainebleau, where Lawson met Alfred Sisley. Shared a studio in Paris with Somerset Maugham (whose novel *Of Human Bondage* presents an artist called Frederick Lawson who also painted at Moret). 1894, exhibited two paintings in Salon des Artistes Français. Returned to U.S. and married Ella Holman. Traveled briefly to France, Canada, and Columbus, Ga. where he taught for short time before settling in New York in 1898. Lived in Washington Heights neighborhood for next eight years, primarily painting this urban landscape. 1904, won first award for painting, silver medal from St. Louis Universal Exposition. 1906, moved to Greenwich Village, met William Glackens, who became lifelong friend. Also met Albert Barnes, later a major benefactor to both artists. (John Sloan, George Luks and Everett Shinn also lived in this neighborhood.) 1905, Lawson's nomination for membership in National Academy of Design rejected. 1906, Luks, Glackens and Shinn also rejected. 1908, Lawson one of group known at The Eight who exhibited independently at Macbeth Gallery in protest against academic conservatism. Sold one painting at this show to Mrs. Gertrude Whitney. April, 1910, Lawson featured in exhibition of Independent Artists, first non-juried show in America. 1913 helped organize Armory Show, serving on Committee on Foreign Exhibitions and exhibiting three works. Soon after, included in Paris exhibition of modern American painters. 1916, cash award from Corcoran Gallery of Art, Washington, D.C., gave artist incentive to take family to Spain. 1917, returned to U.S. Nova Scotia Museum of Art exhibited eighteen of his paintings, June, 1919. Appointed to faculty of Kansas City Art Institute in 1926 and accepted teaching assignment at Broadmoor Art Academy, Colorado Springs, Colo., in 1927. Again used cash award, this time from National Academy, to travel to France to visit family. 1936, moved to Coral Gables, Fla. 1937, Metropolitan Museum bought painting entitled *The Beach, Miami;* commission to paint mural for Federal Art Project in Short Hills, N.J., Post Office (now destroyed). Mural installed in Short Hills early in 1940, shortly after artist drowned in Miami on December 18, 1938. *See color, page 44.*

DA

The Stylistic Diversity of the 20s and 30s

For the American artists who came to artistic maturity in the 1920s and 1930s, European modernism was an inescapable background for all that they did. Those who did not adapt to the new trends reacted to them in characteristic ways. For most it was a liberating influence. Even the society portraitist Louis Betts, who painted his early *Self-Portrait* (p.139) of 1907 in a style close to that of William Merritt Chase and Irving Wiles, employed a much lighter palette and a larger, more decorative brushwork in his portraits of the 1920s and 1930s.

The work of Leon Kroll moved parallel to the development of his friend George Bellows between 1910 and 1925, picking up first the brighter palette and then the stronger sense of geometry that transformed Bellows's style as he indirectly absorbed the new currents from Europe. In Kroll's *Portrait of Ernest O. Roth* of 1920 (p.143) one senses a firm compositional structure that controls the direction of angles and balance of masses. The large forms, which would be further simplified in Kroll's later work, likewise reflect these artists' quest for purity and order in response to the new expectations that abstraction had awakened within the art world. An insistent structure is also evident in the *Self-Portrait* (p.154) by Robert Brackman. A sense of abstract geometry subtly shapes its forms.

The legacy of the Ashcan School found in Kroll's work can also be seen in Reginald Marsh's preference for subjects drawn from the neighborhoods and amusements of New York's lower classes, but his critical point of view differs sharply from the indulgent fascination of the earlier artists. Marsh's edge of satire relates more to the attitude of George Grosz, whose early drawings and prints expressed his horror of the First World War and the rise of Nazi power in his native Germany. Grosz came to New York to teach in 1932, becoming an American citizen in 1938. Both he and Marsh achieved fame while favoring the graphic media and the more fluent, sketchy style they encouraged. The distortions and explosive energy of Grosz's Expressionist style in his *Self-Portrait* (p.141) find an unmistakable echo in the rippling forms and conspicuous technique of Marsh's *Portrait of Kenneth Hayes Miller* (p.145), his mentor and friend and the influential teacher of many of Marsh's generation.

Thomas Hart Benton experimented with abstraction as a young man, while also studying such Old Masters as El Greco for their expressive power. Benton initially shared Marsh's interest in city life as he prepared for his large mural project of 1930 for the New School of Social Research in New York. During the later thirties, however, he drew his themes from rural life and became known as one of the Regionalist painters, celebrating traditional American life. As he turned from modern life, Benton also replaced the remaining evidence of an abstract conception in his work with a new style of emphatic plasticity. This strongly sculptural feeling shapes his late *Self-Portrait* (p.146) of 1963.

Michael Quick

Louis Betts

Born Little Rock, Ark., on Oct. 5. Left school at early age to study painting with father. Worked as an illustrator of books. Traveled to Chicago to study at the Art Institute and subsequently to Pennsylvania Academy of the Fine Arts; also studied under William Merritt Chase in New York. Received Cresson Fellowship for travel from Pennsylvania Academy of the Fine Arts, 1903. Spent two years abroad studying Frans Hals in The Netherlands and Velázquez in Spain. Received first portrait commission while in Haarlem. Returned to New York and had first work exhibited, 1908, at Macbeth Galleries. Exhibited and received Honorable Mention at Carnegie Institute, 1910. Spent most of ensuing year painting commissioned portraits. Married widow of painter George Gardner Symons, 1930. Lived in Bronxville, New York, spending summers in Shelbourne Falls, Mass. Served as president of Salmagundi Club, 1933-35 and vice-president of National Institute of Arts and Letters. Member of National Arts Club and Century Association. Retrospective of his work held at John Herron Art Institute, Indianapolis, Ind., 1942. Died Bronxville, N.Y., on Aug. 13.

BSK

Gertrude Fiske

Born Boston, Mass., Apr. 16. Studied at Museum of Fine Arts, Boston, under Edmund C. Tarbell, Frank Benson, Philip Hale, and in Ogunquit, Me., with Charles C. Woodbury. Began exhibiting at National Academy, 1913, annually until 1952. Awarded a Silver Medal at Panama-Pacific Exposition, 1915. One-woman exhibition at Rhode Island School of Design, 1916. Awarded the Shaw and Clarke Prizes at National Academy, 1922. Active involvement as exhibitor and member with artists' associations, mainly in New England: Guild of Boston Artists, Concord Art Association, Connecticut Academy of the Fine Arts, and National Association of Women Artists. Paintings in collection of Pennsylvania Academy of the Fine Arts and John Herron Art Institute. Died in Weston, Mass., Apr. 18.

BSK

Lilian Westcott Hale

Born in Hartford, Conn., on December 7. First studied painting at Hartford Art School and then privately with William Merritt Chase. 1899, on Chase's advice, entered Boston Museum School, studying with Edmund C. Tarbell and Philip Leslie Hale. 1902, married Philip Leslie Hale, painter and art critic; settled in Dedham, Mass., living there until 1953. Maintained a studio at home and frequently chose scenery of surrounding area for charcoal drawings. Achieved great prominence as portraitist between the two world wars, frequently depicting daughter Nancy Hale, who became known as writer. Painting style deeply influenced by her husband and other Boston Impressionists. Earned several honors at national exhibitions, including a Gold Medal and Medal of Honor at Panama-Pacific Exposition in San Francisco, 1915, and First Altman Prize for Portraiture at National Academy of Design, 1927. Widowed in 1931. Exhibited frequently at National Academy from 1924 through 1949, and then occasionally until her death. 1953, continued to paint portraits after moving to Charlottesville, daughter Nancy's home. 1963, traveled for first time to Italy, visiting Venice, Florence and Rome. Died shortly after returning to U.S., in St. Paul, Minn., on November 7.

DA

John E. Costigan

Born in Providence, R.I., on February 29, orphaned at early age. 1903, sent to New York to work in H. C. Miner Lithographing Company, printers of theater posters; served as press boy, then as sketch artist preparing poster plates for silent screen epics, including D. W. Griffith's *Birth of a Nation*. Residing in a theatrical boarding house, frequently attended rehearsals of productions of his first cousin, playwright George M. Cohan. Attended evening classes in life drawing at the Kit Kat Club, an informal organization of commercial illustrators who sketched as a group without instruction. Briefly attended Art Students' League, receiving instruction from William Merritt Chase. 1915, first exhibited in small group show at Macdowell Club, New York, where exhibition facilities were available to anyone for a fee. 1916, Corcoran Gallery of Art, Washington, D.C., exhibited one of his paintings. Contributed to National Academy of Design annual exhibitions, 1917 and 1918. Served for short time in World War I with Pioneer Infantry Company overseas, returning to H. C. Miner Lithographing Company in 1919 as full-fledged sketch artist. 1919, moved with his wife to a farmhouse in Orangeburg, N.Y., where he spent many years painting rural surroundings. Eschewed portraiture because "the subjects want flattering pictures." Began to receive awards from National Academy and other arts organizations for paintings, watercolors, etchings. During Depression, worked as magazine illustrator and during World War II as machine operator in defense plant. 1941, Corcoran Gallery of Art exhibited his watercolors. Continued to paint and sketch prolifically in the 1950's, also teaching painting at his farm in Orangeburg. Late 1960's, Smithsonian Institution's Traveling Exhibition Service circulated retrospective exhibition of Costigan's work to twenty cities throughout U.S. Died in Nyack, N.Y., August 5.

DA

Louis Betts (1873-1961) A.N.A. 1912, N.A. 1956
SELF-PORTRAIT
Oil on canvas
32½ x 27⅛
Signed upper right: Louis Betts / by / L. Betts 07-

Gertrude Fiske (1879-1961) A.N.A. 1922, N.A. 1930
SELF-PORTRAIT
Oil on canvas
30½ x 25⅜
Signed lower right: Gertrude Fiske 1922

Lilian Westcott Hale (1881-1963) A.N.A. 1927, N.A. 1931
SELF-PORTRAIT
Oil on canvas
30¼ x 25¼
Signed lower left: Lilian Westcott Hale

George Grosz (1893-1959) A.N.A. 1950
SELF-PORTRAIT
Oil on canvas board
23¾ x 19¾
Signed lower right: GROSZ

George Grosz

Born in Berlin on July 26, lost his father at an early age; to support family his widowed mother managed a Prussian officers' club. Attended grammar school in Stolp, Germany, 1902-09, before enrolling at Royal Saxon Academy of Fine Arts, Dresden. 1910, scholarship to Academy of Applied Arts, Berlin, where he remained for several years. While still a student, began to sell caricatures to German humor magazines. Traveled to Paris to study at Atelier Colarossi for six months. 1914-15, served as infantryman in German army, but released after battle injury. Resumed career as caricaturist, gaining public recognition through articles by heodor Daubler in *Weissen Blatter*. Worked in close association with brothers, John Heartfield and Wieland Herzfelde, who started Malik Verlag. 1917-18, called up again by army. Court-martialed for insubordination, but death penalty waived through intervention of a German count. 1918, settled in Berlin, joining Dada movement. Art dealer Hans Goltz arranged first one-man show. Together with Heartfield and Herzfelde, founded magazine *Die Pleite* (Bankruptcy), which ran 1919-1924. With Heartfield, staged satirical marionette shows at cabaret "Schall und Rauch" in cellar of Max Reinhardt's theater. 1920, married Eva Louise Peter. Traveled via Scandinavia to Russia, 1922. 1923, accused of blasphemy for publication of *Ecce Homo*, etching series combining images of destructive technology of warfare with scenes from life of Christ. Certain plates removed, Grosz fined 6,000 marks. 1924-27, traveled to Paris and south of France. Awarded Gold Medal by City of Dusseldorf and, several years later, Gold Medal of Exhibition of the Olympic Games, Amsterdam. Invited by John Sloan to teach at Art Students' League, New York, left Germany with his family only months before Hitler's rise to power. Taught at Art Students' League intermittently for rest of life. 1933-37, ran art school in New York. Traveled to Europe in 1935 and spent first summer on Cape Cod in 1936. Began to paint in oil, eschewing subjects of social criticism in favor of landscapes and nudes. Bitterly denounced by Nazis, his work shown in "Degenerate Art" exhibition in Munich, 1937. Became an American citizen in 1938. Taught at Art School of Columbia University, 1941-42. Received several awards from arts institutions in early 1940's. 1951, traveled again to Europe, this time also visiting Berlin and Munich. Designed costumes for the Berliner Komodie in 1954, then traveled elsewhere in Germany and to London, Monte Carlo and Switzerland. Returned to New York in 1955. 1958, elected to Akademie der Kunste, Berlin. 1959, awarded Gold Medal, American Academy of Arts and Letters. June, returned to Berlin intending to stay permanently. Died there several weeks later on July 6. *See color, page 45.*

DA

Abraham Leon Kroll

Born in New York City on December 6, where father was professional cellist, began formal art training under John Twachtman at Art Students' League in 1899. From 1901, continued studies at National Academy of Design. Won a scholarship to study painting with Jean-Paul Laurens at Académie Julian, Paris. Returned to New York in 1910, exhibiting for first time at the National Academy. Exhibited extensively in early 1900's, participating in Armory Show of 1913 where his work was praised by Theodore Roosevelt. 1919-1923, served as visiting critic at Maryland Institute of Arts; 1924-25, at Art Institute of Chicago; 1929-1930, at Pennsylvania Academy of the Fine Arts. Later held same position at National Academy and again at Maryland Institute. 1929, appointed to serve on International Jury for 28th Carnegie International Exhibition, Pittsburgh. 1936, awarded first prize for painting, *The Road From the Cove*, in Carnegie International. Commissioned along with ten others to paint a mural in Department of Justice Building, Washington, D.C. Also commissioned to decorate Memorial Chamber of Worcester War Memorial, Worcester, Mass., 1938. Received several other mural commissions, including Senate Chamber dome in Indianapolis, Ind., and U.S. Military Cemetery, Omaha Beach, France. Kroll maintained his studio in New York City, spending summers in Maine and Massachusetts with an occasional trip abroad. Received numerous awards beginning in 1922. Died in New York City on October 5.

DA

Ernest David Roth

Born in Stuttgart, Germany, Jan. 17, came to U.S. with family in 1884. Worked for an art business by day and in evening attended classes at National Academy of Design, studying etching under James David Smillie, NA. Later studied in Spain, France and Italy. Married Elizabeth MacKenzie, an artist, and lived in Greenwich Village, New York, for many years. A member of many arts organizations in New York. 1915-1935, received important prizes in both painting and print exhibitions. Most noteworthy among his later awards was Benjamin West Clinedinst Memorial Medal given by the Artists' Fellowship in 1949, an organization established in 1869 (as Artists Aid Society) by ten National Academicians living in 10th Street Studio Building. Roth moved to Redding, Conn. shortly before he died, Aug. 20, 1964. That year the Silvermine College of Arts in New Canaan, Conn., purchased the "Ernest Roth Memorial Press". The artist had expressly wished that his printing equipment be given to a school dedicated to advanced training in graphics.

DA

(Abraham) Leon Kroll (1884-1974) A.N.A. 1920, N.A. 1927
PORTRAIT OF ERNEST D. ROTH (1879-1964) A.N.A. 1920, N.A. 1928
Oil on canvas
30 x 25¼
Signed upper left: Ernest D. Roth / by / Leon Kroll 1920

143

Reginald Marsh

Born in Paris on March 14 to American artists Fred Dana Marsh and Alice Randall Marsh. Came to New York with his parents in 1900. Lived in New York State and New Jersey, attending Riverview Military Academy in Poughkeepsie, 1914-15, and Lawrenceville School, 1915-16. At Yale University for next four years, contributed illustrations to the *Yale Record,* serving as Art Editor in 1920. In New York after graduation, free-lanced as an illustrator for New York *Evening Post,* New York *Herald* and *Harper's Bazaar.* 1922-25, worked as staff artist for New York *Daily News,* principally covering vaudeville, night clubs and trials. Began illustrating for the *New Yorker* in 1925, working actively for it through 1931, and occasionally afterwards. Lifelong free-lance illustration for books and periodicals *Esquire, Fortune* and *Life.* 1923, married sculptress Betty Burroughs. Moved to Flushing, N.Y., his home until his divorce in 1933. Studied at Art Students' League for short periods with John Sloan, Kenneth Hayes Miller and George Luks, 1920-24. Joined Whitney Studio Club where he had first one-man show of oils and watercolors in 1924 and another show of lithographs in 1928. Made first of seven trips abroad in 1925, spending most of the time in Paris often copying the Old Masters. Studied again with Kenneth Hayes Miller, now a friend, at Art Students' League during 1927-28 season. 1928, in Europe again; New York set up studio on 14th Street and there associated with realist artists, among them, Isabel Bishop and Raphael Soyer. Held several one-man shows of watercolors and paintings in New York galleries, 1927-1930. From 1931 included in most national exhibitions of contemporary American art. Experimented with egg tempera in the late 1920's and also worked in lithography. 1934, married painter Felicia Meyer; couple lived in New York and spent weekends in Dorset, Vt. 1935, commissioned by Treasury Department Art Program to paint two frescoes in the Post Office Department Building, Washington, D.C. Also for Treasury, painted mural series in rotunda of New York Customs House. Taught drawing and painting at Art Students' League, summers 1935-1941, and full-time instructor beginning in 1942. 1940-46, studied with Jacques Maroger, learning egg tempera as well as an emulsion technique, based on methods of Old Masters. 1943, war correspondent for *Life,* traveling to Brazil, Cuba, Trinidad and West Indies. 1945, published his book, *Anatomy for Artists.* Second book on anatomy appeared in late 1940's. Recipient of many awards from 1931 and frequent one-man shows till his death of a heart attack in Dorset, Vt., on July 30. 1955, retrospective exhibition held at Whitney Museum of American Art.

DA

Kenneth Hayes Miller

Born in Oneida, N.Y., Mar. 11, the great-nephew of John Humphrey Noyes, founder of the Oneida Community, with which artist was closely associated throughout his life. Spent boyhood in Kenwood, N.Y., later traveling to New York City to study at Horace Mann School; then at Art Students' League with H. Siddons Mowbray, Kenyon Cox and F. Luis Mora; finally at New York School of Art with William Merritt Chase. Traveled to Europe in 1900, returning to New York to teach at New York School of Art until 1911. 1911, married Helen Pendleton, invited to teach at Art Students' League where he remained an instructor, excepting 1936-1944, for rest of life. Taught many well-known figures, among them Isabel Bishop, Marsden Hartley, Edward Hopper, Rockwell Kent and Reginald Marsh. Albert Pinkham Ryder, a close friend, had early influence on his style. By 1920's was actively painting cityscapes, and seldom left New York thereafter, once commenting to Reginald Marsh: "This is one of the greatest landscapes in the world." Recipient of several awards, among them a gold

medal for painting from National Academy in 1943. 1949, exhibition at Art Students' League commemorating his thirty-eight years of instruction there. Died in New York City, Jan. 1. In September, 1953, Art Students' League sponsored memorial exhibition at National Academy; another memorial exhibition held at Munson-Williams-Proctor Institute in Utica, N.Y.

DA

Thomas Hart Benton

Born in Neosho, Mo., on April 15, son of Congressman Maecenus Eason Benton, and grandnephew and namesake of famous Missouri senator. 1896-1904, studied at Corcoran Gallery of Art during father's four terms in House of Representatives. 1906, worked in Joplin, Mo., as cartoonist for Joplin *American.* Briefly attended Western Military Academy in Alton, Ill., before leaving to study at Art Institute of Chicago, 1907-08. Spent next three years in Paris, studying at the Académie Julian from fall, 1908, through spring, 1909, and then daily at Académie Colarossi. Experimented with Impressionist techniques under guidance of John Thompson. Abandoned formal classes to study masterpieces of Louvre. In these years, associated with fellow artists Leo Stein, John Marin and Jacob Epstein, among others, in Montparnasse. 1911, returned to United States, setting up a studio in New York. 1916, participated in "Forum Exhibition of Modern American Painters," Anderson Gallery, New York. 1918-19, served in U.S. Navy as architectural draftsman, stationed at Norfolk Naval Base. Returning to New York, began making clay and Plastilene models for his paintings, a procedure that became a permanent feature of his technique. Worked intermittently from 1919 to 1926 on *American Historical Epic,* a ten-panel mural series of which he exhibited the first five panels at Architectural League, New York, 1923-24. Established permanent summer residence on Martha's Vineyard and, in 1922, married Rita Piacenza, a former student from his Chelsea Neighborhood Association classes. 1926-1935, taught at Art Students' League, New York; exhibited in several New York galleries; traveled many times through rural South and Middle West. 1930, completed set of eight murals, *America Today,* for New School for Social Research, New York. Exhibited at Art Students' League in 1931 and at New School for Social Research in 1932. Completed *The Arts of Life in America,* series of five murals for library of Whitney Museum of American Art. 1933, awarded gold medal for decorative painting by Architectural League of New York; completed series of twenty-two mural panels, *Social History of the State of Indiana,* for Indiana's Pavilion in the Century of Progress International Exposition, Chicago. Commissioned by U.S. Treasury Department to paint a mural in new Post Office, Washington, D.C., but abandoned project when Missouri legislature commissioned mural for Jefferson City, Mo. Permanently moved to Kansas City to work on capitol mural and teach at Kansas City Art Institute. 1937, published autobiography, *An Artist in America.* 1939-1947, exhibitions in Kansas City, Dallas, New York, Philadelphia and Chicago. 1948, began to paint imagery of Far West. 1948, received honorary Doctor of Arts from University of Missouri, in addition to two honorary memberships in the Academies of Florence and Siena. 1957, second honorary degree, from Lincoln University, Jefferson City. 1953-1962, mural commissions in Missouri and New York State. 1959-1962, completed mural for Harry S. Truman Library, Independence, Mo. 1969, received a third honorary degree, from New School for Social Research; published *An American in Art: A Professional and Technical Autobiography.* Retrospective exhibitions in New York City; Brunswick, N.J., at Rutgers Art Gallery; and Kansas City at Nelson Gallery-Atkins Museum, 1968-1974. 1974, awarded Diamond Jubilee Gold Medal, National Arts Club, New York. Died in Kansas City on January 19.

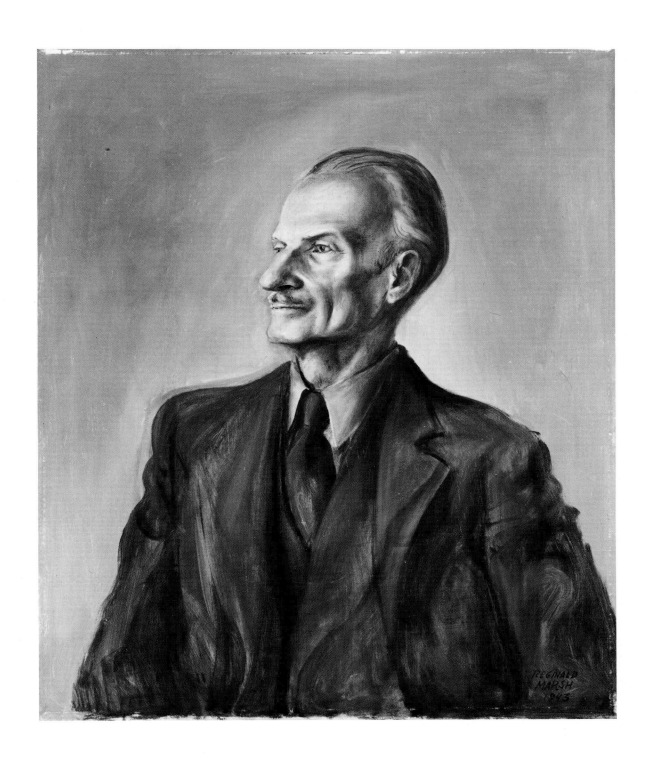

Reginald Marsh (1898-1954) A.N.A. 1937, N.A. 1943
PORTRAIT OF KENNETH HAYES MILLER (1876-1952)
   A.N.A. 1942, N.A. 1944
Oil on canvas
30⅛ x 25¼
Signed lower right: REGINALD / MARSH / 1943

Thomas Hart Benton (1889-1975) A.N.A 1954, N.A. 1956
SELF-PORTRAIT
Oil on canvas
20¼ x 16⅛
Signed lower left: To N.A.D. / from / Benton '63

The Modern Figurative Painters

WHILE SOME AMERICAN ARTISTS BECAME ABSTRACTIONISTS DURING THE EARLY TWENTIETH century and all to some degree reflected a new consciousness of abstract design in their work, realistic figurative painting remained by far the dominant form until about 1950. At that point, the tendency toward native abstract styles that had been building during the previous years became irresistible, drawing most emerging artists away from the figure, until representational painting was revived around 1970.

The degree of the influence of modernism upon the figure painters of the 1930s, 1940s and 1950s is the critical issue that defines them. At one extreme of seeming obliviousness to modernism is the dynastic tradition of the Wyeth family, founded by Newell Convers Wyeth and continued in his son Andrew Wyeth, his grandson James Wyeth and his son-in-law, Peter Hurd. N. C. Wyeth was an illustrator of children's books, and Peter Hurd's Western landscapes seem a continuation of that dreamlike ideal world. Both their *Self-Portraits* (p. 15 and p. 150) suggest a realm of blissful make-believe. Change enters the tradition in the work of Andrew Wyeth, whose impeccably crafted *Self-Portrait* (p. 46), like that of his son (p. 160), contains great depths of psychological resonance.

In this respect, the work of Andrew Wyeth is akin to that of a group of Academy artists who used an apparent realism to heighten a feeling of uncomfortable disquiet, a device derived from the Surrealist movement of the 1930s. In contrast to the Wyeth tradition, however, their realism is highly stylized and distorted, as is readily seen in their *Self-Portraits* (p. 153, p. 48 , p. 151, and p. 47). The grotesque corporeality of Ivan Albright's image (p. 153) is the complete opposite of the boneless disembodiment of George Tooker's ghostly, overgeneralized figure (p. 48), and yet they project a similar sense of threatening unreality. A feeling of painful isolation is conveyed both by the emptiness surrounding the sharply defined figure of Walter Stuempfig (p. 151) and by the shifting planes and uncertain boundaries of the figure and environment of Edwin Dickinson (p. 47). Whether they create an impression of false solidity or explicit uncertainty, all four of these artists use realism to express disorientation.

One does not return to a comfortable order even in the works of such recognizably traditional figurative painters as Robert Brackman (p. 154), Robert Philipp (p. 157) or Raphael Soyer (p. 155). Although relatively subdued in color and faithful to accepted norms of representation, all three *Self-Portraits* belong to the middle of the twentieth century and eloquently express the uncertainty of the age.

Michael Quick

Walter Ufer

Born in Louisville, Ky. July 22. Encouraged by principal, began drawing in elementary school, his only formal education. Apprenticed in lithographic firm, took art classes under student of Meissonier in Louisville. Visited World's Columbian Exposition, Chicago; invited to join lithographic firm in Hamburg, Germany, 1893. Moved to Dresden to study at Royal Fine Arts Academy, 1894. Returned to U.S. 1898. Settled in Chicago, began studying at J. Francis Smith School (affiliated with Académie Julian, Paris) 1900. Began teaching at school, 1904. Employed in advertising division at Armour and Company; married Mary M. Frederiksen, 1911. Traveled abroad: France; Italy; North Africa; Scandinavia; Germany. In Munich, studied under Walter Thor until 1913. Returned to U.S. traveled to Taos, N.M. and became associated with Taos Society of Artists, 1913. Elected active member there, 1917. Lived mainly in Taos, and traveled annually to Chicago and New York, 1914-20. Invited to exhibit with other American artists at Luxembourg Museum, Paris, 1919. Elected Secretary-Treasurer of Taos Society of Artists, 1920. Exhibited at Venice Biennale, 1922 and 1924. Elected President of Taos Society of Artists, 1922. One-man exhibition at Corcoran Gallery of Art, Washington, D.C. 1923. Suffered severe alcoholism early 1930's, Died Aug. 2.

BSK

Newell Convers Wyeth

Born in Needham, Mass., Oct. 22. Studied at Mechanic Arts High School, Massachusetts Normal Art School, Eric Pape School of Art and privately with Charles W. Reed before traveling to Wilmington, Del., to attend illustrator Howard Pyle's school near Wilmington. With Pyle, 1902-04, concentrated on drawing both from the model and antique casts. Possibly Wyeth's first published work was cover illustration of Saturday Evening Post, February 21, 1903. That year visited Colorado and New Mexico, trip providing illustrative material for many years. Soon after return, Wyeth wrote an illustrated article on western sheepherding for Scribner's Magazine. April, 1906, married Carolyn Bockius in Wilmington and settled in Chadds Ford. Among many book and magazine commissions, illustrated eighteen volumes of Charles Scribner's series of juvenile classics, including Treasure Island (1911) and Kidnapped (1913); illustrated for important magazine; Collier's, Harper's, Scribner's and Saturday Evening Post, among them. Awarded gold medal in the San Francisco Exposition, 1915. For relaxation, painted egg tempera easel pictures on wood, often depicting Chadds Ford scenery or, in summertime, coast of Maine near Port Clyde. Raised five children, training them as painters in a small family art school in his studio. 1931, became a director of Wilmington Society of Fine Arts having been a member since its inception in 1912. Late 1930's and early 1940's productive in mural painting as well as book and magazine illustration, expanded his studio space in Chadds Ford to accommodate large-scale mural commissions. Among most noteworthy were two twenty-foot lunettes representing Civil War battles fought in Missouri, for Missouri State Capitol; five large murals illustrating maritime commerce for New First National Bank in Boston; a triptych for Chapel of the Holy Spirit, National Cathedral, Washington, D.C.; and five panels entitled The Romance of Discovery for National Geographic Society, Washington, D.C. Awarded an Honorary Degree of Master of Arts from Bowdoin College in June, 1945. Died in automobile accident in Chadds Ford, Oct. 19. See color, page 46.

DA

Peter Hurd

Born Roswell, N.M. on Feb. 22. Public grammar school, Roswell. 1917-1920, New Mexico Military Institute.

1921, entered U.S. Military Academy at West Point. Sold first painting there, West Point Moon. 1923, resigned to pursue career in painting. Attended Haverford College, 1923-24. Early in 1924, went to Chadds Ford, Pa., to meet N.C. Wyeth, an inspiring encounter. Summer of 1924 returned to Chadds Ford to study with Wyeth; instruction in landscape, still life and portrait painting. Also aided Wyeth with his commissions. Fall, 1924, Hurd entered Pennsylvania Academy of the Fine Arts to work in antique and life classes. Returned to Chadds Ford following summer as student-apprentice to Wyeth, studying composition, landscape and still life. June, 1929, married Henriette Wyeth, eldest of N.C.'s three daughters, herself a painter. Began illustrating, mostly juvenile books, for Scribner's, McKay, Doubleday-Doran and others, until Depression severely limited demand for color illustration. Continued painting, experimenting with different techniques: gesso, tempera and tempera on gesso for mural illustration. 1933, New Mexico Military Institute commissioned mural triptych for new building. 1935, moved back to New Mexico, settling with family on ranch near San Patricio. War correspondent for Life during World War II; working in England in 1942 with U.S. Army Air Forces, and in South America, Africa, India, Arabia and Italy in 1944 with U.S. Air Transport Command. Received other mural commissions from post offices and colleges in Texas and New Mexico. 1967, painted controversial portrait of President Lyndon Baines Johnson. Author and illustrator of several books. Lives in Roswell, N.M.

DA

Andrew Wyeth

Born in Chadds Ford, Pa., July 12, the son of illustrator N.C. Wyeth and Carolyn Bockius Wyeth. A delicate child, was educated at home, learning rudiments of art from father in a strictly disciplined apprenticeship. Taught to draw from model and then, turning his back, to draw figure from memory. Also drew from casts and studied Rimmer's Art Anatomy. Trained in still life painting as well. Learned use of egg tempera from his brother-in-law, Peter Hurd, who had studied with N.C. Wyeth, 1924-26, and married his daughter, Henriette. This exacting technique, demanding innumerable small brushstrokes contrasted sharply with the fleeting impression he achieved in watercolor. 1929, earliest public examples of his work done at age twelve: pen-and-ink head and tail pieces for essay by his father, a recollection of Howard Pyle in the Brandywine Edition of Pyle's The Merry Adventures of Robin Hood (Scribner's, 1933). At fifteen, submitted drawings to Delaware Art Center, winning approval of professional jury. Philadelphia painters Earl Horter and Yarnell Abbott arranged showing of work at Art Alliance in Philadelphia in 1936. The following year, one-man show of watercolors of Maine seacoast at Macbeth Gallery, New York. Exhibition a resounding success, establishing Wyeth's reputation as watercolorist. Subsequently exhibited watercolors and paintings there for several years. 1940, married Betsy James whom he met in Maine.

1941, contributed double-page tonal drawings and pen and ink drawings as illustrations for Henry Seidel Canby's The Brandywine, in Rivers of America series for Farrar & Rinehart. Painted a much admired cover for The Saturday Evening Post but refused contract for steady assignments in order to paint. Awarded several honors in exhibitions, among them Gold Medal from American Watercolor Society's exhibition at National Academy in 1952. Pennsylvania Academy of the Fine Arts organized exhibition of Wyeth's work in 1966, which traveled to Baltimore, New York and Chicago. Metropolitan Museum of Art held comprehensive exhibition, 1976. Wyeth continues to live in Chadds Ford, Pa.

DA

Walter Ufer (1876-1936) A.N.A. 1920, N.A. 1926
SELF-PORTRAIT
Oil on canvas
30¼ x 25
Signed lower left: WUfer

Peter Hurd (1904-   ) A.N.A. 1941, N.A. 1942
SELF-PORTRAIT
Tempera on gesso panel
30 x 25
Signed lower left: Peter Hurd

Newell Convers Wyeth (1882-1945) A.N.A. 1940, N.A. 1941
SELF-PORTRAIT
Tempera on gesso panel
32½ x 27½
Signed lower right: N.C. WYETH / 1940

Walter Stuempfig, Jr. (1914-1970) A.N.A. 1951, N.A. 1953
SELF-PORTRAIT
Oil on canvas
30⅛ x 25
Unsigned

Walter Stuempfig

Born in Germantown, Pa., on Jan. 26. Studied at University of Pennsylvania one year, then at Pennsylvania Academy of the Fine Arts, 1931-34. Received Cresson Traveling Scholarship there, 1933. Became professor of composition at Pennsylvania Academy, 1934. Married Lila Agnes Kennedy Hill, sculptor, 1935. Showed work at major national juried exhibitions Pennsylvania Academy of the Fine Arts; Corcoran Gallery of Art, Washington, D.C., won second prize, 1947; Whitney Museum of American Art Annuals; National Academy of Design, won Altman Prize, 1953. Work shown in major exhibition, "United States Contemporary Art," at Art Gallery of Toronto, Ontario, 1949. Work shown at Walker Art Center, Minneapolis, in special exhibition "Realities and Fantasy," 1954. Member of Century Association and National Institute of Arts and Letters. Died in Ocean City, N.J., Dec. 1.

BSK

Ivan Le Lorraine Albright

Born Chicago, Ill., Feb. 20. Early training in painting under father who was student of Eakins. Chose to pursue career in architecture at Northwestern University and University of Illinois, 1915-17. In Army during World War I, served as medical draftsman in France, 1919. Studied while in France at Ecole Regionale des Beaux-Arts, 1919. Returned to United States, studied at Art Institute of Chicago, 1920-23. 1924, studied one term at Pennsylvania Academy of the Fine Arts and one term National Academy of Design. Returned to live and work in Chicago. Showed work in exhibitions of Corcoran Gallery of Art; Carnegie Internationals; Pennsylvania Academy of the Fine Arts; Art Institute of Chicago; Whitney Museum of American Art; New York World's Fair, and Brussels World's Fair. Commissioned to paint portrait for film *The Portrait of Dorian Gray* with twin brother Malvin, 1948. Elected to National Institute of Arts and Letters, 1957. Traveled annually among Chicago, Woodstock, Vermont and Wyoming, 1963-65. Retrospective organized by Art Institute of Chicago, traveled to Whitney Museum of American Art, 1965. William Benton became his patron, purchasing paintings sight unseen. Albright traveled with wife to Morocco, 1967; Later that year to Russia with letters of introduction to Ambassador Llewellyn Thompson and Russian artists from Benton who had become U.S. Ambassador to UNESCO. Named to American Academy of Arts and Letters, 1967. Moved permanently to Woodstock, Vt., 1967. Became professor Dartmouth College. Honorary degrees of LL.D. conferred by Columbia College, 1969; Ph.D., Lake Forest College, Ill., 1972; Ph.D., Art Institute of Chicago, 1977; Ph.D., Dartmouth College, 1978. Lives in Woodstock, Vt.

BSK

Robert Brackman

Born Odessa, Russia, on Sept. 25. Came to U.S. at early age. Studied at National Academy of Design, 1919-1922, under Leon Kroll and Ivan Olinsky and privately with George Bellows and Robert Henri. Traveled with friend and classmate Robert Philipp to England. First one-man show at Milch Gallery, N.Y., 1925. Represented by Babcock Gallery, 1926-29. Exhibited at Art Institute of Chicago; Connecticut Academy of Fine Arts; won Thomas B. Clarke Prize, National Academy of Design, 1932. Began teaching at Art Students' League, 1934. To support himself, painted commissioned portraits, including Charles Lindbergh, Mr. and Mrs. John D. Rockefeller, John Foster Dulles, as well as many other official portraits for the State Department, Air Force Academy and U.S. Military Academy, West Point, N.Y. Served as Art Consultant for the U.S. Air Force. Painted draped nudes and still lifes. Became active in New York artists associations such as Allied Artists of America, American Watercolor Society and Audubon Artists. Received Saltus Medal for exhibit in Annual Exhibition of National Academy, 1941. Began teaching at American Art School, 1951 (Philipp also on faculty, at one time). 1957, opened Madison Art School, a summer school for painting in Conn. Elected to International Society of Arts and Letters and to Royal Society of Arts, London, 1962. Received Ford Foundation Grant, 1965. Continued to teach at Art Students' League until 1975. Died in Noack, Conn. on July 16.

BSK

Raphael Soyer

Raphael and his twin brother Moses were born on Dec. 25, 1899, in Borisoglebsk, Government of Tambor, Russia, the first of six children of Abraham Schoar, teacher of Hebrew literature and history, and Bella Schneyer Schoar. Boys attended local schools with additional instruction from their father and his pupils. From early childhood, the twins and brother Isaac were constantly encouraged to draw. Ordered to leave Russia, family left for U.S. in 1912. Lived briefly in Philadelphia before moving to New York to settle in the Bronx. Raphael went through public grammar school in two years, then entered Morris High School, continuing to draw and paint at home. Also studied drawing at Cooper Union at night, 1914-17. To earn money, Raphael and Moses left high school and went to work. Raphael began serious art training, entering National Academy of Design in fall, 1918, to study first under George W. Maynard and then Charles C. Curran. Remained at Academy four seasons, through spring, 1922. Also studied at Art Students' League briefly in 1920, 1921, and 1923 under Guy Pène du Bois and in 1926 with Boardman Robinson. First exhibited in a group exhibition in 1926, where painter Alexander Brook first saw his work and helped sell a picture. Brook introduced Soyer to Whitney Studio Club, where he exhibited from 1927. Club's director later bought five of Soyer's paintings. 1929, first one-man show at Daniel Gallery was so well received that Soyer could give up outside jobs and paint full-time. Began teaching career at the John Reed Club of artists and writers, 1930. Married Rebecca Letz in February, 1931. Beginning early 1930's, showed fairly regularly in large annual and biennial American exhibitions of Whitney Museum, Carnegie Institute, Pittsburgh, and Art Institute of Chicago, Corcoran Gallery of Art, National Academy of Design, Pennsylvania Academy of the Fine Arts. Also had series of one-man shows in New York galleries. First award in 1932 followed by numerous others. Worked in Graphics Arts Division of WPA Federal Art Project. With brother Moses, painted two murals for the Kingsessing, Pa., Post Office, 1939. Taught at Art Students' League 1933-34 season and successively from 1935 through 1942; at American Artists School for several years after World War II; at New School for Social Research, 1957-1962, sharing classes there with Julian Levi and Camillo Egas, as well as teaching independently; and at National Academy, 1965-67. Soyer founded the magazine *Reality* in the 1950's, with fellow-artists Edward Hopper, Ben Shahn and Yasuo Kuniyoshi, among others. Frequent travels to Europe during summer, generally three months in London, Paris and elsewere on the Continent. These travels and the works of art studied have inspired several books, *A Painter's Pilgrimage, Homage to Thomas Eakins, Etc.* and *Self-Revealment.* 1977, published *Diary of an Artist,* an illustrated collection of memorable experiences. 1966-67, Whitney Museum of American Art held retrospective exhibition, subsequently shown in six other American museums. Raphael Soyer continues to live in New York City.

DA

Ivan Le Lorraine Albright (1897-   ) A.N.A. 1942, N.A. 1950
SELF-PORTRAIT
Oil on canvas
24 x 20
Signed lower left: Ivan le Lorraine Albright 1948

Robert Brackman (1896-1980) A.N.A. 1932, N.A. 1940
SELF-PORTRAIT
Oil on canvas
30 x 25
Signed lower right: Brackman

Raphael Soyer (1899-   ) A.N.A. 1949, N.A. 1951
SELF-PORTRAIT
Oil on canvas
24½ x 20⅛
Signed lower right: RAPHAEL SOYER / 1950

Robert Philipp

Born in New York City, Feb. 2. Family moved to Germany where he attended school. Returned to New York, an unsuccessful student, removed from school, enrolled at Art Students' League, studied under Frank DuMond and George B. Bridgeman, 1910-14. Transferred to National Academy of Design, studied under Douglas Volk, George Maynard and Charles C. Curran, 1914-17. While a student, exhibited at Academy annual, won Hallgarten Prize, 1916. Upon death of father discontinued schooling; in Newark, N.J., painted posters for movie theaters. Traveled to Paris, upon return met wife-to-be Rochelle Brackman. Began exhibiting and receiving awards in juried exhibitions: Art Institute of Chicago, 1936; Carnegie International, Pittsburgh, 1937; Corcoran Gallery of Art, Washington, D.C., 1938. First patron, J. Paul Getty. Taught American Art School, 1940. Visiting professor of art, University of Illinois, 1941. Traveled to New Orleans, trip inspired series of paintings. 1941-42, represented by Findlay Galleries, Milch Gallery, Grand Central Art Gallery, N.Y. and Vose Gallery, Boston. Painted portrait commissions. Elected to Lotos Club 1945. Instructor High Museum of Art, Atlanta, Ga. 1946. Offically changed name from Moses Soloman Philipp to Robert Philipp, 1947. Exhibited at A.A.A. Gallery, New York and Chicago, 1952. Elected to International Institute of Arts and Letters, 1959. Became Fellow of Royal Society of Arts, 1965. Began teaching at Art Students' League and National Academy of Design, 1966. Exhibition at A.C.A. Galleries, 1970. Death of wife, 1971. Traveled frequently to Europe, mainly England, in 1970s. Died in New York, Nov. 22.

BSK

Edwin Dickinson

Born Seneca Falls, N.Y., Oct. 11. 1897, moved to Buffalo when father accepted pastorate of North Presbyterian Church there. 1899, Dickinson began drawings of battle formations. Appointed to U.S. Naval Academy, rejecting family wish that he become a minister. Was not reappointed to Academy after second failure at mathematics entrance exam, 1909. Study at Pratt Institute, Brooklyn, 1910-11. Classes at Art Students' League under William Merritt Chase, Charles W. Hawthorne, Frank Dumond, 1911-12. 1912-13, studied at Buffalo Fine Arts Academy and National Academy of Design; suspended from National Academy for not submitting drawing for examination. Studied summers of 1912-14 at Cape Cod School of Art, Provincetown, with Hawthorne, the teacher who most influenced Dickinson. Lived in Provincetown throughout winter, 1913. Began exhibiting paintings, 1914, in Provincetown and subsequently at Corcoran Gallery of Art, Washington, D.C., Pennsylvania Academy of the Fine Arts and National Academy 1916-18. Returned to New York to study telegraphy and radio, enlisted in U.S. Navy and upon completion of studies received rating of radio electrician second class. Entered active service, 1917. 1919-1920, discharged from Navy; traveled to Paris and enrolled at Académie de la Grande Chaumière; invited by French government to exhibit at the Luxembourg Museum; traveled to Spain, influenced by El Greco; returned to U.S. and rented a studio in Provincetown, 1919-20. Received first portrait commission, 1921. Taught at Art Students' League, 1922-23. First one-man show, Albright Art Gallery, Buffalo, 1927. Married Frances Foley, who was also a student of Charles Hawthorne, 1928. Taught at Provincetown Art Association, 1929-30. Worked for Federal Emergency Relief Administration (later known as Works Progress Administration), 1933. Returned to France, spent winter in Provence, summer in Brittany, 1937-38. Purchased home in Wellfleet, Mass., 1939, and thereafter usually summered there, wintering in New York. Taught at Brooklyn Museum Art School, 1949-1957. Included in exhibition at Museum of Modern Art, "Fifteen Americans," 1952. Received grant from National Institute of Arts and Letters, 1954. Metropolitan Museum of Art purchased Ruin at Daphne, 1955. Elected member of National Institute of Arts and Letters, 1956. Taught at Skowhegan School of Painting and Sculpture, Maine, 1956-58. Won Creative Arts Award from Brandeis University, received Ford Foundation Grant, and had retrospective at Boston University, 1959. Elected Vice-President National Institute of Arts and Letters, 1958-60. Traveled summers of 1959 and 1960 to Mediterranean by freighter. Elected to American Academy of Arts and Letters and awarded Honorary Degree of Fine Arts by Pratt Institute, 1961. Spent summers in Greece, 1963-65. Executed last paintings, 1964. Retrospective organized by Whitney Museum of American Art, New York. Awarded Florence Brevoort-Eickemeyer Prize by Columbia University and National Academy of Design, 1965. Retired from teaching. Lived principally in Wellfleet in summers and Athens in winters, 1966-1976. Senior American painter represented in U.S. Exhibition at the XXXIV Biennale in Venice, 1968. Stroke in 1972. Awarded Honorary Degree of Doctor of Fine Arts from The Maryland Institute, College of Art, 1973. Died at home in Wellfleet, Mass., Dec. 2. See color, page 47.

BSK

David Levine

Born in Brooklyn, N.Y., Dec. 20. Attended art classes at Pratt Institute and Brooklyn Museum School, 1936-38. Studied at Tyler School of Fine Arts, Temple University, 1943-49. Drafted into military service, 1946, stationed in Egypt and Europe. Sent illustrations to Stars and Stripes, became member of staff, based in Germany. Released from service, resumed studies at Tyler. Enrolled in Hans Hoffman School, New York, a classmate of Aaron Shikler, 1949. Leroy Davis, fellow student at Tyler, became art dealer, formed close friendships with Levine, Shikler, Burton Silverman, Harvey Dinnerstein and other realists, exhibiting their work when Abstract Expressionism was more fashionable. First one-man show at Davis Gallery, New York 1953 (continued to show regularly until 1963). Exhibited at annuals of Whitney Museum of American Art, New York, Butler Institute of American Art, Youngstown, Ohio, in late 1950s and early 1960s. Received Tiffany Foundation Grant, 1956. First awards and purchase prizes at National Academy of Design in 1958 and 1960, continuing through 1970s. Contributed caricatures of prominent politicians, literary figures and artists to illustrated magazines such as Time and Newsweek; staff illustrator for New York Magazine and New York Review of Books. Drawings included in exhibitions at Hirshhorn Museum and Sculpture Garden, Washington, D.C., 1976; American Cultural Center, Paris, 1979; and Pierpont Morgan Library, New York, 1981. One-man exhibitions at Forum Gallery, 1963-present; paintings and watercolors exhibited at National Arts Club, New York, "A Realist View," 1961; Brooklyn Museum, two-man show with Aaron Shikler, 1971. Solo shows at Frye Art Museum, Seattle, Washington, 1977; Claude Bernard Gallery, Paris, 1979; University of Connecticut at Storrs, 1979; and Phillips Gallery, Washington, D.C., 1980. Illustrated and published The Man from MALICE, 1966; Pins and Needles, 1969; No Known Survivors: David Levine's Political Plank, 1970; and The Fables of Aesop, 1975. Has been on Board of Trustees for Brooklyn Museum since 1973; elected to American Academy and Institute of Arts and Letters, 1983. Lives in Brooklyn, N.Y.

BSK

Robert Philipp (1895-1981) A.N.A. 1934, N.A. 1945
SELF-PORTRAIT
Oil on canvas
13⅛ x 13¼
Signed upper right: Philipp / 1950
Gift of Art Students' League, New York, 1983

Burton Silverman

Born in Brooklyn, N.Y., on June 11. Attended classes at Pratt Institute and High School of Music and Art, a New York City school for students of academic and artistic distinction, graduating 1946. Other students at the high school were Harvey Dinnerstein, Wolf Kahn, David Levine, Paul Resika and Aaron Shikler. At urging of parents, studied art history rather than painting at Columbia University, also attended classes at Art Students' League, 1946-49. First exhibited paintings at Pennsylvania Academy of the Fine Arts, 1949. Drafted into military service and upon release, under GI Bill enrolled at New York University's Institute of Fine Arts. After attending three classes, he quit to devote his career to painting. Traditional realists, such as Thomas Eakins, most influenced his painting. 1961, he and ten other artists organized exhibition "A Realist View" at National Arts Club, N.Y., for which he wrote the catalogue introduction, stating "tradition is not to be venerated out of nostalgic indulgence, but as source of learning. . . . We consider it to be the mainspring for the production of great art—past, present and future." First one-man exhibition of paintings held at Davis Galleries, N.Y., 1962. Subsequently represented by FAR Galleries, N.Y., Kenmore Galleries, Philadelphia, Pa., Capricorn Galleries, Bethesda, Md., Doll and Richards, Boston, Mass., and Sindin Galleries, N.Y., where he had one-man shows, 1962-1983. Wrote articles for magazines such as *ArtNews* (in collaboration with Harvey Dinnerstein) and *Book World*. Like Levine and Dinnerstein supported himself by commissions and illustrations, such as drawings for *Esquire* and design of "Aqualung" album cover for English rock musician Jethro Tull. 1964-67, taught painting and drawing at School of Visual Arts, N.Y. 1950s-1983, showed work in invitational exhibitions across the country and annual exhibitions of Butler Art Institute, Youngstown, Oh., and National Academy of Design, winning numerous prizes and purchase awards. Elected to Council of National Academy and served, 1980-83. Authored books, *Painting People*, 1977, and *A Watercolor Journal*, 1983. Summers in Westchester County, N.Y., where he built a studio; lives in New York City.

BSK

James Wyeth

Born in Chadds Ford, Pa., July 6, the youngest child of painters, Andrew Wyeth and Betsy James Wyeth, and grandson of illustrator N.C. Wyeth. After completing sixth grade, Jamie left public school in Chadds Ford to study at home with tutor. 1958, began formal art training with his aunt, Carolyn Wyeth, doing charcoal still life drawings in N.C. Wyeth's old studio. Then worked for three years as apprentice to his father, much as Andrew had served his own father, N.C. To better his understanding of anatomy, moved to New York City where he set up studio in morgue of a major metropolitan hospital. 1963, began to paint in oil. At age nineteen, held first one-man show at Knoedler Gallery, New York; exhibition was very successful, his early pictures evoking the tight linearity of his father's work. 1967, posthumous portrait of John Fitzgerald Kennedy brought significant public recognition. 1968, married Phyllis Mills of Middleburg, Va., and settled on his own farm in Chadds Ford called Point Lookout. Like his grandfather and father, paints Chadds Ford landscape, people, animals and objects, often focusing on a single motif in landscape composition. 1968, bought Rockwell Kent's old house on Monhegan Island, Me., summers there regularly. Elected an Associate of National Academy of Design in 1969, one of youngest members in institution's history. Has recently worked in color lithography, in addition to producing a series of paintings in a combination of acrylic paint and watercolor. Exhibited paintings, watercolors and drawings at William A. Farnsworth Library and Art Museum in Rockland, Me., 1969. Held one-man shows at Coe Kerr Gallery in 1974 and 1977; with other family members, exhibited at Brandywine Museum in Chadds Ford. Major exhibition organized by Pennsylvania Academy of the Fine Arts in 1980; circulated to Greenville, S.C., and Fort Worth, Tx. Jamie continues to live with his wife, Phyllis, in Chadds Ford and on Monhegan Island.

DA

George Tooker

Born in Brooklyn, N.Y. on Aug. 5. Early schooling at Phillips Academy, Andover, Mass.; graduated 1938. Received Bachelor's degree from Harvard University, 1942, and spent the next year in U.S. Marine Corps Officers Candidate School. 1943-45 studied at Art Students' League with Reginald Marsh, Kenneth Hayes Miller and Harry Sternberg. Began painting in egg tempera under Marsh's influence, encouraged by artist friends Paul Cadmus and Jared French to work in the medium. Under Miller's direction, Tooker began to paint compositions using repetitive figure types. Most influential upon his work were Sienese Renaissance school and Giotto. Group exhibition organized by Lincoln Kirstein, including Cadmus, French and Andrew Wyeth, held at Edward Hewitt Gallery, then traveled to England, 1950. Commissioned to design stage sets for Gian Carlo Menotti's production of his play, *The Saint of Bleecker Street*, 1954. Awarded grant from National Institute of Arts and Letters, 1960. Taught at Art Students' League, New York, 1965-68. Exhibited at Museum of Modern Art, Whitney Museum of American Art, Metropolitan Museum of Art in New York, Corcoran Gallery of Art, Washington, D.C. and Art Institute of Chicago. He was included in the 24th Venice Biennale, 1967, and retrospective at Dartmouth College, 1967, and circulating retrospective organized by Fine Arts Museums of San Francisco, 1974-75. Work included in recent exhibitions of figurative and realist art, "From All Walks of Life," 1979, at National Academy of Design, and "Realism and Realities: The Other Side of American Painting, 1940-1960," organized by Rutgers University Art Gallery, 1982. Elected to American Academy of Arts and Letters, 1983. Lives in Hartland, Vt. *See color, page 48.*

BSK

David Levine (1926-   ) A.N.A. 1967, N.A. 1971
PORTRAIT OF BURTON SILVERMAN (1928-   ) A.N.A.
   1969, N.A. 1972
Oil on canvas
24 x 20⅛
Signed lower right: D. Levine 69

James Wyeth (1946-   ) A.N.A. 1969
SELF-PORTRAIT
Oil on canvas
24¼ x 20¼
Signed upper left: J WYETH

Inventory of Portraits of Artists and Architects in the Collection of the National Academy of Design

The following list includes all portraits of artists and architects held in the Academy's collection without distinction as to whether artist or subject was, or is, a member of the Academy. The medium of all works is oil unless otherwise stated.

Abeles, Sigmund:
Self, etching

Adams, Kenneth Miller:
Self

Adams, Wayman:
Jay Connaway
Floyd Gahman
Abbott Fuller Graves
Edward Sheppard Hewitt
Hayley Lever
Hobart Nichols
Eliot O'Hara
Ulysses Ricci

Agopoff, Agop:
Self, bronze (relief)

Aitken, Robert Ingersoll:
Self
Cass Gilbert, bronze
forty pencil sketches:
Edwin H. Blashfield
Kenyon Cox
Emil Carlsen
Cass Gilbert
DeWitt Lockman
Hobart Nichols
Charles Platt
Douglas Volk

Albano, Salvatore:
Edwin White, bronze

Albee, Percy F.:
Self
Grace Albee

Albright, Ivan Le Lorraine:
Self

Albright, Malvin (Zsissly):
Self

Alexander, John White:
Self
Edwin Austin Abbey

Allen, Junius:
Self

Ames, Joseph:
Self

Anderson, Harry:
Self, watercolor

Anderson, Karl:
Self

Andrea, Gerald:
Archimedes Giacomantonio, pastel

Andrew, Richard:
Richard Recchia

Anisfeld, Boris I.:
Malvina Hoffman

Anshutz, Thomas Pollock:
Self

Apt, Charles:
Self

Arndt, Paul Wesley:
Henry Mattson

Aronson, David:
Self

Asplund, Tore:
Self

Audubon, John Woodhouse:
Self

Auerbach-Levy, William:
Self

Avery, Ralph H.:
Self

Baer, William Jacob:
Self

Baker, George Augustus:
Self
Albert Fitch Bellows
Charles Loring Elliott
John Frederick Kensett (1)
John Frederick Kensett (2)
Edwin White

Baker, Samuel Burtis:
Glenn Brown
Howard E. Smith

Baker, William R.:
William J. Hennessy

Bancroft, Milton Herbert:
Henry Bacon
Evelyn Beatrice Longman
Hermon A. MacNeil

Barker, Elizabeth:
Thorne Sherwood

Barnet, Will:
Self

Barr, Robert:
Henry Lee McFee

Barse, George Randolph:
Self

Bartlett, Paul Wayland:
Clinton Ogilvie, bronze

Bate, Rutledge:
Ogden M. Pleissner

Baum, Walter Emerson:
Self

Baumgartner, Warren William:
Self

Bausch, Barbara P.:
Madeleine Park, bronze

Beal, Gifford R.:
Reynolds Beal

Beard, James H.:
James C. Nicoll
William L. Sonntag

Beard, William H.:
William Bradford

Beaux, Cecilia:
Self

Beck, Dunbar Dyson:
William Adams Delano
Walker Hancock
William Mitchell Kendall

Beck, Rosemarie:
Self

Beckwith, James Carroll:
Carleton T. Chapman
William Merritt Chase
H. Siddons Mowbray

Beline, George:
Edgar Melville Ward, plaster

Bellows, George Wesley:
Paul H. Manship

Bendiner, Alfred:
George Howe, pencil

Benson, Eugene:
Self

Benson, Frank Weston:
Self

Benton, Thomas Hart:
Self

Berneker, Maud F.:
Louis F. Berneker

Betts, Edward H.:
Self

Betts, Louis:
Self
George Gardner Symons
Frederic Whitaker

Biggs, Walter:
Self, watercolor and gouache

Bittinger, Charles:
Frederick Vernon Murphy

Blackburn, Morris:
Franklin C. Watkins

Blakeslee, Sarah:
Francis Speight

Blashfield, Edwin H.:
Self
George B. Post

Blauvelt, Charles F.:
Self

Blondell, Jacob D.:
Self
Edward Gay

Blos, Peter:
Roi Partridge

Blumenschein, Ernest L.:
Self

Blumenschein, Mary Shepard Greene:
Self

Bogle, James:
Self
William Ranney
Arthur F. Tait

Bohm, Max:
Self

Bohrod, Aaron:
Self (Artist in Residence)

Bolton, William Jay:
Self (1)
Self (2)

Bongart, Sergei:
Self

Bonnen, Aloys:
Donal Hord

Boog, Carle Michel:
Edward McCarten

Borgord, Martin:
Walter Griffin
William H. Singer

Borie, Adolphe:
Self
Paul Cret

Bosa, Louis:
Self

Bosley, Frederick Andrew:
Self

Boston, Joseph H.:
Self

Bosworth, W. Welles:
Self

Botts, Hugh:
Self

Bowers, Edward:
Jervis McEntee

Boyd, Fiske:
Self, woodcut

Boyer, R. L.:
Kerr Eby
Arthur W. Heintzelman

Boyle, Ferdinand T. L.:
Eliza Greatorex
Jacob Lazarus

Brackman, Robert:
Self
Kenneth Bates
Max Kalish

Bradford, Francis Scott:
Chester Aldrich

Brandegee, Robert B.:
Self

Brandt, Carl Ludwig:
Self

Brandt, Rexford Elson:
Self, watercolor

Breckenridge, Hugh Henry:
Self

Bredin, Rae Sloan:
Self

Breinin, Raymond:
Self

Brewster, George T.:
James Carroll Beckwith, bronze

Bridgman, Frederick Arthur:
Self

Brockman, Anne:
Jon Corbino

Brown Henry Kirke:
Asher Brown Durand, marble

Brown, John George:
William Gilbert Gaul
Edward Lamson Henry

Browne, George Elmer:
John Whorf

Browning, Colleen:
Self

Brush, George de Forest:
Self

Brussel-Smith, Bernard:
Self, wood engraving

Buehr, Karl Albert:
Self

Buller, Cecil:
Self, woodcut

Bunn, Kenneth:
Self, bronze

Burnham, Roger Noble:
Frank Tenney Johnson, bronze

Burroughs, Bryson:
Self

Busch, Clarence F.:
Henry Ward Ranger

Butler, George Bernard:
Self
Charles H. Miller

Butler, Howard Russell:
Self
William Bailey Faxon

Cadmus, Paul:
Self, crayon

Cafferty, James H.:
Self
Jasper Francis Cropsey
Samuel R. Fanshaw
William Jacob Hays
John A. Hows
Thomas D. Jones

Calverley, Charles:
Charles Loring Elliott, marble

Campbell, Blendon Reed:
James Earle Fraser

Cardelli, Pietro:
John Trumbull, plaster

Carlsen, Emil:
Dines Carlsen

Carrett, J. E.:
Van Dearing Perrine

Carrigan, William L.:
Self

Carroll, John:
Louis Bouche

Carter, Clarence Holbrook:
Self

Cartwright, L. C.:
Ralph Adams Cram

Castellon, Frederico:
Self, etching

Chafetz, Sidney:
Self, woodcut

Champney, James Wells:
Self
Lockwood De Forest

Chandler, Elizabeth Chandler:
Alphaeus P. Cole, bronze

Chandler, Helen Clark:
Robert S. Peabody

Chapin, Francis:
Self

Chapman, Charles Shepard:
Self
Walter Farndon
Grant Reynard
Keith Shaw Williams

Chapman, John Gadsby:
Self
Alexander Anderson

Chase, Adelaide Cole:
William Lamb Picknell

Chase, Dorothy:
Peter Dalton

Chase, William Merritt:
Herbert Adams
Robert Blum
Thomas W. Dewing

Ben Foster
William Henry Howe
George Inness, Jr.
Walter Launt Palmer
Robert W. Van Boskerck

Chase, William Merritt and Frank Duveneck:
Frederick Dielman

Chen Chi:
Self, watercolor

Choate, Nathaniel:
Self

Churchill, William W.:
Cyrus E. Dallin

Ciampaglia, Carlo:
Self
Gaetano Cecere

Cikovsky, Nicolai:
Self

Clarkson, Ralph Elmer:
Self
Charles Francis Browne
Leonard Ochtman
Lorado Taft

Clemens, Paul Lewis:
Self

Clevenger, Shobal V.:
Washington Allston, plaster

Clinedinst, Benjamin West:
Self

Cobb, Virginia Horton:
Self, watercolor

Coffin, William Anderson:
Self

Cohen, Lewis:
Self

Coiner, Charles:
Self

Cole, Alphaeus P.:
Self
John Angel
Louis F. Berneker
Archibald Manning Brown
Frederick Dielman
Maud M. Mason
Robert K. Ryland
Charles Wellington Walker
John Alonzo Williams

Cole, Walter:
Timothy Cole

Colyer, Vincent:
Sanford Robinson Gifford

Conover, Robert:
Robert Riggs

Conrow, Wilford S.:
Carl Oscar Borg
Arthur F. Brinckerhoff
Electus D. Litchfield
Douglas W. Orr
Ralph Walker

Cook, Howard Norton:
Self, pastel

Cooper, Colin Campbell:
Self (1)
Self (2)

Cooper, Mario Ruben:
Self

Corner, Thomas Cromwell:
William S. Robinson

Costigan, John Edward:
Self

Cotton, William:
Self
Charles Bittinger
John Russell Pope

Couse, Eanger Irving:
Self

Cox, Allyn:
Moissaye Marans
Lorimer Rich
Lawrence Grant White

Cox, Gardner:
Self

Cox, Kenyon:
Emil Carlsen
Elliott Daingerfield
Charles Dana Gibson
Cass Gilbert
Jonathan S. Hartley, pencil
Childe Hassam, pencil
Samuel Isham
William Fair Kline
Christopher Grant LaFarge
DeWitt Lockman, pencil
Henry Augustus Lukeman
Charles Follen McKim
Maxfield Parrish
Augustus Saint-Gaudens
Samuel B. P. Trowbridge

Cox, Louise Howland King:
Allyn Cox (1)
Allyn Cox (2)

Cranch, John:
Self

Crane, Bruce:
Self

Crawford, Mel:
Philip Kappel, crayon

Creifelds, Richard:
George H. Bogert
John Carleton Wiggins

Crimi, Alfred DiGiorgia:
Edmondo Quattrocchi

Critcher, Catherine C.:
Oscar E. Berninghaus
James L. Greenleaf

Csoka, Stephen:
Self

Cummings, Thomas Augustus:
Self

Cummings, Willard:
Self

Curran, Charles Courtney:
Arthur Loomis Harmon
Francis Coates Jones

Currie, Bruce:
Self

Dabour, John:
Arthur Quartley

Daingerfield, Elliott:
Isidore Konti
Frederick Ballard Williams

Daniel, Lewis C.:
Self, mezzotint

Dannat, William T.:
Charles S. Reinhart

Darley, E. Henry:
Thomas Sully

Davey, Randall:
Self

Davidson, George:
Ezra Winter

Davis, Charles Harold:
Self

Davis, Gladys Rockmore:
Self

Deas, Charles:
Self, graphite

De Gerenday, Laci:
Self, bronze (relief)

De Haas, Mauritz Frederik Hendrik:
Self

De Knight, Avel:
Self, watercolor

Delbos, Julius:
Self

De Luce, Percival:
Self
Alfred Thompson Bricher
George H. McCord

De Marco, Jean:
Clara Fasano, terracotta (relief)

De Martini, Joseph:
Self

De Monvel, Bernard Boutet:
Wallace K. Harrison

De Pol, John:
Self, woodcut

Derrick, William R.:
Self

Derujinsky, Gleb W.:
Hobart Nichols, plaster

Dewey, Julia Henshaw:
Charles Melville Dewey

Dickinson, Edwin:
Self

Dickinson, Sidney:
Self
Bryant Baker
Theodore E. Blake
John Carroll
Donald De Lue
Frederick Detwiller
George Wharton Edwards
Otto R. Eggers
Mary Gray
Robert S. Hutchins
Georg Lober
Ernest N. Townsend
Harry W. Watrous
Edgar I. Williams

Dinnerstein, Harvey:
Self

Dobbs, John:
Self
Raphael Soyer (*Sitting for Raphael*)

Dobkin, Alexander:
Self

Dodd, Lamar:
Self

Dodge, William de Leftwich:
Philip Martiny

Dolph, John Henry:
Self

Dufner, Edward:
Self

DuMond, Frank Vincent:
Self

Duncan, Charles Stafford:
Maurice Sterne

Dunn, Harvey:
Self
Howard McCormick

Dunsmore, John Ward:
Self

Dunwiddie, Charlotte:
Self, bronze (relief)

Durand, Asher Brown:
Self
Lewis P. Clover
Francis W. Edmonds
Stephen Alonzo Schoff

Duveneck, Frank:
Louis Henry Meakin
Charles F. Ulrich

**Duveneck, Frank and
William Merritt Chase:**
Frederick Dielman

Eakins, Thomas:
Self
Edward W. Redfield

Eames, John H.:
Self, etching

Earle, Lawrence Carmichael:
Self

Eaton, Joseph Oriel:
Self
James Renwick Brevoort
Alfred C. Howland
Edward J. Kuntze

Eaton, Wyatt:
Self (*The Artist in his Studio*)

Eby, Kerr:
Self, charcoal

Eichenberg, Fritz:
Self, lithograph

Ellerhusen, Ulric H.:
George Elmer Browne, bronze

Elliott, Charles Loring:
Jasper Francis Cropsey
James Edward Freeman
George W. Hatch
Edward H. May
Frederick R. Spencer

Emmet, Lydia Field:
Self

Etnier, Stephen:
Self

Fabri, Ralph:
Self
Self (*In My Studio*)
Vincent Glinsky

Fanshaw, Samuel R.:
Self

Farlow, Harry:
Aldro T. Hibbard

Farnsworth, Jerry:
Self
Helen Sawyer
Edward A. Wilson

Faulkner, Barry:
Gilmore D. Clarke
Frances Grimes
Frederick R. King
William Platt

Fawcett, Robert:
Self, crayon

Fiene, Ernest:
Self
Frank Eliscu

Filmus, Tully:
Mitchell Fields

Finkelstein, Louis:
Self (*Double Self Portrait in Stillwater*)

Fisher, Alanson:
Self

Fiske, Gertrude:
Self
Charles H. Woodbury

Fitz, Benjamin Rutherford:
Horatio Walker

FitzGerald, Edmond James:
Self
Kent Day Coes

Fjelde, Paul:
Jonas Lie, bronze

Flagg, Charles Noel:
Self
Paul Wayland Bartlett
William Bailey Faxon
Robert W. Van Boskerk

Flagg, George Whiting:
Self

Flagg, Jared Bradley:
Seth W. Cheney

Flanagan, John:
Charles Downing Lay, bronze (relief)

Floch, Joseph:
Self
Self (*Self Portrait in Green*)

Florsheim, Richard:
Self

Folinsbee, John Fulton:
Self
Peter Geoffrey Cook

Harry Leith-Ross
James Kellum Smith
William Thon

Foote, Mary:
Thomas Hastings

Foote, Mary, after Ellen Emmet Rand:
Augustus Saint-Gaudens

Fortess, Karl E.:
Self

Foster, William Frederick:
Self

Fowler, Frank:
Frederic Crowninshield
William M. J. Rice
Walter Shirlaw

Frame, Robert:
Philip Dike

Franzen, August:
Self
Harvey Wiley Corbett
Henry Golden Dearth
Alexander Harrison

Frasconi, Antonio:
Self, lithograph

Frazee, John:
Self, plaster

Frazier, John R.:
Albert Harkness

Frazier, Kenneth:
Thomas Harlan Ellett
Bertram Grosvenor Goodhue
John Galen Howard
Charles Locke

Frazier, Richard:
Self, plaster

Fredericks, Alfred:
Self

Freedlander, Arthur R.:
Joseph Freedlander

Freer, Frederick Warren:
Self
Frederick Stuart Church

Freilicher, Jane:
Self

French, Frank:
Self

Fromkes, Maurice:
Self
Frederick W. Kost

Fuchs, Emil:
George W. Maynard, bronze

Fuller, George:
Self

Furness, William Henry:
Elihu Vedder

Gage, George William:
William Robinson Leigh

Garber, Daniel:
Self

Gaugengigl, Ignaz Marcel:
Self

Gauley, Robert David:
  Ernest C. Peixotto
Georges, Paul:
  Self
  Self (Red Self Portrait)
Geyer, Harold Carl:
  Self, etching
Gibson, George:
  Self
Gifford, Robert Swain:
  Self
Gignoux, François Regis:
  Self
Gikow, Ruth:
  Self
Gilbert, John:
  Esteban Vicente
Glackens, William J.:
  Ernest Lawson
Gold, Albert:
  Henry C. Pitz
Gonzalez, Xavier:
  Self
  Stewart Klonis
Gordigiani, Eduardo:
  Harry W. Watrous
Gorsline, Douglas Warner:
  Self
Gove, Elma Mary:
  Edward W. Nichols
Grabach, John R.:
  Self
Grado, Angelo John:
  Samuel Leitman, pastel
Grafly, Charles:
  Paul Bartlett, bronze
  Walter Elmer Schofield, plaster
Gramatky, Hardie:
  Self, watercolor
Grant, Gordon Hope:
  Self
  William Adams Delano, charcoal
  and colored crayon
Granville-Smith, Walter:
  Self
Grausman, Philip:
  Self, pencil
Gray, Henry Peters:
  Self
  Seth W. Cheney
Greacen, Nan:
  Ruth Nickerson
Green, Frank Russell:
  Self
Greene, Daniel E.:
  Self
Greene, Edward D. E.:
  Self
Greenman, Frances Cranmer:
  Burnham Hoyt
Greenough, Horatio:
  Samuel F. B. Morse, plaster

Greenwood, Marion:
  Self
Griffin, Walter:
  William Gedney Bunce
  Edward F. Rook
Gropper, William:
  Self
Groshans, Werner:
  Self
Gross, Chaim:
  Self, watercolor
Grosser, Maurice:
  Self
Grosz, George:
  Self
Groth, John:
  Self
Grover, Oliver Dennet:
  Self
Gruber, Walter:
  Erwin Springweiler
Gugler, Frida:
  Eric Gugler
Guy, Seymour Joseph:
  Self
  James Craig Nicoll

Haggin, Ben Ali:
  Self
Hale, Lilian Westcott:
  Self
Hale, Philip Leslie:
  Self
Hall, Frederick Garrison:
  Katherine Ward Lane (Weems)
Hall, George Henry:
  Self
Halsey, William Melton:
  Albert Simons
Hamilton, Hamilton:
  Self
  Thomas Moran
Harding, George:
  Charles Rudy
Harmon, Lily:
  Self
Harper, William St. John:
  Self
Harris, Charles X.:
  Louis C. Moeller
Hart, Mary Theresa:
  James M. Hart
Hart, William:
  Self
Hartley, Jonathan S.:
  Daniel Huntington, plaster
  George Inness, bronze
  George Inness, plaster
  (model for medal)
Havens, James Dexter:
  Self, woodcut
Hawthorne, Charles Webster:

Self
Wayman Adams
William Jacob Hays, Jr.
Fred Dana Marsh
Healy, George Peter Alexander:
  George Harvey
Hechenbleikner, Louis:
  Self, casein
Heintzelman, Arthur W.:
  William Truman Aldrich
Heitland, Wilmot Emerton:
  Self, watercolor
Helck, Clarence Peter:
  Self
Heliker, John:
  Self
Heller, Helen West:
  Self, woodcut
Henri, Robert:
  George Wesley Bellows
  Alexander Stirling Calder
  Charles Grafly
  Walter Elmer Schofield
Hermes, Allen:
  Nan Greacen
Herter, Adele:
  Grosvenor Atterbury, pastel
Herter, Albert:
  John Jay Cunningham
  Douglas Parshall
Hicks, Thomas:
  Self
  Vincent Colyer
  Christopher P. Cranch
  Jasper Francis Cropsey
  Alfred Jones
  John Francis Eugene Prud'homme
Higgins, Eugene:
  Self
Higgins, Victor W.:
  Self
Hildebrandt, Howard Logan:
  Self
  Solon H. Borglum
  D. Putnam Brinley
  Edmund W. Greacen
  Harry Hoffman
  Thomas H. Jones
Hinton, Charles Louis:
  Self
Hirsch, Joseph:
  Self
Hoelzel, Elise E.:
  Ernest Hubert Deines
Hoffman, Edward Fenno, III:
  Self, bronze (relief)
  John F. Harbeson, bronze
Hoffman, Irwin D.:
  Samuel E. Homsey, pastel
  Hazel Brill Jackson
Hoffman, Murray:
  Francis Burrall Hoffman
Homer, Winslow:
  Homer Dodge Martin

165

Honig, Mervin:
Self

Hopkins, James R.:
Self

Hopkinson, Charles Sydney:
Self
Robert P. Bellows
William Graves Perry

Horn, Milton:
Self, bronze

Hovenden, Thomas:
Self

Hubbell, Henry Salem:
Self
William A. Boring

Hughes, Robert Ball:
Henry Inman, plaster

Huntington, Daniel:
Self
Victor Gifford Audubon
Henry Kirke Brown
Thomas Cole
George Inness
James Augustus Suydam

Huntley, Victoria Hutson:
Self

Hurd, Peter:
Self

Hyde, William Henry:
Self

Iles, Terry:
Joseph Kiselewski, terracotta

Ingals, Eileen B.:
Abram Garfield

Ingham, Charles Cromwell:
Self
Thomas Seir Cummings
William Dunlap

Inman, Henry:
Edward Ludlow Mooney
Cornelius Ver Bryck
Charles Cushing Wright (miniature)

Inman, John O'Brien:
Self (1)
Self (2)

Inness, George, Jr.:
Jonathan S. Hartley

Ipsen, Ernest Ludvig:
Self
Ernest Albert
Edwin H. Blashfield
Eric Hudson
Robert H. Nisbet
Harry W. Watrous
William G. Watt

Irvine, Wilson Henry:
Self

Irving, John Beaufain:
Self

Irwin, Benoni:
Self
Andrew Fisher Bunner
Harry Chase
Hugh Bolton Jones

Frederic Remington
Dwight W. Tryon

Isenburger, Eric:
Self

Isham, Samuel:
Kenyon Cox

Jacobs, Leonebel:
Luigi Lucioni

James, Sandra:
Syd Browne

Jamison, Philip D.:
Self

Jay, Cecil:
George Hitchcock

Ject-Key, D. Wu:
Linda Wu

Jelinek, Hans:
Self, woodcut

Jennewein, Carl Paul:
Self
William Gehron

Jewett, William:
Samuel L. Waldo

Jewett, William Smith:
Self

Jocelyn, Nathaniel:
Moseley Isaac Danforth
Ithiel Town

Johansen, John C.:
Francis Keally
Richard Kimball
Jonas Lie
Chauncey Foster Ryder
Lawrence Grant White (1)
Lawrence Grant White (2)

Johnson, Avery F.:
Self, watercolor

Johnson, David:
Self

Johnson, Eastman:
Self
Sanford Robinson Gifford

Johnson, Frank Tenney:
Self

Johnson, Joseph Hoffman:
David Johnson

Jones, Dexter:
Self, bronze (relief)
Jack Bookbinder, bronze (relief)

Jones, Mildred:
Theodore Kautzky

Jongers, Alphonse:
Louis Paul Dessar
Henry Ward Ranger

Jules, Mervin:
Self

Kaish, Morton:
Self

Kamihira, Ben:
Self

Kappes, Alfred:
Self

Katzman, Herbert:
Self, sepia chalk

Kayn, Hilde B.:
Self

Keller, B. J., Mrs.:
Joseph Vollmering

Deane Keller:
George Davidson
Herbert J. Gute
Joseph Kiselewski
Everett Victor Meeks
Joseph Renier
George H. Snowden

Kempton, Martha Greta:
Mario Korbel

Kendall, William Sergeant:
Self

Kent, Norman:
Self, woodcut

Kent, Rockwell:
Self, lithograph

Kester, Lenard:
Self

Keyes, Bernard M.:
Self
Andrew Hepburn
Charles D. Maginnis

Kinney, M. West:
Troy Kinney

King, Paul:
Self

Kinstler, Everett Raymond:
Self (1)
Self (2)

Kipniss, Robert:
Self, lithograph

Kiralfy, Verona Arnold:
Janet DeCoux

Kirk, Frank:
Self

Kirschenbaum, Jules:
Self

Kiselewski, Joseph:
Gilmore D. Clarke, bronze

Klebe, Charles Eugene:
Self, watercolor

Kloss, Gene:
Self, dry point

Knaths, Karl:
Self

Koch, John:
Self

Koerner, Henry:
Self

Konrad, Adolf:
Self

Koppelman, Chaim:
Self, etching

Kosa, Emil J.:
Self

Kroll, Leon:
Edward Bruce
Howard Giles
Oronzio Maldarelli
Ernest Roth
Mahonri Young

Kupferman, Lawrence:
Self

Kyle, Joseph:
Self
Jacob A. Dallas

LaFarge, Susan Seidner:
Louis Bancel LaFarge

Lambdin, George Cochrane:
Enoch Wood Perry

Landeck, Armin:
Self

Laning, Edward:
Self

Lankes, Julius J.:
Self

Lascari, Salvatore:
Self
Edmond Amateis
Anthony De Francisci
Karl H. Gruppe
Hilda Kristina Lascari

Lasker, Joe:
Self

Lathrop, Dorothy P.:
Self, woodcut

Lathrop, I. Pulis:
Gertrude K. Lathrop

Lathrop, William Langson:
Henry Bayley Snell
Charles Rosen

Laufman, Sidney:
Self

Lawrence, Jacob:
Self, watercolor and gouache

Lawrie, Alexander:
William J. Linton

Lay, Oliver Ingraham:
Self
Fidelia Bridges
Charles C. Coleman
Casimir C. Griswold
Winslow Homer
Walter Satterlee

Lazarus, Jacob Hart:
Henry A. Ferguson
John Rogers

Leake, Gerald:
Self
Armin C. Hansen

Leason, Percy Alexander:
Henry Gasser

Lechay, James:
Self

Le Clear, Thomas:
Self
William R. O'Donovan
Horace W. Robbins

Lee-Smith, Hughie:
Self

Leiber, Gerson:
Self, lithograph

Leichter, Rhoda:
Leo Friedlander

Leslie, Charles Robert:
Washington Allston

Leutze, Emanuel:
Self
Worthington Whittredge

Levine, David:
Aaron Shikler
Burton Silverman

Levine, Jack:
Self

Lewis, Arthur Allen:
Self, linoleum cut

Libby, William Charles:
Self, lithograph

Limbach, Russell T.:
Self, lithograph

Linton, William J.:
Self

Lippincott, William Henry:
Self
William Henry Drake
William Rutherford Mead

Lockman, DeWitt:
Self
Eliot Clark
DeWitt Parshall

Loeb, Louis:
Self

Logan, Maurice:
Self

Lo Medico, Thomas G.:
Self, bronze (relief)

Loomis, Chester:
Self

Loop, Henry Augustus:
Self
James R. Brevoort
John B. Bristol
Jennie S. Loop
James D. Smillie
John Quincy Adams Ward

Low, Mary Fairchild:
Self
Will Hicok Low

Low, Will Hicok:
Charles F. W. Mielatz

Lucas, Albert Pike:
Self
John Flanagan
Allen G. Newman

MacCameron, Robert Lee:
Self (1)
Self (2)

MacLane, Jean:
Self
Roy Brown
John C. Johansen

MacLaughlan, Donald Shaw:
Self

MacMonnies, Frederick W.:
Self

MacNutt, Glenn Gordon:
Self

Magafan, Ethel:
Self

Magonigle, Edith:
Harold Van Buren Magonigle

Magrath, William:
Self
Arthur Parton

Mankowski, Bruno:
Self

Mannheim, Jean:
William Wendt

Manship, Paul H.:
George Demetrios, terra cotta (relief)

Manso, Leo:
Self

Marble, John Nelson:
Thomas B. Craig

Maril, Herman:
Self

Marsh, Reginald:
Kenneth Hayes Miller

Marshall, William Edgar:
Asher Brown Durand

Marsiglia, Gerlando:
Self

Martin, Eleanor:
Newton P. Bevin, pencil

Martin, Fletcher:
Paul Landacre

Martino, Antonio Pietro:
Self
Paul Wescott

Martino, Giovanni:
Self

Mason, Frank H.:
Self

Mason, Roy Martell:
Self

Mastro-Valerio, Alessandro:
Self, mezzotint

Mattei, Clarence R.:
Belmore Browne

Matteson, Tompkins Harrison:
Jesse Talbot

Maxfield, James E.:
C. Harry Eaton

May, Edward Harrison:
Frederic Edwin Church
Thomas Addison Richards

Mayer, Constant:
Self

Mayer, Henrik Martin:
Self
Henry Kreis

Mayer, Jan:
Frederick James Woodbridge, pastel

Maynard, George W.:
Self (1)
Self (2)
John M. Carrere
Joseph Lyman
William Rutherford Mead
Roswell M. Shurtleff

Maynard, Richard Field:
Will Howe Foote
Everett Warner

Mayr, Christian:
Self

McCoy, John W.:
Self

McIlhenney, Charles Morgan:
Self

McNaughton, Elizabeth B.:
Millard Sheets

Meiere, Hildreth:
Self

Meissner, Leo John:
Self, engraving

Melchers, Gari:
Self

Mellon, Eleanor:
Adolph A. Weinman, bronze

Menihan, John C.:
Self, lithograph

Menkes, Zygmunt:
Self
Abraham Walkowitz

Merritt, Warren Chase:
John W. Winkler

Mestrovic, Ivan:
Self, terracotta

Meyer, Herbert:
Self
Reginald Marsh

Meyerowitz, William:
Self

Miller, Barse:
Self, watercolor

Miller, Edgar:
John Holabird

Miller, Richard Emil:
Self
George Elmer Browne
Henry O. Tanner

Millet, Francis Davis:
Self

Mixter, Felicie Waldo Howell:
Self

Moffat, Salley DeCamp:
Samuel Chamberlain

Moffett, Ross E.:
Self

Molarsky, Maurice:
Albert Laessle

Moller, Hans:
Self

Mollison, Kay:
Harry Russell Ballinger

Montana, Pietro:
Self

Mooney, Edward Ludlow:
Self
Henry Inman

Mora, Francis Luis:
Self
John Taylor Arms
Lillian M. Genth
Albert L. Groll

Moreau-Vauthier, J. Augustin:
Jean Léon Gérôme, plaster

Morgan, William:
Self

Morse, Samuel F. B.:
Self (miniature)
Benjamin West

Moser, Barry:
Self, wood engraving

Mosler, Henry:
Self

Mount, Shepard Alonzo:
Self
William Sidney Mount

Mount, William Sidney:
Self

Mueller, Hans Alexander:
Self, woodcut

Mulhaupt, Frederick John:
Self

Munroe, Marjorie:
Brenda Putnam

Murphy, Alice Harold:
Self

Murphy, Hermann Dudley:
Self
Charles Curtis Allen
Frederick Law Olmsted

Myers, Jerome:
Self
Guy Pene DuBois
Bonnie MacLeary
Harry Wickey

Naegele, Charles Frederick:
Frank De Haven
William Merritt Post

Nason, Gertrude:
Thomas W. Nason

Nason, Thomas Willoughby:
Self, engraving

Nehlig, Victor:
Self

Neilson, Raymond Perry Rodgers:
Self
Francis Scott Bradford
Harriet Whitney Frishmuth
Hayley Lever
Boris Lovet-Lorski
Carl Schmitz

Nelson, George Lawrence:
Self
Chester Beach
Hilda Belcher
Ulric H. Ellerhusen
Gordon Samstag
Eric Sloane

Guy C. Wiggins
Cullen Yates

Nichols, Spencer Baird:
Self

Niehaus, Charles Henry:
Robert Blum, plaster

Noble, John:
Self, lithograph

Noble, John A. H.:
Self, lithograph

Noble, Thomas Satterwhite:
Self

Noci, Arturo:
Ettore Caser

Oakley, Violet:
Self
Frank Miles Day

Oberhardt, William:
Self, charcoal
John Gannam, charcoal
Charles Dana Gibson

Oberteuffer, George:
Self

O'Connor, Gerald W.:
Robert B. O'Connor

O'Conor, Roderic (?):
Andrew O'Connor

O'Donovan, William R.:
William Page, bronze

Oertel, Johannes Adam:
Self

Olinsky, Ivan G.:
Self
Isabel Bishop
Abastenia St. L. Eberle
Rudulph Evans
Emma Fordyce MacRae
Dorothy Ochtman
Tosca Olinsky
Abram Poole
Heinz Warneke

Olsen, Herbert V.:
Self, watercolor

Olson, Olaf J.:
Louis Ayres
Laura Gardin Fraser
Bruce Moore
Albert Stewart

Oppenheim, S. Edmund:
Eliot Clark
Harry De Maine

Orpen, William:
Herbert Haseltine

Osgood, Samuel Stillman:
Self

O'Toole, Cathal Brendan:
Self

Page, Marie Danforth:
Self

Page, William:
Ferdinand T. L. Boyle

Palmer, William:
Self

Paone, Peter:
Self, color lithograph

Paradise, Philip:
Self

Parker, Lawton S.:
Frederick Carl Frieseke

Parker, Robert Andrew:
Self, watercolor and gouache

Parton, Henry W.:
Self

Paxton, William McGregor:
Self
Leslie P. Thompson

Pearce, Charles Sprague:
Self

Pearson, Joseph T.:
Self

Pecorini, Margaret B.:
Janet Scudder

Peele, John Thomas:
Self

Pellew, John C.:
Self, watercolor

Peterdi, Gabor:
Self, etching (1)
Self, etching (2)

Petersen, Martin:
Self

Phelps, Helen Watson:
Charlotte Buell Coman

Philipp, Robert:
Self (1)
Self (2)
Frank Gervasi
Louis Kronberg
Jean Liberte
Louis Ritman
Charles Z. Klauder

Phillips, J. Campbell:
Gifford Beal
Frank A. Bicknell
Jerome Myers
G. Glenn Newell
William Ritschel
Carl Rungius

Phillips, J. Campbell and
Frederick Ballard Williams:
Ralph Albert Blakelock

Phillips, Mel A.:
Everett Shinn

Pike, John:
Self

Platt, Eleanor:
John Flanagan, bronze

Polasek, Albin:
Self
William Merritt Chase, bronze

Pollia, Joseph P.:
Self

Poole, Abram:
Self

Poor, Henry Varnum:
Self

Poore, Henry Rankin:
Self

Pope, John:
Self
Clinton Ogilvie

Potter, Edward Clark:
Self

Potthast, Edward Henry:
Self
Charles H. Niehaus

Powell, William Henry:
Self

Pozzati, Rudy O.:
Self, lithograph

Pratt, Robert M.:
Self
George H. Smillie
Aaron Draper Shattuck

Prellwitz, Edith Mitchell:
Self

Prendergast, Charles E.:
Self

Price, Alice H.:
Louis C. Rosenberg

Prime H. F.:
Margaret Bogardus

Putman, Brenda:
William Adams Delano, bronze (relief)

Pyle, Howard:
Self

Quackenbush, Larry:
Thomas Nicholas

Quinn, Edmond T.:
Sherry E. Fry
Attilio Piccirilli
Furio Piccirilli

Rand, Ellen Emmet:
Self
Jonas Lie
Eleanor Mellon
Walter Nettleton

Rapp, George:
Louis J. Kaep

Ray, Ruth:
Self

Reed, Doel:
Self

Reevs, George:
Thomas Shields Clarke

Rehn, Frank K. M.:
Self

Reid, Robert:
Self

Reinhart, Benjamin Franklin:
Self
Charles Calverly
Edward Moran

Reinike, Charles H.:
Clarence Millet

Reisman, Philip:
Self

Rembski, Stanislav:
Leon Dabo

Resika, Paul:
Self

Ricci, Ulysses:
Jerri Ricci

Rice, William M. J.:
James Carroll Beckwith (1)
James Carroll Beckwith (2)
Frank Fowler
Daniel Chester French

Richmond, Agnes M.:
Cornelia Van Auken Chapin

Ripley, A. Lassell:
Self

Ritchie, Alexander Hay:
Self

Rittenberg, Henry R.:
Self
Alexander Bower
Dean Cornwell
Arthur Covey
Arthur Crisp
Anna Fisher
Cass Gilbert, Jr.
J. Munroe Hewlett
Frederick C. Hirons
Leo Lentelli
John Noble
William Van Alen
Edward G. Volkert
J. Scott Williams
George Wright

Robert, Lucerne McCullough:
John Wheat

Roberts, Morton:
Self
Hugh Gumpel

Robinson, Theodore:
Will Hicok Low

Rogers, Nathaniel:
Self (miniature)

Rolshoven, Julius:
Self
Frank Duveneck

Romano, Umberto:
Self

Rondel, Frederick:
Self

Root, John Wellborn:
Self, pastel

Rosen, Charles:
Robert Spencer

Ross, Alexander:
Self

Rossiter, Thomas Pritchard:
Self
John W. Casilear
Peter Paul Duggan
Richard William Hubbard
Louis Lang

Rouland, Walter Orlando:
Self

Edward A. Bell
Paul Cornoyer

Ruzicka, Rudolph:
Self, pen and ink, and wash

Ryder, Platt Powell:
Self
John George Brown
John A. Parker
Charles Parsons

Ryerson, Margery Austen:
Self

Saint-Gaudens, Augustus:
Jules Bastien-Lepage, bronze (relief)
Francis Davis Millet, plaster (relief)

Saintin, Jules Emile:
Self

Sample, Paul Starrett:
Self

Sargent, John Singer:
Self
Claude Monet

Sartain, William:
Self

Sauter, George:
Joseph Pennell

Savage, Eugene Francis:
Self
Berthold Nebel
Egerton Swartwout

Scheville, William Valentine:
Karl T. F. Bitter

Schlaikjer, Jes Wilhelm:
Self

Schlegel, Fredolin:
Self

Schley, Reeve:
Self, watercolor

Schrag, Karl:
Self (*Paintings and Windows*)

Schreyvogel, Charles:
Self

Schulte, Antoinette:
Cecil Howard

Schultheiss, Carl Max:
Self

Schwartz, Andrew T.:
Charles Keck

Schwartz, Frank Henry:
Self

Schweitzer, Gertrude:
Self

Scott, Julian:
Self

Sellstedt, Lars Gustaf:
Self (1)
Self (2)

Sepeshy, Zoltan Leslie:
Self
Eliel Saarinen

Serwazi, Albert B.:
Self

Setterberg, Carl:
Self

Sewell, Lydia Amanda Brewster:
Self
Robert V. V. Sewell

Seyffert, Leopold Gould:
Self
Dana Pond

Shean, Charles M.:
Henry J. Hardenberg

Shegogue, James Hamilton:
Self
James Smillie

Shepler, Dwight Clark:
Charles Collens, crayon

Sherbell, Rhoda:
Self, bronze

Shikler, Aaron:
Self

Shirlaw, Walter:
Self

Shute, Ben E.:
Henry Johnston Toombs

Silverman, Burton:
David Levine

Simon, Sidney:
Self, terra cotta (relief)

Simpson, Maxwell:
Asa Cheffetz

Sitton, John:
Sidney Waugh

Smedley, William Thomas:
John J. Boyle
William Anderson Coffin
Thomas Hastings

Smillie, James D.:
George H. Smillie, soft ground
etching and drypoint

Smith, Howard Everett:
W. Lester Stevens
Harry A. Vincent

Smith, Wallace H.:
Louis LaBeaume

Smith, William Arthur:
Self
Adolph Dehn, crayon
Dong Kingman

Snell, Henry Bayley:
William Langson Lathrop

Solman, Joseph:
Self

Soyer, Moses:
Self

Soyer, Raphael:
Self
Alexander Brook
Richard Diebenkorn

Spear, Arthur Prince:
Self

Speicher, Eugene E.:
Self
John Fabian Carlson
Leon Kroll

Spencer, Frederick R.:
Charles Loring Elliott
Robert E. Launitz
Thomas Thompson
Edwin White
Alexander Wust

Spicer-Simson, Theodore:
Self, bronze (relief)

Spruance, Benton Murdoch:
Self, lithograph

Staigg, Richard Morrell:
Self
Louis Remy Mignot

Starr, Maxwell B.:
John Gregory

Stearns, Junius Brutus:
Self
Tompkins Harrison Matteson

Sterner, Albert:
Self
Jules Guerin
Edmond T. Quinn

Stevenson, Gordon:
Henry Hering
Harry T. Lindeberg
Wallace Morgan

Stillman, William James:
Self

Stoddard, Alice Kent:
Self
Clarence C. Zantzinger

Stoll, Rolf:
Carl Gaertner
Henry Keller

Stone, Don:
Self

Stone, William Oliver:
Self
John Ehninger
William Stanley Haseltine

Story, George Henry:
Self

Strean, Maria Judson:
Helen M. Turner

Stuempfig, Walter:
Self

Sundblom, Haddon H.:
Charles R. Kinghan

Tack, Augustus Vincent:
Walter Clark
Arthur Hoeber

Tarbell, Edmund C.:
Self (1)
Self (2)
Study for Self
Charles Howard Walker

Taylor, Edwin C.:
Lee Lawrie

Taylor, Prentiss:
Self, lithograph

Teague, Donald:
Self, watercolor

Terken, John:
 Self, synthetic plaster (relief)
Thaw, Florence:
 Birge Harrison
Thayer, Abbott Handerson:
 Self
Thompson, Alfred Wordsworth:
 Self
Thompson, Cephas Giovanni:
 Self
Thompson, Jerome:
 Self
Thompson, Launt:
 Self
 Daniel Huntington, plaster (relief)
 Samuel F. B. Morse, marble
Thompson, Leslie P.:
 Frederick Garrison Hall
Thompson, William J.:
 Self, synthetic plaster
Thorndike, George Quincy:
 Self
Thorvaldsen, Albert Berthold:
 Self, plaster
Tiffany, Louis Comfort:
 Self
Timmons, Edward J. F.:
 Arthur Hill Gilbert
Todd, Henry Stanley:
 William Verplanck Birney
 Benjamin W. Morris
 Alexander T. Van Laer
Tompkins, Frank H.:
 Theodore C. Steele
Toney, Anthony:
 Self
Tooker, George:
 Self
Tovish, Harold:
 Self, bronze (relief)
Treaster, Richard:
 Robert H. Laessig
Trebilcock, Paul:
 Self
Trotta, Guiseppe:
 Victor Salvatore
Turner, Janet Elizabeth:
 Self
Twibill, George W.:
 John Trumbull
Twitchell, Asa Weston:
 James H. Hart

Ufer, Walter:
 Self
Uhlman, Alice:
 George Harding
Unknown artists:
 William F. Lamb
 Benjamin Curtis Porter (?)
 Alfred Wordsworth Thompson
 Hendrick Dirk Kruseman Van Elten
 Robert Walter Weir

Unwin, Nora Spicer:
 Self, wood engraving

Van Soelen, Theodore:
 Self
 John Gaw Meem
Vedder, Elihu:
 Andrew W. Warren
Vickrey, Robert:
 Self
Vinton, Frederic Porter:
 Self
Volk, Douglas:
 Self
von Neumann, Robert:
 Self, lithograph
Vonnoh, Robert William:
 Self
 Thomas Allen
 George M. Bruestle
 Francis Coates Jones
 Alexander Phimister Proctor
 Bessie Porter Vonnoh

Walcott, Harry Mills:
 Self
Waldo, Samuel L.:
 William Jewett
Walker, Gene Alden:
 Margaret French Cresson
 Lu Duble
 Marion Sanford
Walker, Jean:
 Anna Hyatt Huntington
Walker, Henry Oliver:
 Self
 J. Appleton Brown
 Charles A. Platt
Walleen, Hans Axel:
 Self
 Adlai S. Hardin
Waltman, Harry Franklin:
 Self
 Robert D. Gauley
 Frederick W. Hutchison
 Willard D. Paddock
 Arthur J. E. Powell
 Henry M. Shrady
Ward, Edgar Melville:
 Self
 Thomas L. Smith
Ward, Lynd Kendall:
 Self, wood engraving
Warren, Ferdinand E.:
 Self
Washburn, Cadwallader:
 Self
Waterman, Marcus:
 Self
Waugh, Frederick Judd:
 Self
Waugh, Samuel Bell:
 Self

Weidenaar, Reynold Henry:
 Self, aquatint
Weidner, Roswell T.:
 Sydney Errington Martin
Weinman, Adolph A.:
 William Rutherford Mead, bronze
Weinman, Robert:
 Self, aluminum (relief)
Weir, Julian Alden:
 Self
 Childe Hassam
 George W. Maynard
 Robert C. Minor
 Albert Pinkham Ryder
 Olin L. Warner
Weir, Robert Walter:
 John Ferguson Weir
Weldon, Charles Dater:
 Self
Wells, Tom:
 Paul Thiry
Wenzler, Henry Antonio:
 Self
Wessel, Bessie Hoover:
 Edward T. Hurley
Wetherill, Elisha Kent Kane:
 Self
Wheelwright, Robert, Mrs.:
 Robert Wheelwright, watercolor
Whistler, James Abbott McNeill:
 Joseph Pennell, lithograph (1)
 Joseph Pennell, lithograph (2)
Whitaker, Frederic:
 Eileen Monaghan Whitaker
White, Christian:
 Robert White (The Artist's Father)
White, Edwin:
 Self (1)
 Self (2)
White, Victor Gerald:
 Barry Faulkner
Whitehorne, James:
 Self
 John Ludlow Morton
Whitney, Beatrice:
 Bela L. Platt
Whittemore, William John:
 Self
 Charles Aiken
 Charles Courtney Curran
 Charles Warren Eaton
Wickwire, Jere Raymond:
 Self
Wightman, Thomas:
 Self
Wijk, Harry N.:
 Henry Richardson Shepley
Wiles, Irving Ramsay:
 Self (1)
 Self (2)
 Hugo Ballin
 Arnold W. Brunner
 J. Francis Murphy
 Lawton S. Parker

Henry Prellwitz
William Thomas Smedley
William Thorne
Gladys Wiles
Henry Wolf

**William, Frederick Ballard and
J. Campbell Phillips:**
Ralph Albert Blakelock

Williams, Keith Shaw:
Walter H. Kilham
Stow Wengenroth

Williams, Wheeler:
Self

Williamson, Curtis:
Robert Henri

Williamson, John:
Self

Wilson, Matthew:
Self

Wilson, Sol:
Self

Winkel, Nina:
Self, sheet copper (relief)

Winter, Andrew:
Self

Winter, Ezra Augustus:
Donn Barber

Witt, John Harrison:
Self

Woelfle, Arthur William:
Self

Wood, Thomas Waterman:
Self
James Hope

Wooley, Lucy:
Ralph Humes

Worthington, Margaret:
John M. Johansen, pencil

Wortman, Denys:
Self, crayon

Wotherspoon, William Wallace:
Self

Wright, A. Stevens:
Sylvia Shaw Judson

Wright, Catharine Morris:
Self
Clare Leighton
Warren Mack

Wright, George Frederick:
John L. Fitch

Wyant, Alexander Helwig:
Self

Wyeth, Andrew Newell:
Self

Wyeth, James:
Self

Wyeth, Newell Convers:
Self

Yardley, A. T., Mrs.:
Charles Yardley Turner

Yarrow, William:
Carroll Tyson

Yewell, George Henry:
Self
Samuel Colman

Young, Charles Morris:
Self

Zornes, James Milford:
Self, watercolor

INDEX

Design
DANA LEVY

Photography
DAVID ALLISON
STUDIO NINE

Printing
NISSHA PRINTING COMPANY, Kyoto

Composition
LCR GRAPHICS

Typeface
GOUDY OLD STYLE